INSIGHT OF THE MONEY

AF613014

ARVIND UPADHYAY

Copyright © Arvind Upadhyay
All Rights Reserved.

ISBN 979-888521939-6

This book has been published with all efforts taken to make the material error-free after the consent of the author. However, the author and the publisher do not assume and hereby disclaim any liability to any party for any loss, damage, or disruption caused by errors or omissions, whether such errors or omissions result from negligence, accident, or any other cause.

While every effort has been made to avoid any mistake or omission, this publication is being sold on the condition and understanding that neither the author nor the publishers or printers would be liable in any manner to any person by reason of any mistake or omission in this publication or for any action taken or omitted to be taken or advice rendered or accepted on the basis of this work. For any defect in printing or binding the publishers will be liable only to replace the defective copy by another copy of this work then available.

What is this whole business of making money about? How much money do you really need? The answers to these questions depends on your lifestyle and what your material needs are. It is often said that money is not the most important thing in the world. For many people, however, it is right up there next to air in importance. These are not necessarily overly-materialistic people. Rather, they simply understand the true value of money. Money, in and of itself, is not very spectacular. What money can do for you is what is really important. Money gives you freedom and choices. You can decide where and how you want to live when you have a good income or financial resources. On the other hand, when you do not have much money, choice may be something that you cannot afford. The choices available to you may not really be choices at all.

Obviously, you need money to cover your basic expenses: food and shelter. Beyond that, how much money you need will be determined by what kind of life you want for yourself. Most people want a middle class lifestyle. What it means to be middle class varies from source to source though. The general consensus is that those in the middle class typically have adequate access to education as well as goods and services. Also, those in the middle class generally can afford to own property and have a fair amount of discretionary income. That is, they have disposable income or money that is not allocated solely to satisfying basic needs.

So, how do you get money? The best way to achieve your financial and lifestyle goals is to prepare yourself for a good career. And, the best way to do that, in general, is to get a good education. Data shows that college-educated people earn almost twice as much as those without a degree. Your decision about what career path to take should not be solely driven by money, however. Ideally, your career should involve work you find interesting and which you can identify with. Working just for a paycheck is to have a job, not a career.Money is a good servant but a bad master. —SIR FRANCIS BACON Money. Few words have the power to provoke such extreme human emotions. A lot of us refuse to even talk about money! Like religion, sex, or politics, the topic is taboo at the dinner table and often off-limits in the workplace. We might discuss wealth in polite company, but money is explicit. It's raw. It's garish. It's intensely personal and highly charged. It can make people feel guilty when they have it —or ashamed when they don't. But what does it really mean? For some of us, money is vital and crucial but not paramount. It's simply a tool, a source of power used in service of others and a life well lived. Others are consumed with such a hunger for money that it destroys them and everyone around them. Some are even willing to give up things that are far more valuable to get it: their health, their time, their family, their self-worth, and, in some cases, even their integrity. At its core, money is about power. We've all seen how money can have the power to create or the power to destroy. It can fund a dream or start a war. You can provide money as a gift or wield it as a weapon. It can be used as an expression of your spirit, your creativity, your ideas—or your frustration, your anger, your hate. It can be used to influence governments and individuals. Some marry for it—and then find out its real price. But we all know that on some level it's an illusion. Money isn't even gold or paper today, it's zeros and ones in banking computers. What is it? It's like a shape-shifter or a canvas, assuming whatever meaning or emotion we project on it. In the end, money isn't what we're after . . . is it? What we're really after are the feelings, the emotions, we think money can create: that feeling of empowerment, of freedom, of security, of helping those we love and those in need, of having a choice, and of feeling alive. Money is certainly one of the ways we can turn the dreams we have into the reality we live. But even if money is just a perception—an abstract concept—it doesn't feel that way if you don't have enough of it! And one thing is for sure: you either use it, or it uses you. You either master money, or, on some level, money masters you! How you deal with money reflects how you deal with power. Is it an affliction or a blessing? A game or a burden? When I was choosing the title of this book, a few people were actually outraged at the suggestion that money could be a game. How could I use such a frivolous term for such a serious topic! But, hey, let's get real. As you'll see in the pages to come, the best way to change your life is to find people who've already achieved what you want and then model their behavior. Want to master your finances? Find a financial master and imitate how he or she deals with money, and you will have found a pathway to power. I can tell you right now, I have interviewed many of the wealthiest people in the world, and most of them do think of money as a game. Why else would anyone work ten or 12 hours a day after they've made billions of dollars? And remember, not all games are frivolous. Games are a reflection of life. Some people sit on the sidelines, and some play to win. How do you play? I want to remind you, this is a game that you and your family can't afford to lose. My promise to you is this: if you will stay with me and follow the 7 Simple Steps in this book— the steps that have been distilled from the world's most successful financial players—you and your family will win this game. And you can win big! But to win, you have to know the rules and learn the best strategies for success from those who have already mastered the game. The good news is that you can save years of time— and in a few minutes—by simply learning the pitfalls to avoid and the shortcuts to experiencing lasting success. The financial industry often works to make this topic feel incredibly complex, but in reality, once you get past the jargon, it's relatively simple. This book is your opportunity to stop being the chess piece and become the chess player in the game of money. I think you're going to be very surprised at how, with an insider's understanding, you can easily transform your financial life and enjoy the freedom you deserve. So let's get to it. Just imagine what life would be like if you had mastered this game already. What if money didn't matter? How would you feel if you didn't have to worry about going to an office every morning, or paying the bills, or funding your retirement? What would it be like to live your life on your own terms? What would it mean to know you had the opportunity to start your own business, or that you could afford to buy a home for your parents and send your kids to college, or have the freedom to travel the world? How would you live your life if you could wake up each day knowing there was enough money coming in to cover not only your basic needs but also your goals and dreams? The truth is, a lot of us would keep working, because that's the way we're wired. But we'd do it from a place of joy and abundance. Our work would continue, but the rat race would end. We'd work because we want to, not because we have to. That's financial freedom. But is it a pipe dream? Is it really possible for the average person—more importantly, for you— to make this dream a reality? Whether you want to live like the 1% or just have the peace of mind from knowing that you won't outlive your savings, the truth is you can always find a way to make the money you need. How? The secret to wealth is simple: Find a way to do more for others than anyone else does. Become more valuable. Do more. Give more. Be more. Serve more. And you will have the opportunity to earn more—whether you own the best food truck in Austin, Texas, or you're the top salesperson at your company or even the founder of Instagram. But this book isn't just about adding value—it's really about how to go from where you are today to where you truly want to be, whether that's financially secure, independent, or free. It's about increasing the quality of your life today by developing the one fundamental skill that the vast majority of Americans have never developed: the mastery of money. In fact, 77% of Americans—three of every four people—say they have financial worries, but only 40% report having any kind of spending or investment plan. One in three baby boomers have less than $1,000 saved! Polls show that fewer than one in four trust the financial system— with good reason! And stock ownership has been hitting record lows, particularly among young people. But the truth is, you don't earn your way to freedom. As you'll see later in this book, even multimillion-dollar earners such as Godfather director Francis Ford Coppola, boxer Mike Tyson, and actress Kim Basinger lost it all because they didn't apply the fundamentals that you'll soon be learning. You have to be able to not only hold on to a portion of what you earn for your family, but, more importantly, multiply what you earn—making money while you sleep. You have to make the shift from being a consumer in the economy to becoming an

owner—and you do it by becoming an investor.

Contents

Foreword

Often times, people say that they can live without money. They define money as just one of the tools that enhances peoples living environment. However, in real life money is a very important matter in peoples lives. Although the people in history might have lived through the exchange of goods and not relying to the value of money itself, modern society today could not function without money. Money plays a huge role in the society in variety of ways such as in business, at peoples job, and even in education. Money helps people achieve a better quality of education, larger chance of business success, and higher work output.

Higher quality of education

People value education highly in their lives and a quality education is dependent on the amount of money spent on this type of investment. Every single person in this world has to invest their money on education for them to gain learning. These learning would not just count the education they receive in school but other extracurricular activities such as learning how to play the piano, art, and even dancing. Most of the time, for people to have talents such as playing the piano, they have to devote their money to a teacher who has a high piano professional degree. Similarly at school, people would also like to be taught by a teacher with higher degree of profession in their field. It is believed that teachers who have been highly educated can provide better teaching to their students. The high quality of education brings oneself a higher possibility to succeed in the future society. This is because when people are exposed to high quality of learning they tend to be taught higher educated materials from a well-educated teacher. A higher quality of education also means that one would study in a well structured environment with other educated friends. They would also have a better chance of meeting people with more authority which would contribute to their networking in future career.

In Business World

Money also plays a significant role both in our society and in worldwide business. In the business world, most interactions that people have involve a huge amount of money. One common example of a worldwide business is investment. In the field of investment, people put a lot of their money into a particular market and as the market gets bigger and builds a higher reputation, the worth of money invested grows larger. In this investment, people earn a lot of money but often times they lose all of their fortune. The money they gain from the investment is usually used to build up ones new business or even to invest in different markets. The importance of these businesses in our world is that it helps our economy to function well. These businesses help factories operate properly which in turn allows supply to meet the demands of the consumers. In fact, it is the factories and markets who provides the people with the goods that they need. The society will lose its order if the different types of business happening around the world stops. If one business stops other business will get affected and ultimately the supply would not meet the demands of people.

Quality of living

Even in a smaller scale in business, wages and salaries are important matters when it comes to human. The wages are the proof of peoples effort and devotion to the work they do. The wages vary from one to another depending on the kind of job people do and the position they occupy in the company. People use the earnings they get from their work in many ways. They buy the necessary things that they need to sustain their living such as home, food, and car. As mentioned in the earlier paragraph, these wages are also used to attain high quality of education. There are huge differences between people who work and earn wages and people who do not. People who can earn their livings mostly live a life filled with what they want to have. They eat nutritious food which helps sustain body health and use cars to transport them to wherever they want to go. On the other hand, people who do not have a job and earn nothing often have hard times sustaining their life. They have nothing to support their health. They also do not have a permanent shelter where they could rest on. These people could not live properly because they could not afford any of it. These illustrate a contrasting example of people who earn wages and who do not. Wages are a hugely significant matter for one to maintain certain quality of life. Therefore, the importance of money within humans life could not be doubted.

Preface

While it may be true that money makes the world go around, it is not inherently valuable. Unless you enjoy looking at pictures of deceased national heroes, these colorfully imprinted pieces of paper have no more use than any other piece of paper. It is only when we agree as a country to assign a value to that paper—and other countries agree to recognize that value—that we can use it as currency.

Gold and Silver Standards

It didn't always work this way. In the past, money generally took the form of coins composed of precious metals such as gold and silver. The value of the coins was roughly based on the value of the metals they contained because you could always melt the coins down and use the metal for other purposes.

Until a few decades ago, the value of paper money in many countries, including the United States, was based on a gold or silver standard, or some combination of the two. The piece of paper money was simply a convenient way of "holding" that particular bit of gold or silver. Under the gold or silver standard, you could actually take your paper money to the bank and exchange it for an amount of gold or silver based on an exchange rate set by the government. Up until 1971, the United States operated under a gold standard, which since 1946 had been governed by the Bretton Woods system, which created fixed exchange rates that allowed governments to sell their gold to the United States treasury at the price of $35 per ounce. Believing that this system undermined the U.S. economy, President Richard M. Nixon took the country off the gold standard in 1971.

Fiat Money

Since Nixon's ruling, the United States has operated on a system of fiat money, which means our currency is not tied to any other commodity. The word "fiat" originates in the Latin, the imperative of the verb facere, "to make or become." Fiat money is money whose value is not inherent but called into being by a human system. So these pieces of paper in your pocket are just that: pieces of paper.

Why We Believe Paper Money Has Value

So why does a five-dollar bill have value and some other pieces of paper do not? It's simple: Money is a both a good and a method of exchange. As a good, it has a limited supply, and therefore there is a demand for it. There is a demand because people can use the money to purchase the goods and services they need and want. Goods and services are what ultimately matter in the economy, and money is a way that allows people to acquire the goods and services that they need or want. They earn this method of exchange by going to work, which is a contractual exchange of one set of goods—labor, intellect, etc.—for another. People work to acquire money in the present to purchase goods and services in the future.

Our system of money operates on a mutual set of beliefs; as long as enough of us believe in the value of money, for now, and in the future, the system will work. In the United States, that faith is engendered and supported by the federal government, which explains why the phrase "backed by the full faith and credit of the government" means what it says and no more: the money may have no intrinsic value, but you can trust using it because of its federal backing.

Furthermore, it is unlikely that money will be replaced in the near future because the inefficiencies of a purely barter system, in which goods and services are exchanged for other goods and services, are well known. If one currency is to be replaced by another, there will be a period in which you can switch your old currency for new currency. This is what happened in Europe when countries switched over to the Euro. So our currencies are not going to disappear entirely, although at some future time you may be trading in the money you have now for some form of money that supersedes it.

The Future Value of Money

Some economists don't trust our system of fiat currency and believe we cannot continue to declare that it has value. If the vast majority of us come to believe that our money won't be nearly as valuable in the future as it is today, then our currency becomes inflated. Inflation of the currency, if it becomes excessive, causes people to want to get rid of their money as quickly as possible. Inflation, and the rational way citizens react to it is bad for the economy. People will not sign profitable deals that involve future payments because they'll be unsure what the value of money will be when they get paid. Business activity sharply declines because of this. Inflation causes all sorts of other inefficiencies, from a café changing its prices every few minutes to a homemaker taking a wheelbarrow full of money to the bakery in order to buy a loaf of bread. The belief in money and the steady value of the currency are not innocuous things.

If citizens lose faith in the money supply and believe that money will be worthless in the future, economic activity can grind to a halt. This is one of the main reasons the U.S. Federal Reserve acts diligently to keep inflation within bounds—a little is actually good, but too much can be disastrous.

Supply and Demand

Money is essentially a good, so as such is ruled by the axioms of supply and demand. The value of any good is determined by its supply and demand and the supply and demand for other goods in the economy. A price for any good is the amount of money it takes to get that good. Inflation occurs when the price of goods increases—in other words when money becomes less valuable relative to those other goods. This can occur when:

The supply of money goes up.

The supply of other goods goes down.

Demand for money goes down.

Demand for other goods goes up.

The key cause of inflation increases in the supply of money. Inflation can occur for other reasons. If a natural disaster destroyed stores but left banks intact, we'd expect to see an immediate rise in prices, as goods are now scarce relative to money. These kinds of situations are rare. For the most part, inflation is caused when the money supply rises faster than the supply of other goods and services.

To summarize, money has value because people believe that they will be able to exchange this money for goods and services in the future. This belief will persist so long as people do not fear future inflation or the failure of the issuing agency and its government.

Money can't buy happiness, but it can buy security and safety for you and your loved ones. Human beings need money to pay for all the things that make your life possible, such as shelter, food, healthcare bills, and a good education. You don't necessarily need to be Bill Gates or have a lot of money to pay for these things, but you will need some money until the day you die.

Because money is necessary for obtaining the goods and services you need to survive, an understanding of personal finance is essential. You need to be responsible with the money you earn and save enough for the future to ensure you will still have enough leftover when you can no longer trade your labor for money.The sooner you start saving your money, the more likely it is that you'll never face a lack of money or financial stress. In fact, if you save enough and invest wisely, you could even become financially free

— which happens when you have enough money to live on for the rest of your life.

One reason so many people profess not to care about money is that the love of money has been described as "the root of all evil."

It's true, materialistic people can let an obsession with money drive them to do bad things for their own financial gain. But in reality, money is nothing more than a medium of exchange.

Money makes it easier to trade your labor for a diverse set of goods and services. The following are some things to consider when it comes to the value of money and why money is important.

Without money, if you wanted food, you'd need to find someone who had food who was willing to trade it in exchange for a service you could directly provide, or for a product you could produce. Bartering transactions like this are cumbersome and inefficient, not to mention a less reliable means of getting the things you need.

Thanks to money, you don't have to hope someone wants to give you something you need in exchange for something you have available to trade. Everyone recognizes that money has value, so you can trade it for whatever goods or services you desire. This increases market liquidity, which refers to how easily assets can be purchased or sold.

Of course, this works only in situations where money actually has a stable value — and it derives this value from the fact that it is a scarce commodity. If everyone could obtain as much money as they wanted by printing it, it would no longer have any value.

To guard the true value of money, a central authority needs to make sure the supply of money remains limited. In many cases, a central bank like the U.S. Federal Reserve controls the money supply and makes sure we don't end up with so much money that it is no longer seen as valuable — a process called inflation.

CHAPTER ONE

MONEY DECISIONS: WHO'S IN CONTROL?

Most people make decisions about how to use money every day. It may be to take a bus, or to buy something for lunch, or to put money in a parking meter, or buy a new "app", or go to a movie, or... Like it or not, we need money to get and do a lot of things. Try and think of the last day when you didn't spend money – or make a decision about how to use money – either yours or someone else's. You probably make many such decisions involving money – and you have choices. But what things influence the decisions that you make?

Do you feel different when you pay for something with your own money than when others buy things for you?

Factors Affecting Money Decisions

Think about the last item of clothing that you bought. What factors affected your decision? 1. Emotions: Was it how you felt looking at the item – that is, your emotional response? 2. Friends and Peers: Was it your friends – and what you thought they would think about your choice – that is, some kind of "peer pressure" affecting your decision? 3. Customs, Traditions, and Habits: Was it because it was the style of clothes that you have always tended to wear in the past – that is, your custom, tradition, habit, or just falling in line with past choices? 4. Family Members: Did your parents, siblings, or other family members have any influence on your choice – that is, what they would think and how they would react? 5. Latest Styles and Fads: Was it because of any latest style or fad – that is, trying to stay current and with current trends? 6. Advertising: Was it because of any commercial, ad, promotion, or celebrity endorsement that you saw that had an impact on you – that is, some form of advertising? 7. Incentives: Was it because of a "sale" that was on or a discount coupon that you had – that is, some kind of incentive provided by the store to make you buy that product? 8. Your Values and Confidence: Was it because of what you thought – and what you wanted – and your own sense of values, style, and knowing what you want?

When you make decisions about money, take a moment to think about factors that could be affecting your decision. Are you in control of your decisions – or are other affecting what you do? Try and be in control of your own decision.

Impact Can Be Intentional or Unintentional All of these factors influence the decisions and choices you make about spending. Some may even influence you without really trying. Can you think of a decision you made recently that you think may have been influenced by a movie you saw – or a sporting event or sports celebrity – or someone you met? In the end, you will make the decision – but it is always good to consider the factors that might be having an impact on you. Can You Afford It? Another factor that is important – and often gets too little consideration – is whether or not you can afford it. With so many factors influencing us, and affecting our decisions about money and spending, we may buy something we don't really need or want, and may not use – or won't use for long. Looking Back on Past Decisions Once a decision is made, you can look back and think about whether or not it was a good one for you. If it was, why? If it wasn't, why not? Sometimes we make good decisions – and sometimes not so good. The important thing is to learn from the decisions that weren't so good. In the end, though, each of us strives to make the best decisions we can about money – and that is one of our goals with "Money and Youth."

Can you think of something you bought that you never used – or didn't use much at all? If so, think about why you bought it. What can you learn from that decision?

Tips for Making Good Money Decisions Here are a few tips to consider when making good money decisions. 1. "Think about your thinking": Take a moment to "think about your thinking." That might sound a little weird but to make a good decision it helps to take a minute or so to think about the choice you are making – and why you are making it. Many people make decisions without really thinking about why they are making that particular decision. Is it because it's the kind of decision you have always made – because you are trying to make someone happy – because you think it will make you happy – because of what someone taught you – because it's part of who you are and reflects your values ...? 2. Your "Opportunity Cost": Consider your opportunity cost – that is, what are you giving up in making the decision? Every decision has an opportunity cost – giving up one thing to get another. You could be giving up something else you could buy with the money you are spending, or something else you could do with the time you are investing, or another city you could be visiting, or another course at school you could be taking. Among all the possible alternatives, what's the "next best thing" you will be giving up? That is your opportunity cost. 3. Future Trade-offs: Consider the future possibilities. That is, in addition to what you might be giving up today, what might you be giving up in the future because of your decision? What could be different if you waited? 4. Can you afford the cost? Finally, can you afford it? Do you have the money to pay for it? If not, and you are going to use a credit card, will you have the money to pay off the credit card balance when you get your bill? Or will you be "carrying the cost" into the future – and paying interest? If you are going to pay interest you should consider that as part of your costs – and as part of your decision. We have now looked at eight factors that may influence your decisions– and four tips to consider when trying to make good money decisions. But let's not forget about another key factor in all this – and that is, what makes you happy.

To what extent do you take time to "think about your thinking" – and do you think about why you are making that decision?

Try to complete the following activity in less than two minutes. Trying to do this quickly helps you to focus on things you feel most strongly about. Identify the five most important things in your life at the present time and the five things you most hope for in the future.

Your Happiness is Another Important Factor Each of us has to figure out what will make us happy – today, tomorrow, next week, next year, and in the years to come. If you are one who thinks more about today and tomorrow rather than the future, you are probably one who likes "instant gratification" – that is, when you want something you want it now. If You Like "Instant Gratification", Taking Control Can Be a Challenge If you tend to like, and want, "instant gratification" then managing your money will probably be more of a challenge. It will be harder for you to think about your tradeoffs down the road – or the challenge of having to pay for something later if you can't afford to pay today. It may be that some of those influences we just talked about are working on you – and making you want certain things – and wanting them now! If you tend to be one who "acts now and plans later," managing your money – and your money decisions – will be more difficult.

Do you tend to want instant gratification – or are you someone who likes to plan, and can wait to get what you want in the future – and achieve the goals that you set for yourself?

If You Keep the Bigger Picture in Mind, Taking Control Can Be Easier If you are more of a "big picture" person – and take a longer term view of things – you may find it easier to manage your money – and to achieve your goals. When you set goals, you need to think about the present and the future. You have to think about what makes you happy today – and what will make you happy in the years ahead. People often talk about hoping to have a "happy life" – which, in and of itself, is an ambitious goal. Finding the balance between your happiness today and your happiness in the future is key – and not always easy, especially when it comes to how you handle and manage your money.

What, for you, are the key things that you think will help make a "happy life" for you?

Money Can't Buy Happiness – True, But ... The saying "money can't buy happiness" is probably quite true. But it is also true that a lack of money can create problems. Being in debt over one's head, being unable to pay bills, being unable to take holidays, being unable to afford the accommodation one wants can be both frustrating and unpleasant. "Money can't buy happiness" but, let's face it, it helps.

What are your views on the link between money and personal happiness? When are you happiest? What role, if any, does money play in those times?

You Make Your Decisions – But to What End? There is no shortage of advice you are likely to receive about how to effectively manage your money – and what you should be doing with your money. But, in the end, you will decide. A key factor that can affect your decisions are your goals. If you don't have goals then goals won't play a role in your money decisions. But if you have goals, hopes, and things you want to achieve in the future, they will have an impact on the decisions that you make. Therefore, setting goals for yourself can be a powerful incentive which can have an effect on the decisions you make.

Do you think much about what you hope for in the future when you make your money decisions?

Having Goals Can Make a Difference Why can goals make a difference? If you have goals, you'll have to consider the possible trade-offs as you make decisions today. And saving to achieve a goal can be very rewarding, personally satisfying, a real motivator, and a confidence builder. Achieving a goal can help you prove to yourself that you can accomplish what you set your mind to – and inspire you to aim for other goals – and to achieve other things. So, "money doesn't buy happiness", but it does play an important role in most people's lives. We may wish it weren't so, but it's true. Earning money. Spending money. Saving money. Investing money. Making money. Losing money. Giving money away. We make all kinds of decisions, often daily, about money

Money Is a Means to an End But what is money anyway? We don't eat money, wear money, or build buildings out of coins and twenty-dollar bills. Money is a tool. It is a means to an end. It is something created to help our economy work more smoothly. It serves as a medium of exchange, that is, we can use it for purchases. And money can help each of us in achieving our goals – whatever they may be. If we turned on the printing presses and gave everyone twice as much money, would people be better off? The answer is "no". Why? Because with everyone having twice as much money, prices would eventually double as people have more money to spend on things. People would have twice as much money but would be paying twice the price for things – so people wouldn't be any better off. So it is important to remember that money is a tool – and prices will affect the purchasing power of your money and how much you can buy with it. If You Want to be In Control, Have a Plan Money can help us out – but it can also cause problems – getting deep into debt – causing stress, tension, and anxiety – pushing some people to crime – having bill collectors on your back. To avoid money problems, it's best to try and stay in control of your money and how it affects your life. You'll want to maximize the help that money can provide and minimize the problems it can cause. Today is the best time to start to take control of your money. And the best way to take control is to be prepared and plan.

To what degree do you think you are in control of your money?

Identify the top three goals that you hope to achieve within the next year. Identify the top three goals that you hope to achieve within the next three years. Identify the top three goals that you hope to achieve within the next 5-10 years.

Financial Planning is Not Only for Those with Lots of Money Planning how to handle money is not only for those who have lots of money. In fact, the less money you have, the more important it is to plan. You want to get the most from the money that you have. The best way to plan is to set goals

– to know clearly what you want – to know the difference between what you need and what you want – to know the things you care most about – what you want out of life – what you want to achieve and what will make you happy – today and in the future. In setting goals, consider the different "time periods" – the short-term (what you hope to achieve over the next year), the medium-term (1–3 years), the long-term (3–5 years), and the more distant future (5 years and beyond). Short-term goals can be very helpful as they serve as stepping stones to achieving your medium-term goals. Then, use medium-term goals as stepping stones to long-term goals, and so on. Doing this gives you some "check points" to see how you are doing over time – and think about whether your goals have changed and if you want to change direction.

Plan for a Balance between Your Short-term and Long-term Goals As important as it is to keep an eye on the future and your longer terms goals, you want to be happy today too. That is understandable, and should be part of your planning. Finding a balance between today and the future is important. Develop a plan that helps you live as happy a life as you can – today, next month, and into the future.

People Are Different – Their Goals Are Different Different people will have different goals. What one person wants out of life can be very different from what another person wants. Individuals face life and its financial challenges from a wide array of starting points and with different views. Some people have access to a great deal, including opportunities for education, training, working, and acquiring income. Others have access to very little and face different challenges and opportunities. Different cultures also have different attitudes to money and material things. No matter what the differences, however, everyone will face decisions related to their money. To guide these decisions, we need goals. What are yours? Knowing your goals is a key first step in starting to take control of your money.

Five Steps to Saving Money 1. Set a savings goal. Ask yourself: How much money will I need? How soon? Be realistic. 2. Decide how much you will save from your pay. Put aside money to save first, then spend what's left. 3. Track where you spend your money. Learn more about where your money is going. This will help you find ways to cut your spending if you need to – since you will probably be surprised where some of it is going. 4. Build a budget and try to stick to it. 5. Reward yourself when you reach a goal. Give yourself something to look forward to if you do what you set out to do.

Say What? Possible New Terms! 1. Opportunity Cost: the next best alternative given up when you make a decision. 2. Carrying Cost of Debt: the interest charges that you pay on debts that you carry on a credit card over time. That is, credit card debts that you don't pay off right away and result in interest charges. 3. Medium of Exchange: one of the roles of money. Prices can be set in terms of money for goods and services and then money can be used to "exchange" to receive a good or service. 4. Financial Planning: setting goals for things you hope to achieve and acquire over time and making a plan for how to achieve those goals.

Did It Stick? Can You Recall? 1. What factors may be having an influence on your money decisions? 2. What are four things you can do to try and make a good decision? 3. What is the purpose of having a financial plan? 4. How can setting goals help you to make better financial decisions and find a balance in life? 5. What is a key role of money in the economy?

CHAPTER TWO

MONEY AND ME

W hen you think about the things that are most important in your life – and the goals you have for what you want to achieve – do they reflect your "values"? Can you tell? Have you thought much about your values? What are values anyway? Values are those things that make up your character. They represent what you think is important in life. They show up in your decisions, actions, and judgments. How we look on the outside usually tells very little. It's more what's on the inside that will make most of the difference in who we are. And values are a big part of what's inside.

If you were asked to identify three of your "values," how would you answer?

Do you think you are influenced by advertising? Did you make a decision recently that was influenced by advertising?

There are many things that can influence your values. Family members, teachers, and friends are particularly strong influences. Religion, culture and heritage can also have a big impact. Television, movies, videos, and music certainly play a role, too. Advertising can also do a great deal to influence, or try to influence, what you think is important and what you value. Your values govern many of your financial decisions. What material things are important to you? How much money will you need? What will you do to get it? What trade-offs will you make? What will you do with your money when you get it? And so on. There is no denying that decisions related to money are important – they affect each of our lives and those around us. And your values affect those decisions. Let's try to explore the things in life that you value – and the things that have influenced your values.

It is time for brutal honesty. Below are a number of things you may think are important in life. They may be things in life you want for yourself, what you try to be or hope for, or things you respect in others. There are probably other things that are important to you that aren't included. Please add them to the list. Then select the "top ten," the things you value most, and rank them one to ten.

What's Important to You? Happiness Recreation and Travel Maturity Good health Work Status Education Freedom Family Tolerance Love Compassion Sympathy Loyalty Fitness Honesty Reliability Fun Wealth Acceptance Patriotism Responsibility Respect Sense of humour Security Beauty Honour Safety Faith Commitment Religion Being in style Acquiring abilities/skills Independence Excitement Influence Friendship Risk Helping others Community involvement

There are many people, groups, and things that can influence your values. Some may intentionally try to influence your values. Others may do so without even trying. It is important to be cautious about those who are out to influence what you do and the decisions you make

To most people, the figures will appear to be of different sizes. Put a ruler alongside each one. They are, in fact, the same size. But the way they have been drawn makes them appear to be different than they really are. Visual illusions such as this can be fun. They also make a point. We can be fooled. We can be influenced. We can be made to see things differently than they really are. Take a look at the following visual. Did you see both? Both are there. The point is that different people can see things differently. It's not necessarily such that one is wrong and the other is right. Both may be right. So whenever you think something is true, and someone offers a different point of view, consider whether or not there might be other ways of looking at things. Is there another point of view? A better point of view? A view that will strengthen what you believe?

There are many people who make decisions without thinking about their "values." When you make decisions related to money, take a moment to think about your values and if they should play a role in your decision.

Possible Influences Your parents/guardians Your religion Books Camp experiences Other relatives Television Magazines Volunteer experiences Your childhood experiences Entertainers Travel experiences Work experiences Your childhood friends Sport personalities Specific events Sickness or injury Your current friends Radio Community activity Employer Your teachers Music Teammates Coach

The fact is, there are many things in life where others could see things differently than you do. Others may try to bring you around to their way of thinking. And, as you know, what is right for them, may not necessarily be right for you. Consider some instances where people's views have been different. Did you agree with a particular point of view? What is "right" and "wrong" can often be unclear.

Think about the last time that somebody tried to influence a decision that you made. How long ago was it? Why were they trying to influence your decision? Were they able to influence you in any way?

Peer pressure refers to how others around your own age can influence your thinking – on purpose or not. Peer pressure is one of the strongest influences on young people. Friends, classmates, teammates, and workmates are usually very important to you. You may value them and what they think and do. At the same time, they are in the same situation as you are – trying to figure out their lives, trying things, thinking about things, and figuring out what they value and what's most important to them. Many of the decisions that you make in your youth will be influenced by your peers. Situations can arise that involve making decisions related to alcohol, smoking, drugs, clothing fads and styles, courses you take, concerts, schools, careers, jobs, and so on. Many of these are difficult decisions, and peers can apply a great deal of pressure – either directly on you or by the decisions they have made and what they are doing. You will face times and decisions when your values are really put to the test.

In a group situation, discuss the following: • Where does peer pressure push the hardest? For example, is pressure hardest when deciding whether or not to smoke, to dress a certain way, to listen to certain music, to drink, to take drugs, to associate with certain people, to want certain possessions, and so on? When do you feel the pressure the most? • What are the best ways to deal with peer pressure when you disagree with the direction toward which it is pushing you?

As far as money matters go, your peers may seek to influence you – such as how much you spend, what you buy, how much you borrow, what styles you follow, where you shop, and so on. It can be challenging, but it is important to make the decisions you believe are best for you, the ones that fit your values, priorities, and goals – and that make you happy and feel good about your decision.

How have you handled peer pressure in the past? Have you ever made a money decision that was influenced by your peers?

A funny thing about peer pressure – it can pass quickly. You may be in a situation where you are feeling pressure to buy and wear certain shoes – shoes you don't need. If you decide no, the pressure often soon passes and others forget about it. If you decide yes, others may still soon forget about it – but you are out of pocket the money – and may be wearing shoes you don't need – and maybe don't even like. Make sure you use your money the way you think best.

Are you one who tends to make decisions on the basis of what others are doing to try and be "in" or look "cool"? Or are you more of a "do your own thing" person who makes your own decisions based on how you feel and what you think is important?

You probably don't even know anyone by the name of Jones. For you, it may be the Howards, the Garneaus, the Villachis, or others. The "Joneses" is simply a reference to those around us with whom we may struggle to keep up. We may want what they have, or try to live how they live. For youth, the "Joneses" can be friends who wear certain clothes or shoes, go to certain concerts, drive certain cars, have a new possession (such as the latest "iProduct" or computer game), take vacations to nice places, eat at nice restaurants, and so on. No one may be pressuring you to have them – but you may be pressuring yourself to keep up.

Are you an envious person? Does envy play much of a role in terms of your goals, decisions, and actions? On a scale of 1 to 5, rate the influence of "envy" on your economic decisions

Do you feel envy plays much of a role in your life at this time? Do you feel envious of anyone? Is there something that you currently want that is based on envy? Have you made a recent decision or purchase that was based on envy?

Basically, it comes down to how much you are willing to let envy affect your values, decisions, actions, and goals. If you want to be in control, you should avoid envy when you can.

Watch out for envy – it can lead to some pretty crazy decisions – and ones you may regret. It's funny how often others that you envy, may envy you for things you have in your life. Keep in mind the things you value in life – it may make you less envious – and put the brakes on some decisions that you might come to regret.

Advertising is the way producers provide information to consumers about a product or service. They also use advertising to encourage consumers to purchase their products or services. Their goal is to convince you, as a consumer, to purchase their product over that of a competitor. That doesn't mean advertisers can tell you anything they want. Advertisers are governed by rules and regulations (such as those provided under the

Competition Act, the Food and Drugs Act, the Canadian Radio-television and Telecommunications Commission, and other federal and provincial laws) that set standards and guidelines for advertisers. For example, it is illegal for advertisers to provide

untrue or deceptive information. They cannot make false claims about their product. They cannot make untrue statements about their competitor's product. Therefore, within certain guidelines, the advertiser's aim is to influence you and to get you to buy a particular product or service. This is not as deceptive an act as it may sound. As you know, there are many good products and services available. If you don't know about them, you can't make effective decisions about which ones, if any, you want to purchase and use. Furthermore, producers have the right to make accurate claims about how good their product is. If the product is good, they should certainly be able to let you know about it.

On most occasions, have the products and services you bought been as advertised? Have you bought a product that doesn't live up to the advertising?

Advertising is good in a number of ways: 1. Was it how you felt looking at the item – that is, your emotion is a source of information about new products, existing products, and improvements or changes to products. 2. It encourages competition, which can lead to product improvements, lower prices, specials, improvements in supply and availability, and more. 3. As you are probably well aware, advertising pays for many media presentations. Advertising sponsors TV and radio shows, magazines and newspapers, concerts, and so forth. Increasingly, through "product placement" it also helps sponsor movie production. 4. Advertisers sponsor these activities according to how many of their potential customers they believe will watch the show, listen to the show, read the magazine or paper, or come to the concert. Through sponsorship, some of these activities, such as TV and radio programs, are provided free to us (even though we do end up paying for the advertising in the prices we pay for what we buy – and we may also pay cable or satellite fees for the programming). Some (such as a newspaper) are provided to us at much lower cost than would otherwise be the case, and some (such as a concert) might not have come to town without the sponsor. 5. Advertising helps consumers to compare the different products and services that are available and hopefully to help them make better consumer decisions.

How can advertising influence your buying decisions? Advertising may lead to impulse buying (buying on the spot without much thought) or fad buying. It may lead you to buy something you really don't want, or don't need, or shouldn't buy at this time. In other words, it may help lead to a consumer decision that you might come to regret. But whose fault is that – the advertiser's or yours? There is a saying – caveat emptor – which means "let the buyer beware." In the end, you are responsible for your own decisions. If you make a bad buy (one that is not in your best interest), then, unless an ad has been false, misleading, or illegal, you have only yourself to blame. Therefore, when making your buying decisions it is important for you to be aware of some of the ways in which advertisers may try to influence you to buy their product. The advertiser's job is to put the product forward in the best light possible and hope you will buy their product or service. Your job, as a wise consumer, is to make the decisions that you think will be best for you.

There is one further point to mention in this section. As a consumer, you do have certain "rights." The Consumers' Association of Canada states that its goal is to help uphold the following consumer rights: • the right to choice • the right to consumer education • the right to be informed • the right to participate in marketplace decision making • the right to safety • the right to have access to basic services • the right to be heard • the right to a sustainable enviroment1 • the right to redress

You may believe that, on some occasion, your rights have been abused. Or you may have a complaint about a good or service you purchased. If so, identify who you can speak with and voice your complaints. For those times (which we hope will be few) when you have legitimate complaints, you need to learn the "art of effective complaining." Most producers will welcome the chance to turn an unhappy customer into a happy one. After all, if you leave unhappy, you'll probably never return. They lose your future business. And you will probably tell others about your bad experience. Give them a chance to fix any mistakes or problems. You may find you end up quite happy. Sometimes you may even come out ahead. If you find you are not satisfied, and you feel you have a legitimate complaint that was not dealt with properly, you can contact the Better Business Bureau and put in a complaint. But do give the producer or retailer a chance to fix the problem first.

Have you ever bought a product and had a problem or reason to complain? If so, did you – or did you just let it go? How would you assess yourself in terms of your willingness to act if you have a problem with a product?

Advertising And You Review each of the advertising techniques described below. See if you can think of one or more product or service ads that you have seen recently that use the following techniques. Rank these techniques from 1 to 10 in terms of which you think is the most effective at influencing your opinion of a product or service. Let "1" represent the most effective and "10" the least. • Repetition: You have heard it said that "If you tell people the same thing often enough, they will come to believe it." Some advertisers will use this method, repeating their message over and over again in an ad or a series of ads over time. [Built Tough!, "Eat Fresh," "I'm Lovin It"] • Conformity: This approach aims to have you "get on board," "be in," "get with it," [Join the "cool crowd."] • Imitation: This is the effort by an advertiser to influence a consumer by having a celebrity associated with the good or service. The advertiser hopes that those who like and respect the celebrity will imitate the behaviour by using the product. [Sports star's running shoes. Celebrity's make-up line.] • Emotional Appeal: This is where the advertiser seeks to draw upon one or more of the consumer's emotions to influence the decision. [Being away from home – kittens and bathroom tissue – beer and being Canadian] • Good Will: Providing something for free – a free sample, a free issue, and so on. However, always remember that "there is no such thing as a free lunch" – someone always pays the cost. It's a question of who pays and why. ["Four free CDs! Just sign up to buy one CD a month and you'll get four free CDs!"] • Scare Techniques: Well, maybe not exactly scare techniques, but who wants to face the consequences of going around with bad breath, blotchy skin, or underarm odor, especially when the ads portray such awful consequences. ["Nick and Lotta were about to kiss when, all of a sudden, Lotta noticed Nick's teeth. If only Nick had used..."] • Snob Appeal: These ads are designed to appeal to those who want to be seen as in the lead, on the move, those who have made it – and want others to know about it. These ads emphasize that if you have the product you are definitely "in" or among the "elite" or "successful." ["If you need to know the price, you're not interested."] • Economic Appeal: This type of ad presents the "great deal" – no money down, no interest payments, and so on. Be on your toes and watch for those that are genuine deals and those that have catches to them or key points in the fine print. There can be very legitimate offers to help you pay for a purchase over time – such as equal payments over 24 months with no interest. But, in the fine print, it can say that if the amount isn't paid in full within 24 months, all interest charges become payable for the full two years. So check that out and, if that's the case, make sure you complete the payments within the 24 months. ["No payments for three years! That's right, it can be yours and you don't pay a cent for three years!"] • Comfort And Enjoyment Some advertisers may attempt to present their product in relation to something that, although enjoyable, is largely unrelated to the product. For example, have you ever sat through a commercial wondering what on earth was being advertised – only to be surprised at the end? The purpose of the ad may simply have been to get your attention – not tell you anything about the product. • Humour One method to attempt to influence your purchase is to present the product or service in a humorous way and hope that your laughter will carry over all the way to your buying decisions. Can you think of any other techniques that are used by advertisers to affect consumer decisions?

Always protect your PINs and security codes. Change your passwords regularly

As you know, there are lots of things that you can do with your money. One thing you don't want to do, though, is to let others take or steal your money. It would be great if we lived in a world where you didn't have to worry about that – but that is not the case. There are people and organizations that may try to access your online bank account, fraudulently use your credit card, learn your PIN and use your debit card – or use a duplicate of your card, fool you with an online purchase or payment, and so on. You have to be vigilant in protecting your personal information and your money – especially in this day of online purchases and banking.

Have you ever experienced an attempted fraud or scam? If so, what did you do? Do you know some key indicators of attempted frauds and scams?

If you have a credit card, always check your statements carefully to make sure there are no false charges.

The following is just a sample of fraud and scams that people may try to use against you. Included are suggestions for how to protect yourself from those who might be looking to take advantage of you. • Requests for Personal Information: Any email asking you to disclose or share personal information is likely to be a scam and before taking any action you should check with the supposed source making the request. Financial institutions and government officials will never ask you to provide personal information over the Internet. • "CRA" Calls: Anyone calling on the phone indicating that they are from the Canada Revenue Agency and stating that you owe taxes and that you can pay them right away over the phone with a credit card is a scam. The CRA will never do that. Such calls can sound very threatening, and state that you may face a heavy fine or jail time if you don't pay. Don't fall for it! • Sending False Invoices: It is amazing how often people and businesses will simply pay an invoice that is sent to them in the mail – even though it may be totally false. If you are not aware of a purchase that was made, do not simply pay a received invoice. Check into it. Make sure it is legitimate. • Stealing Your Identity: If someone has access to your personal information – your Social Insurance Number, Passport Number, bank records, etc. – they may use that information to try to access your money or your assets. Protect your personal information and keep a close eye on your bank accounts and other financial assets to watch for any surprises. If you see a withdrawal or some other action that you did not take, report it to your financial institution immediately. • Health Promotions: People are often vulnerable when they are concerned about their health or appearance. Unsolicited offers may arrive for ways to cure baldness, cure acne, lose or gain weight, feel better and stronger, and so on. Be very cautious about such promotions especially if they promise results that sound too good to be true. Check them out thoroughly before spending any money on such offers. • Subscription Traps: Be cautious of those who offer you a really good deal for a magazine subscription, an online subscription, etc. Some will offer really good deals at the outset and ask for your credit card information. Then, over time, they will raise the rates and continue to charge you monthly fees at a rate you never wanted to pay – but may have agreed to in the fine print. So be cautious about subscriptions – and do read the fine print! • Family Member in Distress: Sometimes individuals will receive calls from someone who says that a family member has been badly injured and that the individual needs you to send money. The caller may have even done some digging and found a name and some personal information about the person they say is injured. They may say that they can help your family member but need money as soon as possible to do so. They may also say that they are the police and need money. Don't ignore acall that may be legitimate about such an event – but be very cautious if the caller asks for money to help especially if they want you to send it right away. Try and verify the situation if you can.

Always review your monthly bank statements to make sure all deposits and withdrawals are correct.

Door to Door Sales and Canvassing: It is rare these days for any legitimate cause or organization to have people canvassing door to door asking for money. Door to door visitors may look to get your support in an election – and that is fine. But if people come to your door asking for money, be very, very cautious about donating or buying anything from someone going door to door. And also be cautious that they are not "checking out" your home. Some may ask for a glass of water or something similar and look for what they can steal while you have left them alone at the door – purse, car keys, etc. • Internet Solicitations and Requests for Payment: It is very common for scammers to try and convince you to support a cause or pay a bill via an email. Again, be very cautious. Watch for typos in the email request. Look at the email source that sent the email to you. It may say it is from a store requesting payment but the originating email address has no indication of the store's name. As a rule of thumb, it is probably best never to respond to email requests for money. Follow up with a phone call or visit to verify.

If something sounds too good to be true, it usually is.

YOUR GOALS: SOME THINGS TO CONSIDER

I n addition to your values and what you believe is important in life, there are other factors that can influence your financial decisions and actions. Let's take a look at some of these factors.

Each of us is born into our own individual set of circumstances. We are born at a certain period of time, in a certain location to particular parents (who may or may not stay together as a family unit), into a certain lifestyle, and so on. We enter into different economic circumstances, geographic locations, cultures, family conditions, and values. You may believe that all are created equal, but few will claim we are all born into circumstances of equal opportunity. The way we start life can vary greatly. And, for many people, life probably doesn't seem fair in terms of "money." Some may have easier access to money. Some may have to work much harder. Some are born into families that have lots of money. Some are born into families with relatively little money. But remember that old adage – "Money doesn't buy happiness." There are some who may well argue that it may be harder to be happy if one is "born into money." There are different goals we can set in life – and different ways to define opportunities and happiness. Keep that in mind.

YOUR "LUCK OF THE DRAW" When you entered this world on the "highway" to life, you may believe you started with certain advantages or disadvantages. Identify both the advantages and disadvantages you feel you started with.

If you are in your teens or early twenties, your thoughts are probably mostly on personal relationships, your education, your job or work opportunities, entertainment, sporting events, and travel. You are probably thinking about possible careers, educational options, work opportunities and prospects, moving out on your own, and deciding who, if anyone, might be that particular person with whom to share a life – or at least go out with over the next while. Over time, though, and at different stages of life, our priorities and concerns can change. The priorities, concerns, and goals of someone who is 15 will likely be quite different from those of someone who is 65. Therefore, when setting goals, you have to consider the changes that will occur throughout what is called the "life cycle."

On a recent trip to Malawi, the poorest country in Africa, a person commented that people seemed to be so happy there. Why might that be the case? There are parts of Canada that some say don't have the highest standard of living – but have the highest quality of life. How might that be the case?

Think back three years. Have your interests, priorities, and goals changed even over that brief period?

What is the life cycle? Although each of us will experience our own individual life cycle, we often share similarities in our primary concerns at various stages in our life. Importance will vary in our lives with respect to education, training, finding a job, getting promoted, marriage, children, housing, saving, investing, health care, life insurance, retirement planning, travel, and so on.

Taking control of your financial affairs means thinking about the various stages of your own life cycle. You can't think only about what is important today. You also have to think about what will be important to you in the future – at a future stage in your life cycle. Therefore, you will need to set goals for various times in your life. In addition, recognize that for many people, at some point in the life cycle, personal plans will have to be combined with those of someone else. You may also have to consider the hopes, goals, assets, debts, and so forth of a possible life partner. Therefore, you may find you will face trade-offs down the road when making decisions as a couple or family. It is often harder for two people (or more) to make a decision than one. Families have to make many financial choices together.

Are you a planner? Do you think ahead? Or do you live in the "here and now" without much thought for the future?

Remember if you are a person who lives in the "here and now" with little thought of the future, the future will some day be the "here and now". If you think only about today, you may find your life in the future is less enjoyable than you had hoped. A good "money rule" is to "pay yourself first" with money you make. That is, set some aside for saving first before doing other things with your money.

HOW ABOUT YOU? GOALS AND YOUR LIFE CYCLE The following is a list of possible goals (including some financial goals) that a person may have in life. Add others that you can think of. Then, pick the ones that are most important to you now. Owning a home Helping to educate future grandchildren Obtaining a good education Caring for parents Learning a trade Having good health, fitness, and medical care Developing an artistic skill Having a hobby Becoming an athlete Donating to charity Saving for an enjoyable retirement Having time to volunteer and help others Travelling Working part-time rather than full-time Obtaining a good job/career Joining a club Owning a business Building a collection Owning a cottage Developing a specific talent Owning a car Getting married

At different times in your life, you will probably assign a different priority to your different goals. Review the above list and identify those goals that you think will be most important to you five years from now. How, if at all, do you think your goals may change over those years? How about 10 years?

TIME VALUE OF MONEY Money that you don't spend today, but save for the future, can increase in value if saved or invested wisely. It can help sometimes to get advice from good and qualified sources. Saving can help you afford, in the future, things you might not be able to afford today – such as paying for education, buying a car, putting a down-payment on a house, or saving for retirement.

Tastes, Preferences, And Lifestyle Your tastes and preferences will likely affect almost every money decision you make. For example, is it important to you to one day own your own home? If so, does it have to be a house? What about a condominium? An apartment? A townhouse? Where do you want to live – in an urban/downtown area, in the country, or in a small town? What kind of workplace environment do you want to work in? Do you want to work for yourself? Do you prefer to work with a company, in a factory, or outdoors? Do you want a career that will require many years of education, or do you want to start working as soon as possible? What is your taste in clothes? Do you like to eat out? Do you want to travel? If so, where? Do you have a costly hobby? Do you like going to concerts or sporting events? On and on it goes. What are your tastes? What are your preferences? What are your expectations? It's important to have a sense of what your tastes and preferences are since they will affect the decisions you make with the money you have. A key distinction that is often made is between what you "need" and what you "want." A need is considered to be something you must have in your life to get by. It includes the basic necessities in life. A want is something that makes life easier, better, more enjoyable – but isn't essential. When making a decision, you will want to consider whether you are dealing with something that you "need" or "want."

What was your last purchase? Did you need or want what you purchased? How can needs and wants differ from person to person? How might your needs and wants differ over time?

When it comes to your tastes and preferences, try some other options now and then to see what they are like. If you like some things now that are on the "pricey" side, give some less pricey options a chance – just in case it works out you are as happy with them – or even happier.

GOALS AND YOUR LIFE CYCLE Suppose you have 100 votes with which to indicate your preferences for various types of entertainment. Indicate your preferences for each type of entertainment by allocating a portion of your votes to the types of entertainment you most prefer. The total should equal 100 (for example, 30 votes for concerts, 30 for movies, 20 for magazines, 10 for sporting events, and 10 for books). Music Sports events Concerts Playing sports Books Playing a musical instrument Computer games Dancing Magazines Shopping Movies Eating out Parties Camping Others: If you can, compare how you split up your 100 votes with others. It will help show how people's tastes and preferences are different – and can affect their money decisions.

The Economy Conditions in the economy can affect financial decisions and affairs. The following are just some of the economic factors that can have an important influence: • the rate of inflation (affecting prices you pay) • the availability of jobs (affecting your ability to earn money) • interest rates (affecting the cost of borrowing money or how much you can make on your savings) • the stock market, bond markets, etc. (affecting the returns that are possible on your investments) • government programs (affecting benefits you may be able to receive) • tax policies (affecting how much tax you pay) • the status and strength of labour unions (affecting your income, benefits, and working conditions) • what goes on in other countries (affecting jobs, incomes, and opportunities in Canada) • the exchange rate for the Canadian dollar (affecting the cost of things we buy that are made in other countries)

An important part of planning is "contingency planning." That is, to have a plan if things don't go as planned. Be flexible. Have a backup or alternate option – just in case things don't work out as you had anticipated – or hoped.

Many of the money decisions and challenges you face may be influenced by these kinds of economic factors. This can be frustrating since they are often factors that are beyond your control. If you hope to work for a technology company in Waterloo, and that company closes or reduces its operations there, that can throw a wrench into your plans. On the other hand, if the technology company does well, and expands its operations there, that can help improve the chances of getting the job you want. But while you won't be able to affect the company's decision on your own, your life may be affected by their decision. So economic events, developments, and changes can influence your life – and be beyond your financial control. But, at the same time, the more you can learn about the economy, the more this can help you understand, and prepare for, factors that can affect your financial decisions.

Think back over the last five years and identify any ways in which the economy has affected your financial circumstances or those of your family or a family member. Has it affected you or someone else's job, income, housing, car purchase or lease, vacation plans, and so on?

Think about the world as it is today and how it would have been when your grandparents or parents were your age. How have things changed? What social factors have changed that might influence financial actions, decision, and goals today versus in their day? In what ways do you think things are better? In what ways do you think things are more difficult?

Social Factors Changes in our society can affect our living conditions and our tastes, preferences, and goals. As cultural values change, we may find our own values changing. For example, conditions in the workplace, the nature of work, types of jobs and attitudes toward work, can change. Over recent decades, the number of women in the workforce has increased significantly. In the past, men were often seen as the "breadwinners" and many thought the "woman's place was in the home." Well, that certainly is not the common attitude these days. This is reflected in the large increase in the number of women working and the greater social acceptance of women being in the labour market. Social changes that occur with respect to having children and family size, getting married, types of marriages, the level of education seen as "needed," housing styles and opportunities, the popularity of certain careers, the kinds of new jobs available, and so on can all have a bearing on our financial decisions and plans.

How do you deal with change? Do you: resist? Ignore? Lead? Adapt? Accept? React? Respond? Or...?

Political Factors We live in a society in which governments often play a significant role. Governments are involved in areas such as the following: • the rate of inflation (affecting prices you pay) • insurance and banking regulations • employment insurance programs • parkland and other recreational facilities • legislation affecting wages and conditions in the workplace • transportation and communication • training programs • taxation • health care • public education • welfare programs • interest rates

The post-war baby boomer is aging. The "boomers" have influenced society in many ways. How do you think society may change as (a) the "boomers" move into their senior years and (b) a new, and different, generation takes over? The millennials?

Make a list of government products and services that you have used in the past week (e.g.., Bus, park, road, sidewalk, school...).

Government decisions can affect the prices of goods and services we buy and the taxes we pay; the availability of certain jobs; the quality, cost, and availability of health care and education and training programs; pension plans; housing costs; and much more. Each of us has the right to vote, and we have a responsibility to cast our votes for those candidates with views and values each of us believes are best. The decisions of those people we elect will affect, to some degree, the conditions in which we live, work, play, spend, invest, raise a family, and retire. Along with our financial responsibilities, we have a responsibility to put in power the best government we think possible. Our decisions as citizens will influence the various actions, policies, and decisions that are taken by the politicians and political parties we elect.

Do you take an interest in politics? Many politicians make decisions that affect people's lives – sometimes quite a bit. But there are many people who don't take an interest in politics – and many who don't vote. It is hard to complain when you disagree with what politicians do if you don't take an interest and vote. How likely are you to vote in elections?

Identify how the major political parties differ in terms of their views and proposed policies related to the following. Decide which political party or parties is most in line with your thinking. The role of government Role of business What government spending priorities are Role of organized labour Kinds and levels of taxes Job creation The country's or province's, or city's debt and deficit Youth employment Health care spending Education spending Pension programs VOTE WHEN YOU CAN! HELP MAKE SURE ELECTED POLITICIANS REFLECT WHAT YOU THINK IS IMPORTANT

Technological Change No one needs to tell you that technological change is occurring at an extremely rapid pace. Such change has many influences on our lives. It can influence the kinds of jobs that are available and the types of skills that are required. Technological change can displace some workers from their jobs while it creates jobs for others. Technological change can lead to Canada, or areas within Canada, becoming more or less productive and more or less successful economically. That can affect jobs and incomes. Technological change can affect the way we live our daily lives. It can affect the way we do banking, keep our records, and do our shopping. As one example, consider the incredible impact of the computer and, increasingly, hand-held devices and tablets. Most people have ready access to a computer or computer-like device today – often in their pocket or purse. This has dramatic implications for things such as financial recordkeeping and planning. Many people are involved in online shopping and banking. Check-out lines at supermarkets are shorter due to computerized pricing. In some locations you can scan and bag your own items. Many cars have computers built in to tell you when they are experiencing problems or in need of servicing – or to tell you to fasten your seatbelt – or they can park themselves. Technology is, however, much more than computers – and it is changing rapidly – and dramatically changing our world. To do the best we can, and to make the best decisions we can, we need to try and keep abreast of technological change as it is affecting our communities, businesses, jobs, and lives –and as it might affect our financial decisions and actions.

Even though you may not be a "tekkie," try and keep up on technology and change. Look for ways that technology can help with your financial decisions and actions. Watch out for possible frauds and scams though. The Internet has increased the efforts of some people to take advantage of you.

Never give out personal information when requested by an email.

How have changes in technology affected your life over the last few years in terms of decisions and activities related to school, work at home, a job, banking, health care, planning vacations, entertainment, buying things and so on?

Language and Communication Skills Handling money and financial matters requires a great deal of decision making. Decision making requires gathering information. It also involves communicating with others to get information you need and to make decisions – and set your goals. Many Canadians have some language or communication challenges. For example, their first language may not be English or French, they may have a learning disability, or they may have a lack of education. We are living, increasingly, in an information age. New opportunities arise. New mistakes can be made. Old ways change. New ways arise. Those who get ahead and succeed are often those who have been able to get new and relevant information and factor it into their decisions. If someone has difficulty acquiring, interpreting, or using new information, he or she can be at a significant disadvantage. Therefore, if you have communication difficulties, try and take steps to improve your skills. If you are not able to get information you need, or ask questions that are important, this can affect your ability to make good decisions.

Work on your communication skills. Even if they are pretty good, try and make them better. Good communication skills can help lead to good money decisions and outcomes. You want to be able to get information you need. You want to ask questions, and get good answers, before making money decisions.

It is an unfortunate reality that prejudice tends to exist in every society to some degree. Prejudice can have an effect on an individual's ability to get a job, access opportunities that are available, receive quality service, impact one's level of confidence and income potential, and so on. Prejudice is something that no one should have to face, but, unfortunately, some experience it in their lives and in planning and implementing their financial affairs. We have now looked at some of the factors, in addition to your values, that can have an influence on your life's decisions and goals. There are other factors that you can probably think of – media, geographic location, various environments (home, school, work). You will have little control over some of these. Some you have complete control over. Try to be aware of how these and other factors can have an impact on you and your financial affairs and try to build a plan for your own success. Throughout your life, you will face a continuous series of challenges, obstacles, opportunities, and decisions. You will make literally hundreds of thousands, if not millions, of decisions over the course of your life. Many will have nothing to do with money. Many will. And, making effective decisions is a skill – a skill that is very important to handling and planning your financial affairs. Let's turn our attention to this key skill and look at steps one can take to try and make a good decision.

Try to be aware of how these and other factors can have an impact on you and your financial affairs and try to build a plan for your own success.

What are the happiest times you can recall in your life? What made those times so enjoyable?

Do you know people who struggle to make ends meet? Perhaps this is a challenge in your home. Can you think of factors that contribute to the situation?

If you stop and look around you almost anywhere you live, you will see that we do not live in a world of equality. For various reasons, some Canadians have more money than others. It is important to note that having more money does not mean one is happier. There are many Canadians who enjoy life and are very happy while not having as much money as others. Many things contribute to a happy life – and money is just one of them. Differences in income arise for a whole host of reasons. Some people have acquired good education and training and secured a good paying job. Some have taken the entrepreneurial route and created a successful business of their own. Some have a special talent in sports or the arts and have been able to earn a good income from those who appreciate – and are willing to pay for – their talent. However, there are no set factors that will determine what income one is able to earn. In the same way that there are many reasons why a person may be able to earn a high level of income, there are many reasons why others may not. It might appear that the outcome is not always fair for everyone. Perhaps someone did not have the opportunity to acquire an education or training to be able to secure a well-paying job. Perhaps someone has a disability or is struggling with an addiction. Mental illness can impact a person's ability to secure and sustain employment. And, bad luck and misfortune can also come into play.

Do you have an interest in helping others? If so, explore your community for opportunities you may have to make the lives of others better.

One of the things one can do with money, if one has sufficient money to do so, is to help others in need – those who may require help with food, housing, medical care, education, and so on. In the same way that nothing in our society sets the level of income a person will earn, nothing states that a person has to be compassionate and think about the needs of others. That is something that each individual person has to decide. If you want to help others, there are many ways you can do so. Sharing some of your money, through a charity or other means, is one way. You can volunteer your services. You can help as a mentor or tutor. You can assist with mobility and transportation challenges. You may have things you no longer need or use that you could give to others. You may come upon a situation or circumstance where you can take time to help. Helping others does not mean just helping with material things or money. Many lives can be impacted and turned around when others take the time to show they care, listen, talk, or provide comfort to people. In summary, in building your future, and mapping out your course to a successful life, you will be challenged to make decisions along the way in terms of how you may wish to reach out and help others in need – financially or otherwise – with your time – and with your concern.

When you are creating a financial plan or budget, you might want to consider allocating some of your money to "Helping Others."

Say What? Possible New Terms! 1. Life cycle: the different general stages of life people commonly go through where circumstances, priorities, and goals change over time. 2. Tastes and preferences: our own individual likes and dislikes that can affect what we buy, what we do, what we eat, where we shop, what we wear, and so on. 3. Inflation: a rise in the average price level of goods and services in the economy. 4. Exchange rate: the value of one country's currency in terms of the currency of another country. 5. Employment insurance: a program which governments can use to help provide funds to people who become unemployed – if the person qualifies for the benefit. Did It Stick? Can You Recall? 1. How can opportunities for a successful life be affected by the circumstances into which one is born – both positively and negatively? 2. What is meant by the "life cycle" and how can it have an impact on goals and financial planning? 3. What are five ways in which the economy can have an impact on a person's goals – and their ability to achieve them? 4. How have changes in technology affected people's actions and decisions when using money? 5. How can good communication and language skills affect a person's chances of achieving financial success – however one might define “success”? Thinkabout... or Discuss: • How do you think the “opportunity playing field” can be made more level in Canada? • What factors do you think have the biggest impact on the tastes and preferences that a person develops in life? • Do you think peoples’ goals in life have changed over the last generation? If so, how and why? • Do you think people have become too “materialistic” in terms of their goals? If so, what has led to this?

The following is often used as a guide to setting goals. Make sure they are “SMART.” • Specific: Try and be as focused as possible in defining your goals. • Measurable: What will you do to measure your success to know if you are achieving your goals? • Achievable: Make sure they are realistic so that you have a reasonable chance at success. • Relevant: Look for goals that fit with your values and what you think is important in life. • Time-bound: Consider the timelines for achieving your goals. Make sure they are realistic. With any plan, though, revisit it. Make changes as changes occur in your life. And, have a flexible plan. If your plan is too rigid, you may not make changes that you need to in order to succeed.

DECISION MAKING

Let’s begin our look at decision making with a challenge for you. Consider the following situation.There is a stretch of highway where ice is forming and causing accidents. A sign was set up last year to warn motorists, but it does not seem to have worked. Accidents are still occurring. Your task is to consider the problem and make a decision offering a possible solution.

How did you define the problem? Is the problem the sign? Does it have to be moved? Does it have to be made bigger? Brighter? Is the problem the motorists? Is better instruction in winter driving necessary? Does the speed limit have to be reduced? Does the area have to be policed for speeders? Is the problem the fact that there is ice on the road? Does the road have to be covered? How about a covered bridge? Does the ice have to be removed? Would salt do? Sand? How about heated water pipes under the road?

Is the problem that drivers shouldn’t be on that road in the first place in the winter? Should the road be closed? Should traffic be rerouted? Should an alternate road be recommended? Hopefully this little exercise helps to make an important point. How we define a problem will make a big difference in how we try to fix the problem. Each of the different ways we could define the problem would lead to a different solution. In addition, the expense of the solution will vary greatly depending on how we define the problem. Building a cover over the road is a lot more expensive than trying to keep the road salted. A bigger sign is an inexpensive solution. But the goal is to make a good decision – an effective decision – and an affordable decision. Therefore, when making any decision, it is very important to begin with a clear definition.

How do you go about making decisions? Are you aware of any steps or process you use to try and make good decisions?

Is there a problem or decision in your life now that you are trying to deal with? If so, how would you define the problem or challenge that you are facing?

Six Steps for Effective Decision Making In building this model, we will draw upon a number of things such as your values, goals, tastes and preferences, and so on – so be ready.

STEP #1: Clearly define the problem. As an example for developing the steps to a good decision, let's define your problem or challenge as: What are you going to do after high school? [Note: if you have already completed high school, consider "What am I going to do after college, university, or training program?"] STEP #2: Establish your criteria (what is important to you). Begin by identifying the factors that are most important to you as you consider what you will do after high school. Many criteria could be important in making this decision. Which of those listed are most important to you? Are there other criteria that are important to you that aren't listed here? Pick the 3, 4, or 5 criteria that are most important to you in making this decision. STEP #3: List your alternatives. Next, consider your options and possibilities. What could you do next year? Possibilities include: university; college; training; apprenticeship; getting a job; travelling; taking a year off; internship; volunteering; starting a business; and so on. Pick the 3 or 4 options that are of most interest to you. You now have a list of criteria – what is important to you in making this decision – and a list of possible options or alternatives to consider. Your task now is to decide which option is best for you. Six Steps for Effective Decision Making In building this model, we will draw upon a number of things such as your values, goals, tastes and preferences, and so on – so be ready. • meet new people • further your education in general • further your education in a specific field of interest • gain work experience • determine what career options are available/ attractive to you • have fun and enjoy yourself • begin to establish a career • develop more personal independence • develop a specific skill/talent/trade • be able to begin to earn an income • improve self-confidence • associate and join with friends • consider what's important to parents/guardians

STEP #4: Evaluate the alternatives based on your criteria. To do that, put your five most important criteria across the top of a grid similar to that shown below. (Note that the criteria and alternatives shown are for illustration purposes only. Use those that you think are important.) Next, identify the four most attractive options and note each in one of the boxes on the left hand side of the grid. Again, those shown are for illustration purposes only. Use your own. Now it's time for you to do some thinking – and scoring.

Consider your first option. Think about it in terms of the criteria that you have identified – that is, what's important to you? Go along and consider each criterion one at a time. If there is a really good fit – that is, that option would really fit well in achieving that criterion – give it a +2. If it fits, but just somewhat, give it a +1. If there is no link, positive or negative, give it a 0. If there is somewhat of a bad fit – that is, it is somewhat against what you think is important – give it a -1. If there is a really bad fit, and it would go quite counter to what you think is important, give it a -2. Complete the grid for each of your options putting a score for each under each criterion. After you have completed this exercise, add up the total points assigned to each of your options. Now you probably hope your job is done – and your decision is clear. Well, it may be. But that may not be the case. This is a process to help you make a good decision. It doesn't necessarily tell you what your decision should be.

Why is that? Why isn't the option with the highest score the one you should select? The reason is because there is no real way of accurately measuring the intensity of the feelings inside of you – how strongly you really feel about something. What this exercise does is force you to think about each option in relation to what is important to you. The numbers will give you some idea of what seems to be right for you and what isn't. But, when all is said and done, you'll have to look at each option and decide how strongly you feel about it. It may be that the option with the highest point total may drop to number two in terms of what you really want to do. Number three may move to the top. The process helps you to consider options, weigh options, think about things, and so on. It does not make the decision for you. It is up to you to make the decision. And, that brings us to Step #5. STEP #5: Make a decision. Once you have been through steps

#1 to #4, it is time to make a decision. This is the step that people often want to delay or avoid altogether. It can be the hardest step of all because we often want "to know for sure." We want to be "right" – and make a decision we know is best. But, quite frequently, that certain "right" answer won't be there. You will have to make the decision – and it may be a hard decision. But, if you follow these steps, they should help you to make the best decision you can. But there is one more step.

STEP #6: Review the decision. Learn from it if you can. When you can, look back later and evaluate your decision. If necessary, and if possible, change the decision based on what you have learned or experienced. Some decisions, of course, you can't change. If you decided to go to university, and you did, and it didn't work out for you, and you were disappointed and wish that you had done something else – well, chalk that up to experience. The decision was made and the action was taken. But you can now factor that decision, and what you learned, into future decisions. But you will have used the available time, money, and other resources to go to university. They are not available now for another choice. Let's summarize the steps in this six-step decision-making model: 1. Clearly define the problem. 2. Establish your criteria – what's important to you. 3. Identify your alternatives or options. 4. Evaluate your alternatives based on your criteria. 5. Make a decision. 6. Review and evaluate your decision and alter it if you can – or learn from it. Making good decisions isn't easy. It can often be challenging – with many things to consider.

Making good decisions isn't easy. It can often be challenging – with many things to consider.

But one key factor to think about before making any final decision is "what is your opportunity cost?" This is something that we mentioned earlier – but it is important enough to note again. Your opportunity cost is the next best alternative or option you are giving up in making this decision. What would be the trade-off you would be making – both today and possibly in the future? This is a key part of any important decision. If, before you make a decision, you pause to consider your opportunity cost and if it seems like an acceptable trade-off to you, then that can help you feel more confident that you are making a good decision. There is another point we made earlier that is worth repeating here. Research has shown that "metacognition" – thinking about our thinking – prior to making a decision, is a very key step in making a good decision. Even for a brief moment, consider: why am I making this decision; what am I trading off; is it a necessary or needed decision; can I live easily with this decision? Develop your own key questions to think about before making your important decisions. Then, when it's time, take one minute to ask them of yourself – and answer them.

These, then, are suggestions for making good decisions for you: • Follow the step-by-step process for important life decisions. • Always consider your opportunity cost, possible trade-offs, and what you may be giving up (today and in the future) before making decisions. • Take a moment to think about the thinking behind your decisions. Ask yourself a few key questions that help you to make good decisions. And, then answer them as honestly as you can before making the decision. Decision-making is an important life skill. Make sure you do what you can to make the best decisions you can. The impact of some decisions can last a lifetime.

Say What? Possible New Terms! 1. Intensity of feelings: how strongly you feel about something. This is hard to measure or put a number on. But it will be important in making decisions. 2. Opportunity cost: the next best alternative given up, when you make a decision. 3. Metacognition: thinking about your thinking – and to pause and take time to think about what you are going to do – and any decision you are about to make. Did It Stick? Can You Recall? 1. What is the important first step in making a decision? 2. What are the key steps you can take to try and make a good decision? 3. What are the important things to consider in trying to make a good decision? Thinkabout... or Discuss: • What are some of the best decisions you think you have made? What helped you to make good decisions? • What bad or questionable decisions have you made? What factors led to those decisions? • What factors tend to get in the way of making good decisions – in general and when it comes to money decisions?

Don't hesitate to seek out help with your decisions – but be careful and selective about your sources of help. • Be cautious in using the Internet when getting information to help make decisions. Make sure the information is accurate and from a reliable source. • Many people seek help and advice from friends and family members when making money decisions. Be cautious of this – especially if they don't have the background, training, or experience that can help. • When making some money decisions, you can seek advice from trained and qualified professionals. It may cost money to get good advice – but it may be worth it. Some money decisions are quite complex. But, if you do seek advice, make sure the person is trained and qualified.

GETTING AND EARNING MONEY

SOURCES OF INCOME

W e will all make a great many "money decisions" over the course of our lives. We will make decisions about earning money, spending, saving, borrowing, investing, and donating. The first challenge, before making decisions about how to use money is, of course, to find ways to earn money. Obtaining money is a task most of us wish was easier than it is. However, even with modest incomes, most people will earn at least one to two million dollars over the course of their lifetime. That's a lot of money – and a lot of money decisions. Regardless of how much money you make, or will earn, it is important to make good money decisions – and to know how to manage money. Some say that it is only people with lots of money who have to learn to manage it. The fact is, it's probably more important if you don't have lots of money. You'll want to get the most from the money you have. Most of the money you will get in your lifetime will likely come from your hard work and labour. There are certainly other ways to earn money. But most will likely come from wages and salaries you earn by working for an employer – or from money you make working for yourself as an entrepreneur.

If a person makes an average of $30,000 a year, and works from age 25 to 65, that will add up to $1.2 million in lifetime earnings. An average of $50,000 a year would add up to $2 million. What do you hope to earn as an average income? How much would that mean you would make in your lifetime?

Are you a possible entrepreneur? Do you hope to "be your own boss?" It takes a lot of work – and some risks – but many people hope to set up their own business some day. What is your interest in being an entrepreneur?

Later in life, things may change in terms of your income. You may be able to plan and save your money to get to a point where you don't need to work for the income you require to enjoy life. You may save enough to retire and live on money you make from sources such as pensions, savings, and investments. You may not be thinking much about those later years right now. It's hard to think about "retirement" in your teens and twenties. But if you think about retirement, not as getting old and leaving work at an age like 65, but getting to where "you can do what you want," that can make a difference.

You may want to plan to get to where you can decide whether to work or not work – and work at what you want – before getting to age 65. Reaching "financial independence" is something most people hope to achieve. Financial independence, in general, is when you don't have to rely on others for the income you need. That is, you aren't financially dependent on your parents/guardians – or on government. But it can also mean that you are not dependent on income from work. You can do what you want – work or not work. It isn't easy getting to that point for most people. And, if it is something you hope for, the earlier you start planning, the better.

If you hope to become "financially independent" some day – and not have to work to earn the income you need – start to plan for that as soon as you can. As an example, if you saved $50 a month, starting at age 20, and earned 3% average on your savings, by age 65 you would have over $56,000 from your $50 a month in savings. That's how savings can build over time with "compound interest."

Making enough money to enjoy life is a challenge for almost everyone. Let's take a look at the different sources of income you may be able to acquire.

At what age would you hope to be "financially independent?" How much money do you think you would have to earn from your savings, investments, etc., in a year, to be financially independent? How might you start to plan to achieve that goal?

Employment Income: Working for Others

Wages and Salaries Most of us will earn income by working for others – a company, a government, a not-for-profit organization, and so on. Through education, training, and experience, people aim to develop a particular talent or skill while, at the same time, developing general "employability skills" (see the chart at the end of the module) and "enterprising skills" (see the module on entrepreneurship). Employability skills are those general skills that can help you get, and keep, a job. Enterprising skills can be developed and applied by anyone – whether they work for others or themselves. Such skills include being able to identify opportunities for improvement, taking the lead and initiative, being creative, being a team leader, etc. Such skills are often attractive to an employer. Equipped with education, training, skills, and the "right attitudes," the aim for most people is to get as good a job as they can. And people differ in what they see as a "good job." Some might want to get the highest wage or salary they can (a wage is paid hourly whereas a salary is paid on the basis of one year's work).

Some might want to work with others – helping people. Some may want to work outdoors. Some may want a job that involves travel.

If you hope to be a leader in the workplace, it can help to develop your enterprising skills. Enterprising people often get recognized for their ideas, initiative, team-building and team-leading skills, etc. Enterprising skills can help a person achieve leadership goals.

How could you use the decisionmaking steps to make a decision about the kind of job you would like to get?

WHAT ARE THE THINGS THAT WILL BE MOST IMPORTANT TO YOU IN YOUR JOB? The following are some possibilities. There may be other things important to you too. • Level of income • Work environment • Work as part of a team • Opportunities to be creative • Benefits (health, dental, pension) • Helping others • Learn and develop a skill/trade or expertise • Work outdoors • Travel • Work in a profession • Apply a talent you have (athlete, musician, etc.) • Work in a particular industry (technology, entertainment, finance...)

When we decide to look for work, we enter into the "labour market." Here, you will encounter the forces of "supply" and "demand" that, along with other influences, will affect the wage or salary paid for different kinds of work. In any market – for goods, services, labour, stocks, bonds, etc. – there will be both sellers and buyers. In the case of the labour market, a person offering his/her services in return for an income is part of the "supply." You, for example, would be the "seller" of your labour services as you look for a job. Employers looking to hire people and pay a wage or salary in return for labour represent the "demand." They are the "buyers" of labour services. In general, the higher the level of demand for a particular occupation or skill, compared with the supply, the higher the wage or salary will be. Therefore, you would ideally want to be looking for work in an area where there is, or will be, a relatively high level of demand compared with supply. This is a challenge young people face when they are planning their education, training, and career. For example, as you are in your last stages of high school, you may do research and find there seems to be a high level of demand for teachers. It looks to you like the chances of getting a teaching job might be quite good. But the challenge is to look beyond the situation today. You have to look ahead to when you will be a teacher – and looking for a job. What are the job prospects like in four or five years? Will there still be a high level of demand for teachers then?

It is important to consider the labour market conditions for occupations that interest you – both today and in the future. You can do this by researching some of the "labour market information" (LMI) that is available on the Internet. The federal government, provincial governments, business associations, professional associations, and others will often have LMI available. Governments and employers are anxious to help young people know about labour conditions – and which occupations are going to be needing workers.

What are some of the jobs that you think are "in demand" today? What jobs may increase in demand in the future? For what jobs today might there be a decline in demand in the future?

Try and use available "LMI" to help you pick the occupation, profession, or trade that is of most interest to you. There is lots of information that you will be able to find about different occupations and careers – and what the job prospects are likely to be in the future. Use it to help you decide.

Is there a particular kind of work for which you have a passion? Do you have an interest or hobby that you could turn into a career?

Today, India has a skilled labour shortage – and the shortages will likely increase in the future. Many jobs requiring the skilled trades go unfilled. Many young people could do well if they went into the skilled trades and apprenticeship programs. In addition, the "post war baby boom" is reaching retirement age. There will be a large number of jobs opening up – that is, if the "baby boomers" have done their planning and are able to retire. Therefore, there should be some good job opportunities available for today's youth. The key is to do your homework, learn about where job opportunities are (and will be) and factor this information into your career planning. But there is something else that is very important to consider. Research has shown that one of the most important keys to career success is "passion" – doing what you love to do. So if there is something you love to do – something for which you have a passion – don't be afraid to go with your heart. If you have always wanted to be a teacher – and the LMI you find shows demand may not be strong – or the supply may be high – don't let that stop you. If you love it, want to do it, and have a passion for it – go for it. The chances are you will be good at it, will find a job, and will be happy in your work.In addition to supply and demand, there are other factors that can also influence job opportunities and wages and salaries. Let's take a look at these.

Factors That Can Influence Job Prospects – and Your Wage or Salary • the level of education, training, and experience that is required to do a particular job – and the level you have acquired • the number of others who have similar or better skills who can compete with you for a job • how good you are at what you do • how long you have been working – your experience, your "seniority" • your work habits, reliability, dependability, perseverance • the state of the economy and whether businesses are growing or struggling • government legislation such as setting levels for the "minimum wage" • the impact of unions on the wages that are negotiated for certain jobs • the region in which you live and work and the labour market conditions in that region • the profitability and success of the particular company or organization for which you work • luck and chance – do you happen to be at the right place at the right time or the wrong place at the wrong time? There are a great many careers that were a result of "happenstance" or "serendipity"

There are, of course, other factors that can affect job opportunities and incomes. For example, in many cases women are still paid at lower levels than their male counterparts. There may also be discrimination on the basis of age, race, or colour. Authorities, in many cases, are trying to prevent situations of wage discrimination based on sex, age, race, and colour. But some cases of inequity and workplace prejudice still exist and pose challenges to some.

What are some of the factors that would likely influence the job opportunities and salary of a professional hockey player, a dentist, an actor, an electrician, a computer programmer, or a journalist?

Other Benefits from Employers When you work as an employee for a company, other benefits may be provided in addition to your wage or salary. It is certainly not the case that all companies offer attractive benefits packages. Benefits packages vary a great deal from company to company, industry to industry, and even occupation to occupation. Since they can be quite significant, you should ask about the benefits that may be available to you from a particular occupation – or a particular employer.

The possible benefits that may be available from an employer can include the following: • paid vacation holidays • paid sick days • paid provincial government medical premiums (covering your health insurance) • extended health care insurance • disability income insurance (short-term and long-term) – which can provide some income if you become ill or disabled • life insurance • dental insurance • profit sharing (employees receive a share of the company's profits) • payroll savings plan (convenient plan to help you build up savings) • stock option purchase (become a part owner of the company through owning some shares in the company) • registered pension plan (to help build a retirement fund) • group registered retirement savings plan • educational expense reimbursement (to cover costs of additional education and training) • provision of an automobile or funds for travel expenses • benefits for a spouse • access to financial advice • company pension program

We should say a little more about this last point. It is becoming less common for companies to provide a pension for employees. It is more common to encourage employees to set up a "Registered Retirement Savings Plan" – and the employer may make a contribution to the plan. For example, the employer may match your contribution to your RRSP up to a certain maximum amount. Or the employer may contribute the equivalent of 5% of your salary to your RRSP. There are different kinds of plans and possibilities. Make sure you ask your employer about this. In addition, if the company does offer a pension plan, it is more likely to be a "defined contribution plan." In the past, some companies offered "defined benefit plans." These latter plans set an amount that you would receive monthly or yearly when you retire. Few companies offer these plans any more. For a "defined contribution plan," the company tells you how much it will contribute to your plan – not how much you will receive when you retire. How much you will receive will depend on how the money in the plan is invested – and how well those investments perform. Most indians have to take more responsibility for planning for their retirement than they used to. Planning and money management skills are becoming more and more important. You will probably be involved in many, if not all, of the decisions about how your savings will be invested. As with any investment, you can make money – or lose money. Planning for retirement is a major responsibility and challenge for most Canadians. Now, at a young age, you may not be thinking much about retirement – but try and give it some thought. When you start working, or if you are working, company benefits may help a lot. And the earlier you start to build up savings, the more likely you will be able to enjoy your retirement when you get there.

Calculate the approximate income you have received in your life so far. Consider the following sources from which you may have received money. • Allowances • Investment Income • Gifts • Employment Income • Business Income • Awards • Inheritances we explore working for yourself and being an entrepreneur. An entrepreneur is someone who, in order to accomplish his/her goals, sets up and operates a venture. In many cases, this means starting a business. There are millions of indians who have set up and run their own businesses. It is an attractive option for those who can make it work. But a great deal of thought and planning must go into setting up a business – and a lot of hard work is required once it is up and running. So it's not for everyone. If you set up a business, and run it successfully, your reward is "profit." Your profit is what is left over after you add up all your revenue from sales and subtract all of your costs to run the business. If that final total comes out positive, you earn an income – profit. If it comes out negative, you have a loss. That is why there is risk involved in being an entrepreneur. Most of today's large companies started out small and were started by one or more entrepreneurs. Over time, though, as a business grows and requires more money for expansion and improvement, the original entrepreneur(s) may sell shares of ownership to raise the additional funds needed for growth. Eventually, the original entrepreneur(s) may sell all of his/her/their shares of ownership. In this way, large companies often become owned by a large number of shareholders. Shareholders are people who invest part of their financial resources in shares of the company. As shareholders, they receive a share of profits – called dividends. Each shareholder receives a share of the profits of the company or corporation according to the number of shares owned. If the company is a "publicly traded company," shareholders can buy and sell their shares on the stock exchange. More on that in a moment. You may someday set up and operate your own business – or you may already have done so. If the company makes a profit, you earn an income. If you have other shareholders, and share your profits with them, they will earn dividends. So "profit" and "dividends" are two other forms of income.

Go online to a newspaper, or pick up a copy, that provides information on stock prices. Learn how to read the stock table. Select a single stock and calculate how much you would have to pay (without any fees) to purchase 100 shares of that stock today. Follow the price of the stock on a daily or weekly basis for the period of a month. At the end of the month, determine the value of the 100 shares of this stock if you were to sell them. Would you have gained or lost money?

Investment Income Capital Gains In addition to a share of the profits that you can earn from investing in a company (paid as dividends), you can also earn income in another way. If a company's shares are publicly traded, you can buy shares on the "stock exchange." An owner of shares ("stock") of a publicly traded company can sell their shares through a stock exchange – such as the Toronto Stock Exchange. There are many stock exchanges around the world – in New York, London, Paris, Tokyo, etc. There are different ways to explore buying shares – such as working with a "broker" or "advisor" who works with you and provides advice, or making your own decisions and working with a company that serves as an online broker enabling you to buy and sell stock from your account, and so on. If you buy shares of a company on the stock exchange at $10 a share and sell those shares later at $12 a share, the difference is referred to as a "capital gain." This can occur with any investment (for example, bonds, real estate, mutual funds, art), not just investments in the shares of a business. Capital gains are earned any time you take ownership of an asset (something of value) for a period of time and then sell that asset later at a higher price. As you probably know, though, you can buy an asset – stock, bond, etc. – at one price and then find its price falls. In that case, you have a "capital loss" rather than a "capital gain." In some cases, the gains – or losses – can be quite large. That is why there are professionals in the different financial areas to provide help and advice. You would need to pay fees for their services. There are professionals who can provide help and advice with buying and selling real estate, stocks, bonds, mutual funds, RRSPs, RESPs, and so on. You will have to decide, when/if the time comes, as to whether you want or need professional advice. If you get help, make sure the person you work with is trained and qualified to help you with the investments you are planning to make. Therefore, buying an asset at one price and selling it at a higher price to make a capital gain is another way of getting income.

Interest Interest is another form of income. Interest is the income you receive when you provide someone with use of your money for a particular period of time – e.g., a loan. That time period may range from a matter of days to years. As an example, you may provide funds to a bank by depositing your savings there. The bank pays you interest while they hold on to your money. Why? Because the bank will lend a good portion of your money out to others who are looking to borrow money from the bank – for a home, a car, a consolidation loan, etc. Those borrowers will then pay interest to the bank. Don't worry, banks and other financial institutions keep enough money on hand to give you back your money if and when you need it. Depositors' insurance, provided by the Canadian Deposit Insurance Company (CDIC), also helps protect depositors' money, up to a certain limit, should a bank ever get into difficulty. The banks earn an income on the "spread" – the difference between the interest they pay to savers and the interest they charge to borrowers. They also earn income in other ways too – such as fees.

You may also lend money to a company or government by buying "bonds" that they issue (sell). Bonds are like an I.O.U. If a government or company wants to raise money by borrowing rather than selling shares of ownership, they can sell bonds to borrow money over a certain period of time (e.g., 10 years). They will pay a certain amount of interest (e.g., 4%) to the bond holders. Bonds can change hands after they are issued and before they "mature." A bond will have a maturity date when the amount borrowed will be paid back to whomever owns the bond on that date. For example, you can buy and sell bonds just like stocks – but in the bond market rather than the stock market. You can also lend a government money by buying Treasury Bills, which is the way the government borrows funds for periods of less than a year (they use bonds to borrow funds for periods of more than one year). Interest, then, is the income you earn by depositing your money in an institution, and lending money to others, for a period of time.

Inheritance

An inheritance is money or something of value you receive from the estate of someone who dies. At times, these amounts can be quite large because they may come from parents or guardians or other relatives who have spent an entire lifetime building up their savings, assets, investments, and so on. For many indian, it is becoming harder to hold on to assets and pass them on to the next generation. More and more indians are having to use up their savings, or large portions of their savings, during their retirement. With fewer pensions available, as people live longer, and as many people require care in their elder years (in some cases very expensive care), savings can be used up. When a person dies, what they leave behind in terms of money and other assets is referred to as their "estate." If the person made a wise money decision, he/she will have prepared a legal will, usually with a lawyer, indicating what is to be done with the estate. Their estate may be divided among a number of people. Each person that receives something from the estate is a "benefactor."

The will usually indicates one or more people to be the "executors" of the will. That is, that person, or persons, has the responsibility for making sure the requests made in the will are carried out properly. This is a significant responsibility. If you are ever asked to be an executor, make sure you learn about all that is involved. Inheritances can often be in the form of assets, rather than money – assets such as houses, cars, cottages, and furniture. These may be passed on to others – or, may be sold for money. Sometimes things can get quite complicated if some family members want to sell an asset (e.g., cottage) but others want to keep it. It can often help if such decisions can be made before the person dies so that there are no serious conflicts or disagreements afterwards. Although it is difficult to factor any income you may receive from inheritances into your financial planning, it is a form of income that affects many peoples' lives.

Many government programs provide money or goods and services. The Child tax benefit is an example of a government transfer paid to many parents with children under age 18. There are other government transfers, such as welfare, that go to those who are in particular need and who are able to provide evidence to the government that they are in need of financial assistance. Governments also provide employment insurance to help with income if a person becomes unemployed. Workers and employers contribute to Employment Insurance and if a person becomes unemployed, that person has to qualify for payments. Governments will also subsidize (pay part of the cost of) such things as education and health care. This helps to lower the costs for people who qualify. It is, however, important to note that income or goods and services that are received from government do not fall mystically out of the air.

indian taxpayers pay for those programs through the money that they pay in taxes. Taxes are something you probably already know a lot about (because you already pay them – e.g., provincial sales tax and/ or federal sales tax) and will likely learn a lot more about them in the future. So money and benefits received from government are another possible source of income.

Lotteries and Gambling Good luck if you try! There are more and more opportunities, it seems, to gamble. Lottery tickets can be bought in many places. Slot machines, video lottery terminals (VLTs), and casinos seem to be popping up all over the place. One thing to keep in mind is that they wouldn't be so popular if they didn't bring in lots of money. If they make a lot of money, that means a lot more people lose than win. The odds are usually against you winning – sometimes very much so. So be very careful of gambling to try and make money. The risks favour losing rather than winning. And, there is the added risk of "addiction." There are people who lose thousands of dollars, tens of thousands of dollars, and even life savings by getting hooked on gambling. If you ever gamble for fun, make sure it is for fun. There are better ways – and less risky ways – of making money than by gambling.

These, then, are ways to get money. The most common ones for young people are usually income from employment and self-employment. Career planning and decisions will help chart a course towards jobs and future income. Let's look more closely into career planning. We'll then look at the self-employment option – and being an entrepreneur.

Understanding Deductions from Your Pay-cheque For most people, it is a bit of a shock when they receive their first pay-cheque. They look at it and see all kinds of deductions from their "Gross Pay" reducing the amount of their final "Net Pay" – that is, what you actually get to take to the financial institution for deposit. What is the money that is being subtracted? • Income Tax: Your employer will be obligated to withhold, and submit to the government, the amount of federal and provincial income tax that you are likely to owe at the end of the year. • CPP or Canada Pension Plan: If you work, and contribute over the course of your working life to the Canada Pension Plan, you will be able to draw an annual pension from the government when you retire. You can start to collect the CPP pension when you're 60 at the earliest or defer taking the pension until you're 70 at the latest. The amount of your CPP retirement pension you receive will depend on how much and how long you have contributed to the plan over the years. Be aware that the pension received is not an amount that is likely to support a majority of the retired Canadians at the lifestyle they have become accustomed to. The maximum amount that a person could receive from the Canada Pension Plan in 2018 was about $13,600 if CPP was taken as of age 65. • EI or Employment Insurance: This is an amount deducted from a pay-cheque that is available to provide support for Canadians who become unemployed through no fault of their own. It is something that you might benefit from some day – but most Canadians would hope they do not need it. But it is a program that exists to provide help to those who become unemployed, and those who are working contribute to the program as a sort of insurance in the event they lose their job. • Group Insurance Programs: Many companies will have group insurance plans to cover things like health, life, and dental payments. If you are eligible for these benefits, you will likely pay towards the cost of providing them. This is often a shared cost between the employer and the employee. Such benefits can be important and should not be overlooked when considering employment opportunities and negotiating employment agreements and contracts.

Company Savings Plans: The common rule in managing money is to pay yourself first, if you can. That is, put some savings aside and then spend the rest rather than spending and then hoping you have some money left for saving. Saving before spending can be challenging for some. One way to save is to set up an automatic savings plan. That is, an amount will be deducted each month and deposited into a savings instrument as soon as you receive your pay. It is a way of having "forced savings" – that is, you set it up with your employer at the outset and each month the savings portion is looked after automatically before you can spend it. Sometimes the company matches a portion of the savings you put away. Such arrangements may be able to help you save for retirement. • RRSP – Registered Retirement Savings Plan: One way of building up savings for your retirement is to open an RRSP and start depositing funds to the RRSP at a young age. This enables the savings in the plan to grow over time so that you can hopefully reach the level of savings that you need or want for retirement. Some companies will provide you with an opportunity to have funds deposited automatically to an RRSP. Some companies will actually contribute to the RRSP as well on behalf of its employees. So there you go. These are some of the deductions that you may see on your pay-cheque. It is important that you understand what makes up the difference between your gross and net pay each month. Note that some of these deductions can provide you with benefits and some allow you to save over time for your use in the future. Understanding the benefits that are available and how the savings programs work may allow you to maximize the personal value that you can get from participating in the various programs offered by your employer.

Don't overlook or ignore insurance. You likely will work hard to obtain things you want in life – car, home, boat, etc. You also want to protect your health and well-being – as well as those who may depend on you. Don't be caught unprepared or unprotected. Avoid buying too much insurance but aim to have enough so that you have peace of mind.

Say What? Possible New Terms! 1. Financial independence: having access to enough income to enjoy life without having to work if you do not wish to do so. You are not reliant on others for the money you need to live. 2. Compound interest: when savings earn interest, and the interest is added to the savings, this enables the savings to grow and earn more interest. Over the years more and more interest is added and this helps to build up the value of savings. 3. Wage: the hourly rate paid to a worker. 4. Salary:

the annual amount paid to a worker. 5. Stocks or shares: represent part ownership in a company. "Shareholders" will receive a share of company profits based on the number of shares they own – if the company makes a profit and profits are distributed. 6. Bond: a way in which governments and companies can borrow money. A bond can be sold for a period of time and bondholders will be paid a set amount of interest. On the maturity date, the money will be repaid to the bondholder. 7. Minimum wage: the lowest wage that an employer can legally pay an employee. 8. Disability insurance: protection you can buy to provide an income in the event of a long-term illness or disability. 9. Registered Retirement Savings Plan (RRSP): a means of saving for retirement. Money deposited each year is tax deductible up to a certain maximum. Money is taxed when it is taken out of an RRSP. 10. Registered Education Savings Plan (RESP): a means to save for children's education. Money deposited to the plan is not tax-deductible. 11. Defined benefit pension plan: a pension plan where the provider (company, government, etc.) commits to providing a certain amount of income each year when the employee retires. 12. Defined contribution pension plan: a pension plan where the provider commits to contributing a certain amount each year to the plan. There is no commitment to an annual payment in retirement.

13. Capital gain: is earned when an asset is bought at one price and sold at a higher price. 14. Dividends: the shares of a company's profits that are given to shareholders. 15. Stock exchange: where buyers and sellers come together (not physically) to buy and sell stocks with the help of stockbrokers. 16. Broker (or stock broker): a person trained and licensed to buy and sell stocks. 17. Estate: the money and assets left by a person upon death. 18. Benefactor: a person who receives money or assets, as indicated by a will, from someone who has died. 19. Executor: the person or persons responsible for seeing that an estate is settled according to a will.

Thinkabout... or Discuss: • How can you determine if you are a prospective entrepreneur? • How feasible is it to achieve "financial independence" today? What are the keys to being able to achieve financial independence? • What are some of the jobs/occupations where demand is likely to increase over the next decade? Decrease? • How can young people get the best guidance and advice in making education, training, and career decisions? • Why aren't more young people going into skilled trades where there are jobs and good incomes? • Is it true that more and more young people aim to live the lives they lived with their parents/guardians as soon as they leave home? Why? What are the consequences of this? • What factors are leading young people to take on more debt at younger ages these days?

Did It Stick? Can You Recall? 1. What are the different possible sources of income? 2. What are the different ways of looking at retirement? 3. What is the difference between (a) wage, (b) salary, and (c) benefits? 4. Why is Canada experiencing a skilled labour shortage? 5. What are the things most important to you as you consider your career and the kind of jobs you want? 6. How can the forces of demand and supply affect job opportunities and wages and salaries? 7. What is "LMI"?

8. What are some of the factors that affect your job prospects? 9. What are some of the "benefits" you might be able to receive from an employer? 10. Why is it becoming more challenging for Canadians to be able to save for retirement? 11. What kinds of income can be made from investments? 12. Why are opportunities to gamble becoming more and more common?

EMPLOYABILITY SKILLS Communicate • Read and understand information presented in a variety of forms (e.g., words, graphs, charts, diagrams). • Write and speak so others pay attention and understand. • Listen and ask questions to understand and appreciate the points of view of others. • Share information using a range of information and communications technologies (e.g., voice, e-mail, computers). • Use relevant scientific, technological, and mathematical knowledge and skills to explain or clarify ideas. Manage Information • Locate, gather, and organize information using appropriate technology and information systems. • Access, analyze, and apply knowledge and skills from various disciplines (e.g., the arts, languages, science, technology, mathematics, social sciences, and the humanities). Use Numbers • Decide what needs to be measured or calculated. • Observe and record data using appropriate methods, tools, and technology. • Make estimates and verify calculations. Think And Solve Problems • Assess situations and identify problems. • Seek different points of view and evaluate them based on facts. • Recognize the human, interpersonal, technical, scientific, and mathematical dimensions of a problem. • Identify the root cause of a problem. • Be creative and innovative in exploring possible solutions. • Readily use science, technology, and mathematics as ways to think, gain, and share knowledge, solve problems, and make decisions.

Evaluate solutions to make recommendations or decisions. • Implement solutions. • Check to see if a solution works, and act on opportunities for improvement. Demonstrate Positive Attitudes And Behaviours • Feel good about yourself and be confident. • Deal with people, problems, and situations with honesty, integrity, and personal ethics. • Recognize your own and other people's good efforts. • Take care of your personal health. • Show interest, initiative, and effort. Be Responsible • Set goals and priorities balancing work and personal life. • Plan and manage time, money, and other resources to achieve goals. • Assess, weigh, and manage risk. • Be accountable for your actions and the actions of your group. • Be socially responsible and contribute to your community. Be Adaptable • Work independently or as part of a team. • Carry out multiple tasks or projects. • Be innovative and resourceful: identify and suggest alternative ways to achieve goals and get the job done. • Be open and respond constructively to change. • Learn from your mistakes and accept feedback. • Cope with uncertainty. Learn Continuously • Be willing to continuously learn and grow. • Assess personal strengths and areas for development. • Set your own learning goals. • Identify and access learning sources and opportunities. • Plan for and achieve your learning goals. Work Safely • Be aware of personal and group health and safety practices and procedures, and act in accordance with them. Work With Others • Understand and work within the dynamics of a group. • Ensure that a team's purpose and objectives are clear. • Be flexible: respect, and be open to and supportive of the thoughts, opinions, and contributions of others in a group. • Recognize and respect people's diversity, individual differences, and perspectives. • Accept and provide feedback in a constructive and considerate manner. • Contribute to a team by sharing information and expertise. • Lead or support when appropriate, motivating a group for high performance. • Understand the role of conflict in a group to reach solutions. • Manage and resolve conflict when appropriate. Participate In Projects And Tasks • Plan, design, or carry out a project or task from start to finish with well-defined objectives and outcomes. • Develop a plan, seek feedback, test, revise, and implement. • Work to agreed-upon quality standards and specifications. • Select and use appropriate tools and technology for a task or project. • Adapt to changing requirements and information. • Continuously monitor the success of a project or task and identify ways to improve.

CAREER UNDER CONSTRUCTION – INVESTING IN YOU

B efore we get into looking at planning and picking a career, let's start with something very important – you! How are you doing? How are you feeling? What do you see as you look into your future – your options and possibilities? And, let's look at how some things in your past may have had an impact on how you see your future. To begin, let's start with a test. Take a look at the set of figures below and select the one that doesn't belong. This set of figures appeared in a book entitled A Whack on the Side of the Head by Roger von Oech. In that book, he gives the following response to the "test" you just took."If you chose figure B, congratulations! You've picked the right answer. Figure B is the only one that has all straight lines. Give yourself a pat on the back! Some of you, however, may have chosen figure C, thinking that C is unique because it is the only one that is asymmetrical. And you are also right! C is the right answer. A case can also be made for figure A: it is the only one with no points of discontinuity. Therefore, A is the right answer. What about D? It is the only one with both a straight line and a curved line. So, D is the right answer too. And E? Among other things, E is the only one which looks like a projection of a non-Euclidean triangle into Euclidean space. It is also the right answer. In other words, they are all right depending on your point of view. Much of our educational system, however, is geared toward teaching people the one right answer... the "right answer" approach becomes deeply ingrained in our thinking... if you think there is only one right answer, then you will stop looking as soon as you find one."

This is particularly true for those who have come through a school system that focused on "right answer" learning. You probably have taken, and will take, test after test, quiz after quiz, and exam after exam. The student who entered school full of excitement, creativity, and hopes for the future may have had those hopes drift away with "A's" turning to "B's," then to "C's" and then who knows where eventually. As the famed educator Neil Postman said: "Students enter school as question marks and leave as periods." There is no doubt about it, the school system works very well for many students. But it also does not work particularly well for many others. Some students, for example, may have many talents but do not do well in written exams. They often end up on the lower end of the grade scale. They are put on a level somewhat below others – others who were able to take notes, study from books, and score well on tests. What is the impact of this? First, the dreams and hopes of some students are affected. They lose self-confidence. They lower their expectations of themselves. They start to "give less" and as a result "get less." Their overall selfesteem takes a beating. The reality of this is shown by the drop-out rate from many schools. Some young people decide school is not working for them. It isn't providing what they need, or perhaps what they want.

Is your interest in school still high? Are you motivated and inspired and feel you are benefitting from school? Or, have you lost some interest and are struggling to feel motivated?

So your school experience and performance so far may have had an impact on your outlook for the future. And your outlook – and belief in yourself and your potential – is very important when it comes to career planning. It can affect your goals, hopes, and dreams. It can affect what you think you can do and the career options you consider. No matter what your school experience has been, look at who you are. What skills and abilities do you have? Which might you want to develop? Have you had success in sports, dance, acting, music, and so on? These can be very important – and provide experiences and skills to build upon. So consider and value your accomplishments. If you have accomplished some things in life, this can build confidence in what you think you can accomplish in the future. But, many young people have little appreciation for the things in life they have accomplished. Therefore, they lack a sense of accomplishment and a belief that they can accomplish new things. Many young people think only about longer-term goals such as careers, jobs, incomes, and families. They often don't think about many other things in life they may have already achieved – in sports, in school, in theatre, in dance, in the community, with their family, at work, and so on – they may be thinking they don't matter, don't count, or aren't important. But they are. All accomplishments matter. And, if you want to accomplish bigger things, you have to develop skills by accomplishing smaller things. Have you learned to swim, ride a bike, drive a car, use a computer, drive a boat, build a deck, plant a garden, make a dress, or paint a room? The list could go on and on. How long is your list? Recognition of our accomplishments helps to build self-confidence. And, self-confidence is one of the most important things employers look for – and one of the most important characteristics for any entrepreneur. So, hold on to your hopes and dreams. Work on your self-confidence. Think of your successes and accomplishments – large, or small, or anything in between. Set some short-term goals for yourself and work to achieve them. Prove to yourself that you can do what you put your mind – and hard work – to achieving.

Does any of this apply to you? It may not. You may be thriving in school, happy with school, doing well and looking ahead to a bright future. But, on the other hand, you may struggle in school. Your test results may not be the greatest. You may be concerned about where you'll go from here – and what options you may have. How great is the "fit" between you and school.

Career Planning: Some Suggestions To Consider

Apply the decision-making steps that were discussed earlier to help you decide on your career interests. Few decisions are more important for you than selecting the career that's best for you. • Do volunteer work to gain experience, learn more about some occupational areas that are of interest, and broaden your outlook into other areas to learn more. This will help you to determine whether or not you would enjoy working in a particular field. Furthermore, you will probably get personal benefit from the experience, benefit others at the same time, and volunteer experience generally makes a positive impression on a résumé. • Consider careers that might be related to a hobby or something you enjoy (for example: sports, movies, music, science, camp, computers, travel). • Be honest with yourself in assessing your talents and abilities. You should never lower your sights below your true potential. At the same time, you should avoid setting your sights so high that you are likely to be frustrated and disappointed. • Nothing is more important today in getting a job and planning and starting a career than networking. Connecting with people, seeking advice, and getting help is very important. Don't hesitate to use your connections. Others don't. Build a network – then use it. • Set goals. Set your sights on what you want to achieve. Work toward something. Don't meander down the road and occasionally stop to see where you are. That may be a nice way to see Europe, but it's a poor way to find a career. Furthermore, don't set only long-term goals. Set some short-term goals, too. Give yourself a chance to succeed. • Learn from your mistakes and disappointments. Mistakes are powerful learning experiences. They are stepping stones to future success. Apply that attitude to everything you do. • Talk with people who are working in careers that interest you. You can learn a great deal about many career optionsfrom talking to someone who is already involved in a particular career. • Talk with a range of people. Don't judge a career on the basis of discussions with one or two people. People have different talents, different experiences, and different interests. What doesn't work for them may work for you.

Networking is crucial in getting a job and building a career. How effective is your network already? If you had to identify five people in your network to call upon for career or job advice, who would they be? What kind of help would be good for you to have? Who could provide that for you? Who might be good to add to your network? Who could help you build your network? Young people today are very familiar with social networking. Draw upon these skills and experiences to network re your career and finding a job.

Plan for the future, not the present. Look ahead, not to the side. Observe trends. Watch for changes. Look where everyone else is going, and realize that if they are all heading there, it's likely to be pretty crowded. Do you still want to head in that direction? Or, might you want to change course? • Know why you want to work. What do you want out of your career? Are you working strictly for an income? Are you concerned about the working environment, how mobile you can be in the job, opportunities for advancement, job satisfaction, the people you will work with, the benefits that may accompany the income? There are many possible factors that might be related to why you want to work – and the type of work you want to do. Include these in your career plans and decisions. • Regard your career as a path of lifelong learning and development. Keep on top of developments in your field. Pursue new training if you are able and interested. Lifelong learning is a valuable concept. Many, if not most, people will have four or more different careers in their lifetime – or more. • Keep your options open. Make sure you don't slam the door on yourself by making poor course selections in school.

• Look beyond the most obvious career options. Some of the less known careers can be the more interesting ones. Furthermore, far fewer people may be preparing for them, which may help when hiring time comes along. • Look beyond your own front door to see what's going on. Look at what's going on in other communities, other provinces and territories, across the country, and in other countries around the world. • Don't be your own worst enemy. Don't get down on yourself. Don't have a negative state of mind. You have a lot of control over what goes on inside your head. You can affect your attitude and how you act – and how you come across to others. Attitude means so much. It makes a huge impression. Be your own biggest booster. • Know your strengths and work on them. Recognize the talents that you have, and then build on and develop them. • Learn how to cope with stress. Identify what puts pressure on you. Do what you can to minimize those things. Deflect the pressures. Learn how to relax. Avoid burnout. Learn how to keep your cool. That can affect your success in the workplace – and as an entrepreneur.

Identify a "trend" you believe is just getting started. What types of jobs do you think would be helped if this trend really developed? Can you identify two or three trends that have been big over the last two years that led to career and employment opportunities for many people?

Some Tips On Finding A Job There are many different approaches to looking for a job. It would be a good idea for you to read up on some of the different methods. The following represent a number of general tips for your consideration. • Recognize that finding a job is hard work. Develop a plan and a schedule for yourself in terms of what you are going to do on a day-by-day or week-by-week basis to find a job. • Make contacts. Make as many contacts as you can with people who work in the type of business or field in which you are seeking employment. Keep a record of your contacts. You never know when they may come in handy. • Do your research. Learn about a company when you are applying to work there. You might want to take a look at the company's annual report. Try and impress them with what you know about the company. • Don't rely on a résumé (see the next section on résumés). A résumé should be a tool in your job search, it can't do it all for you. • Don't count on seeing ads for employment in the newspaper. The majority of jobs are probably never advertised. That is why networking, and using contacts, is so important. • Don't waste time on gimmicky approaches. They usually won't work and they often have a negative, rather than a positive, impression. Be direct, truthful, and businesslike. • Set non-employment goals for yourself. A job search should not be singularly focused on getting a job. Set targets for number of contacts, number of interviews, and other related tasks. Meet your objectives. Keep at it. Set new dates and targets. • Recognize that finding a job takes time. Don't wait until April or May to find a summer job. Start in January. Don't think finding a job takes a week. It often takes a lot longer. Using "connections" can help shorten the time – if you have connections to use. • Contact local, provincial, and federal government placement centres to explore the programs that focus on youth. • Watch the local papers for announcements regarding the activities, plans, and growth of local businesses and industries. Some developments may indicate that a business will be looking for workers. • Maintain a good appearance. This does not mean that you can't be yourself. However, you may have to face certain realities in the workplace. Some styles popular among youth may not be as popular among potential employers. Just as you have the right to be yourself, they have the right to hire those they feel will be best for the job. You may have to decide on the degree to which certain styles are important to you versus the prospect of getting a job. This is often a difficult decision, especially for youth who are very much involved in trends, fashion fads, and so on. As much as you may be attempting to convey a message about yourself through style, businesses have their own protocols and standards, and dealing with some of the more unusual fads and trends of youth are often not one of them. Once again, it is up to you to make the call on your dress and appearance. • Be confident in yourself. People will be hesitant to hire someone who doesn't convey the message that he/she is able to do the job. If it looks like you don't have confidence in you, they probably won't have confidence in you either. • If you are turned down for a possible job, try to learn from the experience. Follow up on any contact or experience. Ask interviewers for a review of how you did and suggestions for how you could improve your performance in a job interview or on your résumé. • Have references available to provide if needed. Make sure your references know you are providing their names as references and get their permission. If a possible employer is planning to contact your references, let your references know to expect a call.

Don't pressure yourself to "know" what it is that you want to do. Give yourself the chance to fully explore various options and alternatives. Avoid pressure to make some decision at an early age about what you are going to do for the rest of your life. • Be organized. Keep clear and thorough notes and records. Keep track of your contacts. Keep files on companies in which you are interested. Collect articles providing advice on résumés and job search techniques. • Have a good résumé – one that makes a good impression – one that says "put me near the top of the pile." A poor résumé will scream "put me near the bottom" – or in the trash.

Assume that you are about to begin a search for a job. Make a list of the steps/actions you could take that would help you find a job. Note such things as who you would approach, what offices you would visit, what businesses you would contact, whose advice you would seek, or what information you would write, and so forth.

A résumé is a written summary of your work, education, and experience as well as other abilities you have that make you a candidate for a particular job. It is your "ad," if you like, illustrating your strengths and abilities and why you would be a good person to hire for a particular job. Most young Canadians have had little experience in preparing résumés. But yet résumés are an important tool for you in your job search. There is no standard format. You should investigate different approaches and styles to develop the résumé that best suits you and the job for which you are applying. It is important to note that you should never send in your résumé alone. You should always include a covering letter. The covering letter should be specific to the job for which you are applying. You should introduce yourself, state why you are interested in the position, and why you think you are well suited for the job. Your cover letter should be no longer than one page – a page and a half at most. Therefore, conserve words. Be clear and concise. Most employers will have many letters and résumés to read and review. They won't spend a long time on any single one. You will have to have yours make a quick, and good, impression. In addition, check grammar and spelling carefully. Nothing will get a résumé to the bottom of the pile quicker than spelling mistakes and bad grammar.

• Your objective with your résumé should be to sell yourself. It should represent you well, covering all of your strengths, skills, accomplishments, and abilities. You want it to show, as best it can, how you stand out from other applicants. • Don't trivialize your accomplishments. Some things that may seem small to you may be a sign to a potential employer of particular skills and abilities. For example, babysitting may seem like a trivial thing to note. However, considerable babysitting experience shows responsibility. It also shows that you took the initiative to get out and work and earn some income. The responsibility of looking after a child is far from trivial and can reflect the confidence that other adults have had in your abilities. • Be proud of things you have done. Think of what they may imply about you and your abilities. • Avoid gimmicks. They usually do not impress. Furthermore, it is the content, rather than the style or format, that will make your résumé stand out. Therefore, don't go to a

great deal of effort and expense to have your résumé prepared in some fancy fashion. • Although content is more important than format, format is important too. Prepare your résumé neatly on good quality paper and bind it well and attractively if submitting a hard copy. • Do not include a long list of personal statistics such as age, height, and weight. This is excess information. Simply indicate your name, address, contact numbers, and any abilities you have in speaking various languages. • Keep in mind that your résumé should answer the following questions for a potential employer: Why should I pick you? Why are you right for this job? Why are you better than the other applicants? • When you can, present your résumé in person rather than by mail or e-mail. It puts a face to the paper and may provide you with an early opportunity to make a positive impression. • Quantify your accomplishments where possible. How many children did you care for or supervise? For how long? How many children were you responsible for at camp? How many newspapers did you deliver? When the numbers help to convey the scale of your activity or responsibility, use them. • Use action words to describe your responsibilities and accomplishments, words such as: organized, created, demonstrated, supervised, managed, coordinated, developed. These words imply Assume that you are applying for a job as a camp counsellor at Camp Buckhorn. The Camp specializes in offering programs for children with discipline problems. Write a covering letter outlining why you are interested in this job and why you think you are suited for it. Then develop a résumé to accompany your letter. If a school counsellor is available, ask for a review of your letter and résumé. If a counsellor is not available, a teacher or a family member should be able to offer a knowledgeable review. Take Act ion. Take Control! particular abilities and skills. Furthermore, even if the activity that you co-ordinated is unrelated to the job for which you are applying, the fact that you have served as a coordinator could be very relevant. • Keep the structure of your résumé as flexible as possible so that you can easily change it. You may recall something you want to add, or you may want to tailor it for a specific job application. • Keep it up to date. Change it when you acquire more education or experience – or when you develop a new skill. • Offer references upon request; do not include them on your résumé. Do not put a great deal of reliance on letters of reference. Most employers feel that it is the rare person who will not be able to find someone who will say nice things about him or her. Besides, it is often difficult for employers to know if the letters are from friends. On the other hand, some references may be particularly helpful if they are from persons known by the company – or who are with a company in a similar line of work. Often an employer will contact references before making the final decision to hire you. They will do so to make sure your references help support their decision, and to make sure there are no surprises. Suppose now that you have organized your job search, you have prepared an effective résumé, you have developed a network of contacts, and you have been asked in for an interview. The following are some tips related to job interviews.

Tips On Job Interviews The interview is usually the last step in the job search process. Everything up to that point – contacts, cover letter, résumé, and so on – has been designed to give you a chance to meet with the employer and show why you should be hired. Virtually no job will be attained without going through an interview process. It is a fearful experience for some, but an enjoyable experience for others. If it is a fearful experience for you, you have got to change that. When you are fearful or overly nervous, you will seldom put your best side forward. The most important piece of advice regarding interviews is to be you. If you go into an interview trying to give the "right" answers, you will almost always enter in a nervous state as you try and think of "right" answers when you don't even know the questions you will face. If you go in knowing who you are and what you believe in, then you can feel confident that you will always give the best response you can based on what you truly believe. Therefore, be confident about who you are. A key recommendation is to go into an interview prepared to be yourself and answer questions on the basis of what you honestly believe. Now here are some others. • Dress appropriately. You are out to make an impression. Don't work against yourself by giving the impression that you don't care or that you don't respect the people who are interviewing you. • "Mind your manners." Once again, you are selling yourself. • Be prepared for different interview styles. You have to realize that it is not easy to hire good people. Employers will use a variety of methods to try to ensure that they hire the best person for the job. Hiring is an important responsibility for any employer. • Know your rights. There are certain questions that you cannot be asked and certain things that employers cannot do in screening potential employees. Some interviewers use the "good cop, bad cop" technique. This is an interview by two people, one of whom appears to be friendly and supportive of things that you say while the other will tend to disagree with you and be somewhat unfriendly. The aim of this may be to see how you cope in both situations and how you react to criticism. Sometimes you will be interviewed by a team of people. Each member of the team may have something in particular that he or she is looking for. A team interview means that you will face a variety of approaches and objectives all in the same interview. And there are other interview techniques. Be prepared for a variety of approaches. This is another reason to be yourself – you never know the type of situation that you may face.

BE PREPARED: Sample Questions Employers May Ask in a Job Interview 1. Why do you want to work in this field? 2. Why do you specifically want to work for this company? 3. What do you know about our company? 4. Why do you feel you are the right candidate for this job? What do you think you can bring to this company? 5. What things are important to you in the type of position you want? 6. How has your education prepared you for this type of job? 7. Which school courses did you like most and why? 8. Do you plan to continue your education? 9. What are your short-term goals? 10. Where do you see yourself in 5 years? 11. What do you like to do in your leisure time? 12. What are a couple of accomplishments in your life that have given you the most satisfaction and why? 13. What are some skills that you feel you have gained from your past employment and education? 14. What motivates you to put forth your best effort? 15. What is your greatest strength? 16. What is your greatest weakness? 17. What are your salary expectations? 18. What hours are you willing to work? 19. Are you flexible in these hours? Can you work overtime if necessary? 20. Are you willing to travel? Questions Employers Cannot Legally Ask in a Job Interview 1. What health problems do you have? 2. Do you have any disabilities? 3. Have you ever been denied health insurance? 4. When were you hospitalized the last time? 5. Is any member of your family disabled? 6. Do you have AIDS? 7. Have you ever been addicted to drugs? 8. When was your last medical checkup? 9. How old are you? 10. When were you born? 11. When were you married? 12. How old are your children? 13. Where were you born? 14. What church are you a member of? 15. Does your religion prevent you from working weekends or holidays? 16. Are you a member of any religious group? 17. What's your sexual orientation? 18. Are you married, divorced, separated, or single? 19. Were you ever arrested? 20. What is your economic situation or status? 21. What is your race, ethnicity, colour? 22. What is your gender, gender identity, gender expression?

Go to as many interview situations as you can to become familiar with the processes/styles that employers use. This will help you to become more confident. Each interview can be a learning experience. • If you are turned down after an interview, try to follow up. If the interviewer will take the time, ask for suggestions about how you could improve your interview skills; ask if you might be considered again in the future; and so on. Learn as much as possible from each interview experience. • Role play in advance. That is, work with someone if you can to rehearse an interview. Ask a parent, teacher, counsellor, or friend to ask you questions so you can practice your responses. • Be enthusiastic. Appear as if you want the job. • Don't be long-winded. Keep your answers informative, concise, and to the point. Be sure to answer the question asked but don't go on and on. Try to avoid yes and no answers. The interviewer is trying to find out about you and will become frustrated by yes and no responses.

Suppose you have been successful in getting an interview for the job at Camp Buckhorn. Imagine how you would answer the following questions. • Why do you think that you would be able to work effectively with these children? • What do you think are your greatest strengths? • Do you foresee any situations in which you would have problems? • What experience have you had with children? • If you are given the opportunity to develop some programs for these children, give me an example of something you might do. • What would you do if a child refused to do what you told him/her? • Do you feel your education has prepared you in any way for this job? • What would you see as your major responsibilities in this position? • Do you take criticism well? • In which situations are you "your own best friend"? • In which are you "your own worst enemy"?

That concludes our tips on career planning, résumés, job search, and interviews. These will hopefully help if your goal is to get a job working for someone else. But maybe you are interested in creating your own job – and starting a business. That is, maybe you are interested in becoming an entrepreneur. Let's turn our attention to the topic of entrepreneurship. And, even if you aren't interested in starting and running your own business, you may be interested in developing your entrepreneurial and enterprising skills. They can help you in any job or career.

Changes in the Nature of Work A very dramatic change is occurring. But it is not change that is obvious to many people. Those who are on the front lines of change in major industry areas of our economy are witnessing very significant changes – the nature of work, and the skills, attitudes, and attributes that are being sought and valued by employers. The types of jobs that are being created and those that are disappearing also show that the job market is changing. Various aspects of technology impact jobs and how businesses do what they do – robotics, artificial intelligence, virtual reality, and so on all have an impact on the way businesses produce goods and services. For young people in school this is a very significant development. Decisions have to be made about education and training with the outcome being that youth make the right choices so that they can secure and sustain a good job – or create a new business that can succeed in such a changing world. It is extremely difficult for teachers to keep up with or anticipate the dramatic changes going on in the job market. Teachers have a full-time job preparing for instruction, providing instruction, evaluating work, and providing additional assistance to those who need it. That makes it very difficult to keep in touch with all the changes occurring in the job market that are impacting the skills and talent that are in demand. If you want to gain more insight into what is happening in the workplace to help with your education and career choices, the following is a link to help get you started.

If you have the opportunity, talk with family members and friends about their jobs and the places they are working. Do they see changes occurring? Are their jobs changing as a result?

Try not to depend on others to provide you with information on how the world of work and jobs are changing. Be proactive and try to learn about the changes going on. It will help you in making your education and career choices.

The key element is to try and understand the accelerating changes that are underway which could impact your future career and your ability to secure a good income. Understanding the changes that impact the career in which you are interested will help you as you make decisions that will likely affect the rest of your life. Try and talk with those who are already working and experiencing the changes going on. Talk with family members that may help provide you with insight. Encourage your teacher to invite one or more guest speakers who may be able to shed some light on the various changes that could impact your education and career decisions. You, in the end, will be responsible for the education and career choices you make. Get as much help as you can from parents, teachers, other contacts, online references, etc., so that you can make informed decisions and choices. Don't look back in three, four, ten, or 25 years and say, I wish I had made other choices back when I had the chance – now is your chance!

Say What? Possible New Terms! 1. Career plan: the steps and strategies taken to explore career options, set career goals, and obtain the required education, training and experience to achieve career goals. 2. Career path: various career stages over the course of one's life. Many people will have multiple jobs over time building up to a career path. 3. Covering letter: a letter written to accompany a résumé and is written specifically for a job for which you are applying. 4. Résumé: sometimes called a "curriculum vitae," or "CV," this is a summary of your work, education, and experience as well as other abilities you have that make you a candidate for a particular job. 5. References: letters or comments from people you know regarding your abilities, characteristics, skills, etc. that an employer may refer to in making a hiring decision.

Self-confidence is key in getting a job and succeeding in the workplace. Find ways to build your self-confidence. • Don't pressure yourself at an early age "to know" what you are going to do in terms of a career in life. You may know – and that's great. But many people don't get into their ultimate career field until post-secondary years – and beyond. Keep your eyes, ears, and options open. • Do what you can to explore a range of career options. Don't find out years later about a career possibility that you would have loved to pursue.

ARE YOU AN ENTREPRENEUR?

Y ou may or may not be familiar with the term "entrepreneur." Even if you are, you may have some mis-perceptions of entrepreneurs because there are many myths about them. For example, many believe that entrepreneurs only start up small business enterprises. Although many entrepreneurs set up and run small businesses, you can also apply entrepreneurial skills to other kinds of activities – within companies, within governments, running a not-for-profit organization, and so on. Let's take a closer look at entrepreneurs and entrepreneurship and whether or not it is an option of interest to you. Let's start with a quick quiz. The answers follow the quiz – but try the quiz first without looking at the answers. The goal is to help you decide if being an entrepreneur is something of interest to you

Entrepreneur's Quiz

1. Faced with a problem, the entrepreneur is most likely to: a) go to a close friend for help; b) get help from a stranger who is known to be an expert; c) try to work through the problem alone.

2. The entrepreneur is most like the distance runner who runs mainly: a) to work off energy and to keep in good physical condition; b) to gain the satisfaction of beating other competitors in the race; c) to try to better his or her previous time over the distance.

3. Entrepreneurs are motivated most by the need to: a) achieve a goal of greater personal importance; b) gain public attention and recognition; c) control wealth and other people.

4. Entrepreneurs believe the success or failure of a new venture depends primarily on: a) luck or fate; b) the support and approval of others; c) their own strengths and abilities.

5. If given the chance to earn a substantial reward, which of the following would entrepreneurs be most likely to do: a) roll dice with a one in three

chance of winning; b) work on a problem with a one in three chance of solving it in the time given; c) do neither (a) nor (b) because the chances of success are so small.

6. The entrepreneur is most likely to choose a task: a) which involves a moderate level of risk but is still challenging; b) where the risks are high but the financial rewards are also very great; c) which is relatively easy and the risks low.

7. Money is important to entrepreneurs because: a) it allows them to develop other ideas and take advantage of other opportunities; b) monetary measurements provide an objective measure of how successful they have been; c) the main reason they accepted the risks of starting a new venture was to accumulate personal wealth.

QUESTION 1: Entrepreneurs do tend to be independent, self-reliant individuals. They may try to work through a problem alone. They do have a high need to achieve. But successful entrepreneurs are not so focused on doing things alone that they won't seek help when they need it. Being a successful entrepreneur is a challenge and usually requires the help of others. Successful entrepreneurs will seek out those who can be most helpful whether they are friends or strangers. They are usually good "team-builders" and "team-leaders." They put together the talent they need to succeed. And the need to achieve will likely be greater than the social need to work with friends. The best choice is (b)

QUESTION 2: Entrepreneurs often have a great deal of energy and drive. They are usually able and willing to work for long hours. Good general physical health is necessary in order to withstand the stresses of running their own ventures. One of the risks they must evaluate is that their work will likely put physical, social, and emotional strains on them. Few entrepreneurs pursue initiatives for the good of their health although many seem to thrive on the work-related stress. Entrepreneurs tend to compete against standards of achievement they set for themselves rather than standards set for them by others. Entrepreneurs are most like the runner who races to beat the clock. To achieve a new "personal best" time will likely be more rewarding than beating others. The best choice is (c).

QUESTION 3: Those who are motivated by a need to gain attention, get recognition, and control others are motivated by power. They are more active in political life or large organizations where they concentrate on controlling the channels of communications both up to the top and down to the bottom so that they are more in charge. By contrast, entrepreneurs are motivated more by their need for personal achievement than personal power. Power and power recognition may be the result of success, but they are not usually the motivating goals for an entrepreneur. The best answer is (a).

QUESTION 4: Successful entrepreneurs likely have a high level of self-confidence and "self-efficacy." Self-efficacy is the belief in yourself that you are able to accomplish things – that you will be able to achieve goals you set for yourself. Therefore, entrepreneurs tend to believe strongly in themselves and their own abilities. They also believe that what happens to them in their lives is determined mainly by what they do – not by what others do. They are not reluctant to place themselves in situations where they are personally responsible for the success or failure of an operation. They will take the initiative to solve a problem and provide leadership where none existed before. The best choice is (c).

QUESTION 5: The entrepreneur is thought of as a risk taker. There are many risks involved in entrepreneurial activity. But psychological testing of entrepreneurs has indicated that they are no more motivated to do something that involves risk than anyone else. They are not daredevils or reckless gamblers. Successful entrepreneurs are very good at assessing the amount of risk involved in a venture and will choose to accept that risk if they feel their personal chances for success are relatively high. They may well choose to do something when the odds of success are only one in three if they believe they have the abilities and experience needed to succeed. The entrepreneur would most likely choose (b), to work on the problem even though rolling dice is obviously less work. Entrepreneurs avoid situations where the results depend mainly on chance or the efforts of others. The opportunity for personal achievement is more important than the size of the reward offered.

QUESTION 6: Entrepreneurs tend to be positive, optimistic types who focus their attention on their chances of success rather than the chances of failure. Individuals who fear failure tend to select tasks that are either very easy or where the risk is very high. By selecting an easy task, the chances of failure are reduced. By selecting a task with little chance of success, failure can be rationalized, "Oh well, it was just a long shot anyway." The entrepreneur avoids both extremes and selects those tasks that are challenging but where the opportunities for success are reasonably good. The best choice is (a).

QUESTION 7: It is a popular misconception that entrepreneurs are, at heart, greedy individuals who enter into ventures for the purpose of accumulating personal wealth. Such a description would be more aptly applied to some promoter who's a "fast buck" artist. Entrepreneurs are driven to build a venture rather than simply to get in and out in a hurry with someone else's money. They will enjoy the benefits of a higher income but will usually spend only a portion of their gain on personal consumption. Entrepreneurs are primarily interested in the creation, not the consumption, of wealth.

So, what is entrepreneurship? The statement below provides one definition. Entrepreneurship involves the recognition of opportunities (needs, wants, and problems) and the use of resources to pursue an idea for a new, thoughtfully planned venture. Does that describe something that interests you? Might you be a prospective entrepreneur?

What motivates you most – the desire to make money or the desire to accomplish your goals and make a difference?

Contributions Of Entrepreneurs To Society In addition to your own personal interest, everyone should probably know something about the contributions entrepreneurs make. Even if you never become an entrepreneur, you will probably have the opportunity to interact with a great many. In our society, entrepreneurs may: • create new ventures that provide new, improved products and services • find new ways of making products and services available to more people • compete with each other to be the "best," which improves the quality of goods and services and keeps prices down • create jobs for others in the community through the new ventures they create • increase the quantity of products and services we produce in our economy (that is, help us to achieve "economic growth") by creating new ventures • create new opportunities for others through their initiatives and innovations • provide a spirit of energy, initiative, and potential for progress to a community Can you think of others? Do these spark an interest? Do they motivate you? To help you consider the entrepreneurship option, it would probably be helpful to review some of the key characteristics and skills associated with entrepreneurship.

One important point to note is that it is possible for virtually anyone to develop and apply entrepreneurial or enterprising skills. You can also be an entrepreneur by starting with/or running an entrepreneurial not-for-profit company – or a government department. You don't have to set up and run your own business to be entrepreneurial or enterprising.

What entrepreneurs do you know of in your community? What contributions are they making to your community?

Do you think you take an entrepreneurial or enterprising approach to your work? Do you take initiative? Are you creative? Do you look forward to making things better?

You can be an enterprising employee. You can Think About It even apply many enterprising skills in the home – or, to how you run a sports team, or an acting company, or .....the list could go on and on. So, while entrepreneurs look to start and build successful businesses, entrepreneurial or enterprising skills can be developed and applied by virtually anyone – and applied to any kind of endeavour.

Who do you know who is very entrepreneurial or enterprising – but who doesn't run their own business?

"The Entrepreneur's Dozen" Next, let's consider what an entrepreneur actually does. It sounds simple to say "starts and builds a business." But the reality is far from simple. One way to consider what an entrepreneur does is via "The Entrepreneur's Dozen" – or the 12 steps in entrepreneurial or enterprising activity. An entrepreneur: It is important to emphasize that one of the most essential ingredients of entrepreneurial success is making sure you have found a good opportunity. An entrepreneurial opportunity is a need or want that needs to be satisfied (or that can be satisfied in a new or better way) or a problem that needs to be solved. You may have a good "idea" – but if few want it, need it, or see it as a problem, your chances of success will be low. How do entrepreneurs seek out, find, and assess potential opportunities? The following are some suggestions for you to consider. Examines needs, wants, and problems for which he/she feels something can be done to improve the way things are. Narrows the possible opportunities down to one specific opportunity. Thinks of an innovative idea. Researches the opportunity and idea thoroughly. Enlists the best sources of advice and assistance that can be found. Plans the venture and looks for possible problems that might arise. Ranks the risk and the possible rewards. Evaluates the risk and possible rewards and makes a decision. Never hangs on to an idea, as much as it is loved, if research shows it's not likely to work. Employs the resources necessary for the venture if the decision is made to go ahead. Understands that any entrepreneurial venture will take a great deal of long, hard work. Realizes a sense of accomplishment from successful ventures and learns.

SAFARI TIP #1: Recognize patterns as they are forming. The entrepreneur has an advantage if trends, patterns, and changes are detected before others have noticed them – perhaps even before they have happened. SAFARI TIP #2: Look at the small things. Many of the best opportunities lie in what has been overlooked by others. SAFARI TIP #3: Don't overlook the obvious. There is a saying that "only a foolish mouse would hide in a cat's ear, but it is the foolish cat that fails to look there." SAFARI TIP #4: Watch for good ideas that are poorly executed. Some people find good opportunities but just don't know how to take advantage of them. You may know how to.

SAFARI TIP #5: Combine two or more things/thoughts together. Somebody came up with the idea for combining a bar and a laundromat. Someone else came up with a coffee shop and book store. Opportunities can often arise when two things are brought together for examination and thought – and a possible new venture. SAFARI TIP #6: Look for new, generally unknown information. The best information is what is new and/or generally unknown – or that most others are unaware of. SAFARI TIP #7: Talk with people. What better way is there to identify needs, wants, and problems than by talking to people and finding out what they have to say. SAFARI TIP #8: Read journals, trade magazines, and so on to keep on top of things and to gather new information that may give rise to an opportunity or idea.

SAFARI TIP #9: Look for what has worked elsewhere. It may be needed and could work where you are. SAFARI TIP #10: Look for new ways to meet old needs and wants. SAFARI TIP #11: Look for ways to overcome barriers that blocked a good idea in the past. People tend to resist change, and some other entrepreneur may have been unable to overcome the resistance to a good idea. You may find the way. SAFARI TIP #12: Look for "left-behind" markets – products that are no longer produced but many people still have. As long as people continue to use certain things, they continue to have needs. SAFARI TIP #13: Look for good ideas that others have had that can be improved.

SAFARI TIP #14: Look at "why" people buy something rather than "what" they buy. The idea is to get at what motivates people – what prompts them to buy something – what the underlying needs and wants are. Therein lie the opportunities. SAFARI TIP #15: Look for new uses for old products – old tires, end pieces of lumber, old TV antennas, and so on. SAFARI TIP #16: Look for what's not working. You may find a way to make it work.

SAFARI TIP #17: Look for unhappy, dissatisfied people. Here you will find needs and wants that are still to be addressed. SAFARI TIP #18: Look for happy, contented people. Here you will find insight into what has worked and what might work better. SAFARI TIP #19: Keep your eyes and ears open to things that are around you – what people say – what you see – what you read. There is no more important tip than this one!

Look around your community. What needs, wants, or problems exist? Identify five opportunities that you believe exist right in your local community.

Once you have found an opportunity, it is important to assess it. Is it a good one? Is it a great one? Is it the best one that can be found? To start out as an entrepreneur, the most important thing to have is a good opportunity. Your idea is also important. But, as we have noted, if your idea doesn't fit with an opportunity, it will be hard to succeed. The following represent some of the key questions you can consider when assessing an opportunity you have found. "Assessment" Actual: Is it really an opportunity? Seen: Has it been seen by others? Selected: If seen, have others acted upon it? If not, why not? Enduring: How long will it last? Satisfied: Are you satisfied that you have accurate and sufficient information? Specific: Have you specifically defined the opportunity? Many: Do, or will, many care about the product or service you will provide? Experience: Do you really know what you're doing in this area? Number 1: Is it the best opportunity you can see? Think: Can you come up with a good idea that fits with the opportunity? Once you have a good opportunity, you need a good idea.

Generating Ideas Armed with a good opportunity, you also need a good idea. Most entrepreneurs start with finding a good opportunity. Then they look to develop a good idea. How can you look for, find, and create ideas? Here are some tips for generating, and evaluating, ideas. 1. Believe you are creative and don't be afraid of being wrong. 2. Listen, really listen, to what others have to say. 3. Listen to, accept, and think about criticisms you receive from others. 4. Break with your habits and routine. Force yourself into something new to gain a new perspective. 5. Role play. Pretend you are someone, or something, other than who you are. 6. Relax. Have fun. Kid around. Humour and fun allow the mind to venture down new, previously untraveled pathways. 7. Practice coming up with ideas for every problem, challenge, etc., you see, hear about, or come up against. 8. Daydream. Let your mind wander and see where it ends up. 9. Look at two things that are totally unrelated. Can you link them together in a new, innovative way? 10.

Ask lots of questions – and then listen to the answers. 11. Ask new and different questions – ones that are unexpected, perhaps illogical, perhaps a little crazy – perhaps ones that will make you think. 12. Try to come at a problem from an entirely new perspective. 13. Write all your ideas down. Don't let them get away.

It has often been noted that one of the biggest blocks to creativity is thinking you are not creative. Do you think you are a creative person?

Once you have an idea, or a bunch of ideas, you have to evaluate or assess them – just as you would evaluate an opportunity. The following are some suggestions for evaluating the ideas you are able to generate. Are you a planner? Have you planned something in your life? If so, how did it go? What did you learn from the experience? How About You? 1. What do others think of the idea? 2. Has the idea been tried before? 3. If not, why not? 4. If so, with what success? Can you improve on that? 5. What information was used to generate the idea? Was it accurate, dependable, reliable information? Was it sufficient? 6. How confident do you feel about the idea? 7. What are the risks associated with the idea? Are they controllable? 8. Is the idea directly related to an opportunity? Specifically define the opportunity. 9. Is there a "user-market" for the idea? Define it. How large is it? 10. Will there be much resistance to the idea? From where? Why? Can such resistance be overcome? 11. Is much money necessary to finance the idea? Will it likely be available? 12. Have you made any questionable assumptions in formulating your idea? 13. Is there a better idea available?

The Importance of Planning Once you have a good opportunity and a good idea, the important next step is to put together a good plan. Having a good plan is crucial to being a successful entrepreneur. You can find sample plans at the Canadian Foundation for Economic Education's (CFEE) website – "Entrepreneurship: The Spirit of Adventure." You can get to it via CFEE's site – www.cfee.org or www.cfeespiritofadventure.com. It will show you the different parts of a plan that you can include in a "Venture Plan." One thing to remember though is to keep your plan flexible. You don't want it to be too rigid. You don't want it to be a strait-jacket on you as you try to succeed. Very seldom will things ever go exactly as planned. You will have to adapt to the things you didn't expect – or that you encounter. So have a plan – but have a plan that can change as your venture unfolds

A key part of your plan will also be to identify the resources you need. Entrepreneurs can fail by trying to do too much themselves. Be honest about the talent and skills you have. Then make sure you partner with, or hire, people with the other skills you need. The quality of the resources you employ, acquire, and use will affect the success of your venture. Finally, if you try your hand at being an entrepreneur, be prepared for success. Some entrepreneurs fail because they didn't plan for success. What if things go well? What if things go very well? Are you prepared for the impact that success may have? Experiencing success, and handling growth and expansion, are some of the biggest challenges entrepreneurs can face. So be prepared, and plan for, success. And be cautious in managing the challenges of growth. Getting a venture started is one thing. Managing its success is a whole other set of challenges. There you have it – a basic primer on entrepreneurship and what it takes to be an entrepreneur – or an entrepreneurial person. Of course, there is much more you can learn about being an entrepreneur or an enterprising person. There are many other resources that can help you.

SPENDING MONEY AND TAKING CONTROL

U sing money wisely is a skill – and a skill that will usually pay off. Any skill, like being a plumber, an auto mechanic, a doctor, or a dentist requires learning – what's important to know, how things work, how to do the work, what can go wrong, and what to do in certain circumstances. That's the case with money too. There are things to learn about money that can help you to take better control, make better decisions, and have a better chance of achieving your goals. To help you take better control of money in your life, let's cover a few of the "basics." These can help build your basic understanding as you get more and more involved with money and money decisions.

In the old days, what people used as money often had value in and of itself. For example, some money was made from metals like gold and silver. The coins were actually valuable because of the metal they contained. A gold coin had a value based on the worth of the gold used to make it. Money made of material like gold and silver is said to have "intrinsic" value. There was actual value in the money itself. That is not the case today. A $100 bill doesn't contain $100 worth of metal or any other material worth anything close to that. The $100 bill doesn't "contain" $100 in value – it "represents" $100 in value. You can use a $100 bill to buy $100 worth of stuff. Stores, for example, will provide you with products worth $100 in return for that colourful (and now plasticized) little piece of paper. You don't have to give them gold, or a goat, or bushels full of grapes. One little piece of paper and you can walk out with $100 worth of product – with nobody chasing you. But why are they willing to accept it? They accept it because they know others will accept it from them. They will be able to get something else, from someone else, worth $100. The $100 bill has become "legal tender" – along with the quarter, the loonie, the ten dollar bill and all our other coins and currency. Legal tender is what we officially use as money.

Money that doesn't have "intrinsic value" but, instead, "represents value" is called "fiat money." That is what we use today. A dime isn't made of anything worth 10 cents. The same is true for the loonie, the toonie, the $5 bill and so on. They don't have "intrinsic value" – but they do have "purchasing power." You can use them to buy things. In the course of history, a variety of things have served as money – gold, cows, shells, playing cards, and other things in countries around the world. But, in today's world, what is used as money has become pretty standard from country to country. That doesn't mean we all use the same money. Canada's money is different from money used in the U.S., Japan, Europe, Russia, and so on. What is common is that all countries, for the most part, use fiat money. There aren't countries using cows as currency anymore. However, in some countries you can probably still trade a cow for some things. Trading one item in exchange for another without using money is called "bartering." Bartering is basically another word for trading – trading one thing for something else. The problem with bartering for a modern economy is that with so many goods and services produced, setting prices would be a nightmare. What is one computer worth – 500 towels? Or 3 bicycles? Or a six-person tent? Or ½ of a good lawnmower?

Have you ever bartered or made a trade – and exchanged one thing for another without using money? If so, how did that come about? Was it easy?

Have you ever had to exchange indian rupees for the currency of another country? If so, how did you do that? What was the cost to make the exchange? Why was there a cost? Did you use the money when you visited another country? If so, how did the costs for things compare with the costs in india? If costs were different than in india, why do you think that was the case?

So different countries use different kinds of currencies as money. But, for something to serve as money, it has to have some specific characteristics. • It has to be durable. If we used apples, they would rot. That wouldn't work. • It must not be easily reproduced. We could use chestnuts. They're pretty durable. But soon everyone would be planting chestnut trees.

There would soon be so many chestnuts, and prices would rise so high, you'd need a wheelbarrow full of chestnuts to buy a loaf of bread. • While it must be relatively scarce and not easy to reproduce, it can't be too scarce. If it was, we wouldn't have enough for all the exchanges that have to take place. So we could use whooping cranes – but we'd never have enough for the money we need. • It also has to be easy to transport and carry around. We could use elephants but just try putting a couple of them in your pocket or purse. • And finally, it has to be divisible into fractions. We use a dollar as our basic unit of currency but we also have 5/100 of a dollar (nickel), 10/100 of a dollar (dime) and so on.

So money needs to be durable, not easily reproduced, available in sufficient quantity for transactions in the economy, easily carried, and divisible. But more than anything, it has to be widely accepted as money. So what we use as money has changed over time. How we use money has also changed. Today, we have a pretty sophisticated financial system – one in which you often don't actually need to hold or handle much money. Why? Because we have things like debit cards and online banking. We can transfer money through our computers from the comfort of our homes – or in our car – or on the bus. We can send money to someone overseas in a flash. Things have changed dramatically over the last thirty years or so in terms of money and how we use it.

How do you like to pay for things you buy? Do you carry much money on you? Why or why not?

There are three basic roles. First, money serves as a "medium of exchange." As we have noted, it helps us buy things from one another. It is a lot easier to use money than to barter and try to exchange one item for another. We all use money to buy things – as a medium of exchange. But this brings us to another role of money – it makes it easy to set prices. Rather than having to set prices in terms of all sorts of things, prices are set in terms of money. How much money does it cost? What is the price? Everything has a price – in terms of money. Money is said, then, to serve as a "unit of account." That makes things easier too. Finally, money serves as a "store of value." That means we can save it and use it in the future. We can store money for the future in different ways – and in different places. We can even try and do things with the money we set aside to try to increase its value – by saving or investing it.

So let's review a list of some key things to note about money: • Our money isn't valuable in and of itself. Its value is in what we can get with our money – it's "purchasing power." • Prices will affect the purchasing power of our money. If prices, on average, rise, that will lower what we can buy with the same amount of money. Rising prices therefore reduce the purchasing power of money. • If prices, on average, rise in an economy, that is called "inflation." The job of trying to control inflation in india lies primarily with the Reserve Bank of india. You can't do your banking at the Reserve Bank of india. It is an agency of the federal government. The banks deal with the Reserve Bank of india – individual indians and businesses do not. An important job of the Reserve Bank of india is to try and influence the levels of spending, the money supply, and interest rates so that prices are kept pretty stable. There is probably no more important role for the Bank than to keep the rate of inflation under control to help protect the purchasing power of india's money.

• Most of us keep much of our money in financial institutions. We have a variety of ways to get and use our money – cash, cheques, debit cards, online transfers – if, for example, we want to make a purchase – like buying a book, a meal, a car, a computer, etc. • Credit cards are not a form of money and they don't help us get and use our money. They help us get and use someone else's money – such as money that a bank has made available to you on a credit card if you need it. • Most of us "store" our money in financial institutions by putting it in different kinds of accounts – savings account, chequing account, savings-chequing account, tax-free savings account, and so on. We may invest some of those savings to try and increase the value of our savings in the future. For example, we might invest some savings in stocks, bonds, mutual funds, treasury bills, and so on. Therefore, by putting our money in a financial institution, we can store our money to protect it, be able to get it when we need it, and hopefully find ways to increase its value over time. • Inflation makes it harder to increase the value of our savings. If you are able to earn 3% interest on your savings in a year, but inflation is 3%, your savings will have trouble increasing their "purchasing power." Inflation can eat away at the value of our money and make saving for the future more difficult. • At the same time, if inflation is 3%, gaining 3% on your money is better than earning nothing at all. If you don't earn 3%, the purchasing power of your savings may actually fall. So it is a good idea to put your savings to work to try and earn some more money for you – and to protect its value and purchasing power from inflation.

Before we wrap up this brief primer on money, there is another key point to make. In addition to the other key role we mentioned about the

Reserve Bank of india – that is, influencing interest rates, the money supply, and level of spending to keep inflation under control – the Reserve Bank of india also produces our currency – our paper money. (Note: the Canadian Mint produces our coins.) Since the Reserve Bank of india can print money, the question may come to mind – why not just print more money and give it to people and make everyone better off. Sounds like a good idea. Unfortunately, here's why it won't work.Think of the game "Monopoly." If you have never played Monopoly, get someone to briefly explain the game. In essence, though, here's how it works. Players role dice and move their player pieces around the board, buy "properties" that are available for sale, trade to form "monopolies," (get all the properties that are of the same colour or type) and build houses and hotels to try and make more money than the other players – and win the game. At the beginning of the game, players are given a certain amount of money. They use this money to buy properties, to buy and sell properties to form their monopolies, and to buy houses and hotels. Now what if we doubled the amount of money in the game? Would the players, overall, be better off?

No. Why not? Because there is no added "value" in the game that the money can buy. There are the same number of properties, houses, and hotels. The added money can't be used to buy anything new. The players may have more money but they will need more money, due to higher prices, just to buy the same things as they would in a game with half the amount of money. In terms of "real value," players are no better off having twice as much money. What will be the result? Prices in the game will increase. In fact, on average, they would likely double. The added money would be "chasing after" the same quantity of goods. With more money in the game, prices will be bid up as players look to build their monopolies and make exchanges with one another. The same is true in our economy. If we add more money to the economy, but don't produce any more, the added money will just push up prices. This brings us to a key point. Money is of little value in and of itself. We can't eat it, wear it, or build houses with it. Its value is in what it can buy – its purchasing power. So if we have twice as much money – but prices double and we have nothing more to buy – we are no better off.

Things are different when the economy produces more. More money will be needed by the economy when there are more goods and services produced. More money will be needed so that the new items can be bought. But if it's just the same quantity of stuff in the economy this year as last year, any added money will just lead to things costing more. And inflation will just eat away at the purchasing power of our money.

So keeping inflation under control is a key job for the Reserve Bank of india.

To review – money is a "medium of exchange" (we use it for spending), a "store of value," (we use it for saving and investing), and a "unit of account," (it enables us to set all prices in terms of money.) When it comes to what we do with money, everyone faces a variety of money challenges and decisions. These decisions include: • Getting money • Spending money • Overall budgeting, planning and managing money • Borrowing money • Saving and investing money • Protecting money • And donating money – giving some of our money away to others

We have looked at ways of "getting money" in earlier modules. We have also looked at how to make good decisions when it comes to spending money. We'll soon look more closely at some of the "major expenses" – the bigger things that many people spend money on. As we continue, we will look at each of these other money challenges and decisions as well. We will try and help you develop your money skills – take more control over your money – and have a better chance of reaching your financial goals. Let's turn our attention to the overall challenge of budgeting, planning, and managing your money

How Financial Institutions Work

The Business of Banking Banks Aim to Earn a Profit for Shareholders Banks operate as businesses and, as such, aim to make a profit. The profit earned by the banks can be reinvested, saved for reinvestment in the future, or distributed to shareholders – the owners of the bank. Most indian banks are privately owned by many shareholders and the shares are available for purchase on the public stock exchange. The shareholders receive a share of the profits, which are distributed as dividends.

What Do Banks Do With Their Deposits? In managing their deposits, banks will allocate their deposits in three general areas: • Cash reserves: These are held to cover day-to-day needs for cash, and some are held for precautionary reasons to cover potential, unforeseen needs. • Highly liquid assets: These include treasury bills, which earn interest but are quickly convertible to cash if the bank should find that it has additional cash needs. Liquidity refers to how quickly an asset can be converted to cash at a predictable value. • Less liquid assets: These include commercial, consumer, and mortgage loans, which return a higher rate of interest to the bank but are less easily converted to cash and represent greater risk.

Can you think of times when banks may need to have more cash on hand to respond to depositors wanting to withdraw cash?

Do you have money deposited in a bank? If so, how did you decide which bank to use?

Do you actually use much cash these days to handle your purchases? How do you prefer to handle your purchases? Do you know of any costs you incur when you use other forms of payment?

Banks will hold on to sufficient funds as cash or highly liquid assets for those clients with deposits to feel confident that they can always access their funds when needed. The decisions made by banks about the quantity of liquid assets, such as cash, to hold in reserve are determined by a variety of factors. For example, during the Christmas season, people tend to withdraw more funds and spend more. The banks will need to have a higher quantity of liquid assets available at such times. But not all of the banks' deposits need to be held as cash or in highly liquid form. Why? Since the vast majority of payments made today are not in cash, but via cheque, debit card, or online transfers, the banks only need to hold a relatively small portion of all their deposits to service the needs of their depositors on a day-to-day basis. The rest of the deposited funds are then put to work by financial institutions as loans or investments to earn interest – with profit being the goal. We noted that banks will aim to earn a profit for their shareholders. Profit is defined as Total Revenues minus Total Expenses. Let's look closer at the expense side of the banking business.What costs does a bank incur in operating its business affairs? We know that a bank incurs a cost for the funds held as interest-bearing deposits. That is, a bank has to pay interest on its deposits. In addition, a bank faces costs such as salaries for employees, property expenses for its branches and offices, advertising, branch operations, and taxes. In other words, a bank faces most of the normal operating costs that other businesses face. Another potential expense for a bank is not as obvious – and that is the allowance for possible losses on loans. As you can imagine, banks make loans on the assumption that they will be repaid. Extensive checks are done on a borrower before the bank provides a loan in order to try to ensure the loan will, in fact, be repaid. But sometimes things don't go as planned or forecasted and some borrowers may find that they can't meet their payments. They may even encounter such hardship that they may not be able to repay the loan – or a portion of the loan. The banks have to plan for the possibility of such situations and the possible cost of loan losses. That's the cost side of the banking business.

What about the income side?

The Income Side Banks earn income on the spread (or the difference) between the interest rate they pay to depositors and the interest rate that they charge to borrowers. But that's not the only way in which the banks can earn income. Banks invest in assets such as bonds and treasury bills that pay interest to the banks. Banks also earn income from foreign exchange commissions as people and businesses pay a fee to convert money from the currency of one country to the currency of another. They also earn significant income from a variety of possible fees that may be charged, such as those charged on/for: • certain bank accounts as maintenance fees • providing hard copies of bank statements • requesting a deposit slip • returned deposit fees (if someone writes you a NSF cheque) • overdraft charges • ATM fees • notarizing documents • lost card fees • and others As with any business, if a bank's total revenue exceeds its total expenses, it earns a profit. Generally, the better a bank is managed, the higher its profit and its stock price will be. However, if a bank is not managed well, and if its performance doesn't meet expectations, disgruntled shareholders may exert pressure for changes in the bank's management.

What fees might you be paying to a bank for services the bank provides?

TAKING CONTROL OF YOUR MONEY

L et's assume you have found one or more ways to get money. You have an income coming in. You have money decisions to make. What are you going to do with your money? How are you going to manage it?

Putting together a basic "budget" can help you manage and control your money. A budget is a plan for how you use your money on a month-to-month basis. It helps you look at your expenses – both those you have each month and those that come up now and then. It helps you work out how you will cover your expenses from your income. A budget also helps you to save, build up your savings over time, and achieve your financial goals.

Do you already have your money under control? Do you know where it's going – how you are using it? Are you able to save money or do you always tend to be short of money? How are you as a saver?

How will you afford some of the bigger things you hope for some day if you don't save for the future? Is there anything you want you know you will have to save for?

Interestingly, survey after survey shows that most people think that having a budget is important – and budgeting is a wise thing to do. But, as surveys also show, most Canadians don't work with a budget. Why not?

Many people don't budget because they feel that they don't earn enough money to need a budget. In reality, the less money you have, the more likely it is that a budget can help you. You will want to get the most out of your money. You won't want to waste any. You'll want to make as many "good" money decisions as you can. Budgeting can help – and can help most people regardless of how much money they have.

There are also many people who don't budget because they fear that a budget will put them in a "financial strait-jacket." They think a budget will have too much control over what they do. Actually, a person who fears that a budget will control them too much is often a person whose spending is out of control. If you fear a budget, you probably need to budget. A budget helps you gain control – not lose it. Deciding to budget is a sure sign you have decided to take control of your money. But have you any idea how your money is being used – where it is going?

Did you ever think of having a budget to help you? Do you already have a budget? Do you know if your family works with a budget?

Whether or not you use a budget, stay in control of your money. Know where it's going. And make sure it's going where you would like it to go.

The best way to start taking control of money is to "track your expenses." And that isn't hard today with how easy it is to carry a little notebook or use the note pad on a cell phone or other hand-held device. All that you have to do is, over a month or two or three, write down what you spend your money on: $12 movie; $35 scarf; $19 book; $80 bus pass; and so on. Then, take a few minutes at the end of that time and write down a number of categories. These might include: • Transportation • Snacks, eating out, and food in general • School supplies • Movies, music and entertainment • Your hobby • Cell phone or Internet • Savings • And so on

Based on how you use your money, what categories of spending would you list?

Next, before you add up how much you have spent on each category, write down the percentage of your money you think you spend on each category.

Then add up how much money you actually spent on each category. See if the results surprise you. Or see if the results come close to what you expected. This will give you one sign as to whether you know where your money is going – and if you are in control. There is one other thing you can do too. Look at how much you are spending in each category. Is that the way you want to be using your money? Are you spending more in some areas than you would like to – or think you should? Are you saving as much as you would like – or need to?

Going through this exercise – seeing where your money is going – and thinking about where you want it to go – should tell you pretty clearly if you need to budget. If you are pleased with how things are, and happy with how you are using your money, you may not need a budget – at least not yet. It may be that you are in control of your money and managing it well. However, as you make more money, take on new expenses, and life becomes more complicated, you may find that a having budget will help you stay in control. At the very least, on a regular basis, you should do a check on how you are using your money. Track your expenses over a period of time. See if things are still on track and how you would like them to be. Your goals may change. You may start to build a household and family. You may lose your job – or get a job – or get a better job – or get a raise. Life is always changing. So keep in touch with how you are using your money – and check whether it is being used as you would like.

Save some of your money! If at all possible, get into a habit of saving – even if it isn't a lot. There is a saying that "few people get rich off their income." Build up some savings if you can. It can make a big difference.

As your life circumstances change, think of the changes this may have on how you use your money. Do you need to change your budget? Or do you now need to budget if you didn't before?

Now, on the other hand, when you track how you are using your money, you may not like what you find. You may find you are spending more on one area than you would like. You may find you aren't saving enough – or that you are charging too much on credit cards – or that you aren't able to spend money in some areas that you would like. Maybe you would like to join a club or a workout program and don't have the money to do so – based on how you are currently using your money. If you find things are not as you would like – or if you would like to change things for some reason – or if things have changed in your life – you may find that budgeting your money will help. And even if you are happy with what you find, you may want to use a budget too – to keep you on track and to keep you in touch with where your money is going. A budget is a great way to keep control of your money – or gain control if things are not going as you would like. Let's take a closer look at what a budget is and how it can help you.

Controlling Your Money – Budgeting

A budget is not a strait-jacket. If anything, it can help give you greater financial freedom. A budget helps you know where your money is going. As you work out your budget, you may find ways to cut back or ways to save more. If you can, use your budget to pay yourself first. If you pay yourself last, it often ends up that there is nothing left. Put some of your money in savings when you get it and budget how you will use the rest. Even if it is a small amount, try and start by paying yourself – with savings. And try and make saving a habit from a young age. It is a great habit to develop. It can be an important way to achieve your goals. Basically, a budget involves comparing your income with your expenses. It gives you a picture of your financial situation – and where you may be heading. And it should give you a very clear indication of whether or not you are on the road to accomplishing your longer-term goals. The first thing to work out is your monthly income. That will tell you what you've got to work with. The second step is to list your monthly expenses. Some expenses you will be able to control (for example, entertainment). Others you can't control as readily (for example, your housing costs/rent – at least you can't control them today). You can always take more control of a cost like rent by moving to less expensive accommodation or getting a roommate to help share the cost – but that will take some time. You will usually have two categories of expenses in your budget. First, you will have your regular monthly expenses. These are expenses you know you will have each month. Second, you will have your irregular expenses – those that come up every now and then or perhaps once a year. For example, you may have an annual car insurance bill you will need to pay – or a club membership – or a new cell phone you know you are going to need soon. You will want to plan for such expenses in your budget and allocate some funds each month so that you can pay them when they are due. As shown below, you can divide the total of these occasional expenses by 12. This will give you a target amount to set aside each month so that you are able and prepared to cover them. The monthly amount you need to set aside to cover both your irregular expenses, and your regular monthly expenses, make up your total monthly expenses. When you add up your total monthly income and your total monthly expenses, you will see whether you are able to save money or not. You will find if you are spending more than you would like in certain areas. You will quickly see if you are in control of your money – or heading toward money problems. In short, you can learn a great deal about you and your money by creating – and using – a budget.

Do you have a credit card? Do you have more than one credit card? If so, are you paying off the balance each month? Or are you carrying a balance from month to month? Is that balance growing? Do you know the interest rate that you are paying on money you owe on the credit card? One of the fastest ways to have money problems is to charge more on a credit card than you are able to pay that month. Then it happens the next month... then the next... and, before you know it, you have a large balance of debt on which are you paying a lot of interest. Does this describe your situation? Or are you in control of your credit card(s)?

Sample Costs When Moving Out on Your Own

When you are about to move out on your own, it is often difficult to estimate the various costs that you will face. You may be aware of such costs including rent, hydro/electricity, gas, food, leisure activities, and so on. Talking with parents and friends can help you get a sense of the costs you will face – and how much those costs might be each month. But, if you would like some online help, you can go to the following link provided by Numbeo. Numbeo, as their website states, "is the world's largest database of user contributed data about cities and countries worldwide. Numbeo provides current and timely information on world living conditions including cost of living, housing indicators, health care, traffic, crime and pollution." Numbeo has cost estimates for living in Canada and you can access the site via the following link: https://www.numbeo.com/cost-of-living/country_ result.jsp?country=Canada There is also a drop-down menu where you can enter your city and it will provide you with local cost estimates. Many factors will, of course, affect the costs you will pay. But the site does give you a sense of the costs and it also shows ranges from the lowest cost to the highest cost. It may help you, in addition to the help you will get from parents and friends, in estimating the costs you will face and what you might have to put in your budget for each expense. Be sure to build in a cushion in your budgeted costs especially when you are still figuring out what the exact costs could be and don't forget to set aside money regularly to establish an emergency fund if you don't already have one. You can also get cost estimates from whomever is renting you the place you will move into. But those are not always precise either since people behave and act differently and therefore also use different amounts of electricity, water, internet, and so on. In the end, when you move out and move in to your own place, you will quickly find out what the actual costs you will incur will be and you can then adjust your monthly budget accordingly.

You hope they won't arise, but what unexpected or surprise costs can you think of that could come up – and that you should be prepared for?

If you are planning on moving to another town or city, check out how costs can differ from one location to another – sometimes by a great deal.

Everybody knows about taxes. Usually you hear people complaining about taxes. Why do we pay taxes anyway? Taxes are payments that we make to governments – federal, provincial, and municipal. It is the means by which governments receive the money to provide goods and services. The primary goods and services provided by governments are called "public goods and services" – that is, goods and services that everyone should have access to regardless of their ability to pay. That includes things like public schools, hospitals, sidewalks, roadways, sewer systems, defense, judicial systems and courts, and so on. Governments can also decide to produce goods and services that are not necessarily public goods and services but that they think should be provided. Different political parties will differ in terms of the kinds of goods and services they believe governments should provide – and voters will determine which party will form the government and put their policies in place. If a government spends more than it takes in revenue, it runs a deficit and will need to borrow money to cover its spending. If a government brings in more in revenue than it spends, it runs a surplus. Over time, the overall level of government debt or surplus will rise or fall based on the outcome of each year. Just so you know, the federal debt, as of 2018, was over $650 billion. If you add in the debt of the provinces, the total debt is about $1.4 trillion. You can see that governments, over time, have been running deficits much more than they run surpluses. You can follow the level of federal debt via the Canadian Taxpayers Federation "National Debt Clock" at http://www.debtclock.ca/. We pay taxes to fund government spending. You will have the opportunity to exercise your right to vote in elections as you make decisions regarding which political party's views and policies you support. We pay both federal and provincial income taxes in Canada based upon the level of income we make. For example, in 2018, the following were the federal tax rates: • 15% on the first $46,605 of taxable income • 20.5% on the next $46,603 of taxable income (on the portion of taxable income over 46,605 up to $93,208), + • 26% on the next $51,281 of taxable income (on the portion of taxable income over $93,208 up to $144,489), • 29% on the next $61,353 of taxable income (on the portion of taxable income over 144,489 up to $205,842), • 33% of taxable income over $205,842.

What "public" goods and services do you use on a daily, weekly, or monthly basis?

If you can, talk with your parents/guardians about tax credits they have been able to use to reduce taxable income and the amount of tax they need to pay.

When you are employed, try to make sure your employer deducts, and submits to the government, the right amount of tax that you will have to pay. This is done on a monthly basis. You probably don't want to find at the end of the year that you have to pay more taxes than was deducted.

your taxable income. Tax evasion is against the law. In contrast, tax avoidance refers to legal steps you can take as permitted within the tax laws to reduce your tax burden. One way that you can reduce your tax burden is by making sure that you claim all the tax deductions and tax credits you're entitled to. You can also reduce your tax burden by contributing money to an RRSP or setting up a TFSA. These are referred to as "tax avoidance" strategies but they are perfectly legal.

SPENDING ON MAJOR PURCHASES

A t some time in their lives, many people will face a number of major expenses or purchases. Three of the most common ones are: • Education and/or training • Buying or leasing a car • Housing Another area of spending that is often a major one for youth is for a cell phone or hand-held device of some kind. Let's take a closer look at each of these major purchases.

A good education can affect your ability to get the kind of job you want and the level of income you can earn. To get a good job, some post-secondary education or training is almost a requirement these days. Dropping out before completing high school, or not getting any further education or training after high school, can make it very difficult to compete with others in the job market. The cost of post-secondary education and training is one of the first major costs many people face in life. It is the first reason many people go into debt. And many young people are completing their education and training today with $15,000, $20,000, $25,000 or more in debt. To prevent this, it's best to plan ahead – and to start saving early. The earlier you start saving, the more time your savings will have to grow.

How can you prepare for the cost of postsecondary education and training? Will you need to pay for your own education and training? Will parents, guardians, or other family members be able to help? Are you likely to need a loan to help out? Everyone's situation is different. In any case, to prepare for the cost, it's good to have a sense of what the cost will be.

Do some research on the Internet to see how many jobs require postsecondary education or training today – and which jobs are available to those with high school graduation only.

The Costs of Post-secondary Education and Training Let's take a look at some of the more common costs. TUITION Tuition fees vary from school to school and program to program. They also vary across the country. You will need to do some research to see what the costs are for programs that are of interest to you. APPLYING It costs money to apply to post-secondary institutions. You only pay these fees once, when you apply. But costs can vary. Check with the guidance staff at your school to find out more.

The Investor Education Fund has information on their web site on the average tuition fees at the different indian universities and colleges.

Buying Or Leasing A Car You may not need a car now. You may not need a car at any time in your life. But at some point, you may decide to get one. If you do, will you buy or lease a car? Let's take a look at both options.

Leasing A Car Leasing a car involves making monthly payments for the use of a car for a certain period of time – e.g. 3 or 4 years. It involves signing a lease agreement – and these can vary quite a bit. A lease agreement usually includes things such as the following. • The length of the lease (e.g. 36 months or 48 months, etc.) • The estimated value of the car at the end of the lease. This will determine how much of the car's value you will be paying for. • The down-payment – the amount you pay at the time you sign the lease. This will lower your total lease payment and your monthly payment. • The interest or financing amount you will pay. The interest rates on leases can vary greatly and some companies will offer lower interest rates to encourage people to lease their cars. • The number of kilometers you can drive without extra charges – e.g. 20,000 or 24,000 kms. a year. You can pick from different "mileage" allowances. The less you drive, the lower the cost. But, if you go over your allowance you will be charged a certain amount per kilometer. Your lease will tell you the cost for each km. over. • The warranty that applies to the car. • The total monthly cost you will pay. • The total cost you will pay for the whole lease.

Advantages Of Leasing Lower monthly payments: When you "buy" a car you are paying for the total value of the car. When you lease a car, you are only paying for "part of the car" – that part you "use up" over the period of the lease. From the moment a car is sold, it "depreciates" in value. Its value will decrease each year over time. In a lease, you will pay for how much it is estimated the car will depreciate in value while you have it. By paying only for that part of the car that you will use over three years, your monthly costs will be lower than if you bought the car. Lower down-payment: Whether you buy or lease a car, you may have to make a down-payment – or you may want to make a down-payment. The larger the down-payment you make on a lease, the less you will have to pay back and the lower the monthly cost. You may be able to make a lower down-payment by leasing a car than by buying a car.

Lower repair costs: If you lease a car and return it after 3-4 years, you can often avoid expensive car repairs that can come up for older cars. Use of a newer car: If you prefer to stay in a newer car, leasing means you will likely get a new car every three or four years. You can also choose a different kind of car when your lease is up if you like. Tax advantages: For some people, for example those who need to use a car for business, they may be able to get a tax deduction based on how much the car is used for business. Disadvantages Of Leasing You don't own the car: At the end of the lease you turn the car back in. You don't own the car – you aren't acquiring an "asset." As a result, you won't get to a point where you own the car and no longer have to make monthly payments. You have to return it as you got it: The car is not yours to do with as you like. You will need to return it as you got it. You are sort of locked in: If things change for you, and you want out of the lease, it can be difficult – and maybe costly – to get out of the lease. There are some possible options – for example getting someone else to take over your lease – but it will be more difficult than if you bought a car and could sell it. Higher insurance costs? Maybe. Maybe not. Check this out prior to making your decision to see if insurance rates will be different if you lease or buy. The "extra" charges: As noted, if you drive more kilometers than those in your "allowance", you will pay for the extra kilometers.And if there is any damage beyond "normal wear and tear" you will probably have to pay for those repairs.

If you find you are facing a decision of buying or leasing a car, you may want to look into leasing if: • You don't have a lot of money to use to spend on a car or want to make lower monthly payments • You don't want to worry about expensive car repairs • You like staying in a newer car • You need to use a car for your business • You don't drive more than say 20,000–24,000 kms. a year • You have a reliable source of income • You don't care that much about owning the car and having the car as an asset

If, on the other hand, you decide you want to buy a car, the following are some general tips to help. Tips When Buying A Car • Explore various possible sources for a car: dealers; private sale; cars that were repossessed and are being sold off; car rental companies and taxis and police vehicles (be aware, though, that used cars that served as taxis or police vehicles may have received pretty hard use.) • Never buy a used car without having it inspected by a good mechanic. • If you buy a used car, check for things such as: is there rust on the surface and under the car; how is the compression in the engine; has the car been painted or been in an accident; are the tires worn unevenly indicating a problem with the alignment; how is the smoke from the exhaust – is it white, which is normal, or is it black or blue indicating problems; are there any leaks under the car – let it sit in one spot for a while, then move it and check; do the gears shift smoothly? • Set a limit on the amount that you are going to spend for a car and stick to it. • If you buy a used car, make sure that there are no liens against it, that is, someone might have taken out a loan and used the car as collateral. If they did, and the lien still exists, then the car can be taken from you and sold to pay off the debt. • Check the history of a used car if you can. Contact past owners if you can by tracing the history of the car through provincial records. • Negotiate the price. Car dealers will bargain – and usually expect to. You may also be able to bargain if you have a car to "trade in" as part of the deal. The dealer may be able to bargain on the "trade-in allowance." • Buy in the winter, if you can, when fewer cars are purchased. Demand is lower and you may be able to strike a better deal. • Keep up regular maintenance on a car – it more than pays for itself in the long run by helping to avoid major repairs. • Read all contracts carefully. • Never sign an offer for a car until you are absolutely sure that you want to buy it. • Don't be pressured into a sale. If you feel you are being pressured, back away and think about it. People are especially likely to be influenced by a friendly or aggressive salesperson. Most car dealers won't want you to leave if they feel they are close to a deal. But if you feel uncertain – walk away and take some time to think. • Check any warranties that are offered to see who backs them – the manufacturer? the dealer? an insurance company? • Don't buy a used car without seeing proof of ownership of the vehicle. • Check the consumer reports publications and other books to research the record and reputation of the car you are considering. • Get a receipt for any sale, and make sure that it states any equipment on the car that is to be included that might be removed by the current owner. • Should you get a new or used car? Do you have a choice? Used cars are cheaper, depreciate less quickly than new ones, and usually cost less to insure. On the other hand, used cars often aren't backed up by a dealer who you can go back to if you have a problem, they usually cost more to operate, and you may not know how a used car has been handled or driven by previous owners. • Make sure that you really need a car. What are the options (bicycle, public transportation, etc.)? Is it worth the expense? And, if you get one, enjoy it and drive safely!

Housing Moving Out On Your Own One decision many people face when they leave home is whether to move out on their own or move in with one or more roommates. Both can have their challenges. If you move out on your own, the cost will usually be higher than if you were able to share the cost with others. However, living with others – including friends – can be a challenge. It is usually a good idea to establish house rules at the outset to be prepared for any issues that might arise. For example, you may find that you have differences in terms of work/study habits, or neatness/cleanliness, or how things are organized, or eating or drinking habits and personal values when it comes to things like smoking drugs, etc., or how visiting friends behave, and so on. It is best to think ahead and have a plan for dealing with differences or disputes. Now, what about the costs of moving out? Let's assume you will rent first. Not many young people can afford to buy right away.

Do you prefer living on your own? Or with one or more roommates? What are the benefits of each? What are the challenges? What has your experience been like if you have lived on your own or what can you learn from others who have?

Decide whether you will look for furnished or unfurnished accommodation. Do you have furniture? How about your roommate(s) if you choose to live with others? • Are utilities (oil/gas/electricity/water/cable/Internet) included in the rent, or do you have to pay? • How close will you be to school or work? Does the location add to, or save on, transportation costs? Will it be important to you to live in a certain area? • If you are moving out to go to school, do you want to live on campus or off? If on, can you get into residence? If off, can you afford it? Does it cost more or less than school residences? • What services are provided by the landlord? What are your responsibilities? • If you have a car, is parking available? If so, do you have to pay extra for it? If not, is parking available nearby? • What is the neighbourhood like? Safe? Attractive? One you will be happy living in? • What are the neighbours like? Quiet? Noisy? Friendly? Does that matter to you? • Check things such as the plumbing, wiring, and appliances. They can become very important to you once you move in. Besides, you also want to ensure that they are safe and reliable. • Is there any storage space available if you need it? Does it cost extra? • Check to see what access your landlord has to your place. Usually a landlord can only enter for an emergency or after giving you prior notice of 24 hours. • Check the security of the property. Are you vulnerable to break-ins – or theft? • How much notice do you have to give before leaving if you have to move for some reason? • Be prepared to pay the first and last month's rent. This is a common practice. The landlord holds the last month's rent as protection. However, you should be paid interest on that money. • You may also have to pay a security deposit when you move in to cover any possible damage at the time you move out. If there is no damage, and no repairs that the landlord has to pay for, you should get this deposit back when you move out. • Consider getting insurance to cover any damage that might occur – for example a fire in the apartment you are renting. Renter's insurance is available if you think it is right for you. These are just some of the things to keep in mind when you move out and rent your first place. That first move out on your own can bring many pressures, stresses, challenges, problems, and expenses. Plan it well. Now let's take a closer look at what is involved in buying a home if that's what you may do some day

Purchasing A Home TYPES OF HOMES One of the major decisions you will have to make when you look to "buying" a home is to decide what type you want to buy. The following are possibilities: • Detached house: a house that stands on its own unattached to any other building • Semi-Detached: a house that is attached on one side to another house • Townhouse (Row House): a house that is attached to another house on both sides • Duplex: a house in which there are two separate living areas, for example, one upstairs and another downstairs (triplexes have three living areas, fourplexes have four) – may be detached, semi-detached, or attached on both sides • Condominium: an apartment that you buy rather than rent • Mobile home: many areas in Canada have mobile home parks where people live in mobile homes if they wish • Co-op: a property you purchase in conjunction with others; for example, you may own an apartment that is part of a co-op where the members of the co-op own and manage the building You will have to decide what type of housing you prefer – and what type you can afford. Unfortunately, the two don't always go together. You will likely have to make trade-offs as you look for a home you want to buy. You will have to consider location, size, condition (are renovations needed?), quality of appliances, and so on. Probably the most important factor, though, will be what you can afford. Let's look a little more closely at the financial aspects of buying a home.

Mortgages Most homeowners have a mortgage – at least when they first buy a house. They may eventually pay off the mortgage and own the house outright – but most have a mortgage in the beginning. A mortgage is simply a loan that you take out to use toward buying a home. For many Canadians it can be quite a big debt – hundreds of thousands of dollars. It is not as difficult to borrow quite large sums of money toward a mortgage as you might think. Why? Because the lender is pretty certain of getting the funds back. Why is that? Because the funds are being used to buy an asset – a house, condo, etc. – that has value. If you don't keep up the payments, the home you bought could be sold to get the funds to pay back the mortgage. That is why financial institutions will want to send out an "appraiser" to check the value of the property you are planning to buy. The lender will want to make sure that you are not paying more for the house than it is worth. They want to make sure there is at least enough value in the property for them to be able to get their funds back if you, for some reason, can't pay the mortgage. The lender will not lend you the full amount to buy your home. There are legal limits set in terms of how much can be loaned to a home buyer. This is to try and stop people from buying homes they can't afford.

Go online and check out what the costs are of (a) different homes of different types in different areas and (b) what the cost is to "carry" mortgages of different amounts at different interest rates.

Let's assume a purchaser has managed to save $40,000 and needs a $200,000 mortgage to buy a $240,000 home. The first decision will be where to get the mortgage. It will be good to shop around and compare mortgage rates. There are web sites to help home buyers shop for and compare rates. There is a good chance your bank will match the rates offered by others if you find a lower rate elsewhere. You will need to work with the lender to see if they are willing to lend you the money. The lender will do a credit check and look into your "credit worthiness." Let's suppose you are approved and you can get a $200,000 mortgage. Second, you will have to decide on the "amortization period" – the number of years over which you will plan to pay back the mortgage loan – 25 years, 20 years,15 years? The shorter the amortization period, the lower your total interest cost. Third, the next decision will be the "terms" of the mortgage. Because most mortgages are over many years, lenders will only set the "terms" for a certain period of time – 6 months, 1 year, 2 years, etc. up to about 7 years. You will have to consider the interest rates that are offered for different lengths of time.

There will be a 6 month rate, 1 year rate, 2 year rate, and so on. To make your decision, you will have to think about whether you think interest rates may be headed higher or lower. Every time your term expires, you will have to negotiate new terms. You will do this up to the time your mortgage is paid off. Each time that your term is up, try to get the best terms you can and try and work things out so that you pay as little interest as possible.

The degree to which you own your home (versus how much of it the lender holds) is referred to as your "equity." If you pay $40,000 toward a $240,000 home, then you have $40,000 worth of equity. If the value of that home should rise, to say $260,000, then your equity increases. You still owe the balance of the mortgage, but your equity has increased by $20,000. The more quickly you pay off your mortgage, the more equity you have in your home. In addition, the more valuable your home becomes, the more your equity in your home will grow. Finally, if you ever buy a home, be aware of the costs in running a household beyond the mortgage payments – for example, property taxes, utilities such as water and electricity, repairs, heating, home insurance, and general upkeep. As we said, a home is the largest investment that many Canadians make in their entire lives. If one day you decide to purchase a home, do all you can to make sure that you know what you are getting into and that you make a wise decision. A major purchase for many young people is a cell phone – and not just purchasing a phone but paying the costs for using the phone. That's where the costs can really add up. Let's take a closer look at cell phones and plans.

If you think interest rates may be coming down, go for a shorter term – 6 months, 1 year or 2 years. Then, when your term is up, and if rates have come down, you can work out a new term at a lower rate. On the other hand, if you think interest rates may be headed higher, you may want to "lock in" for a longer period – 4 years, 5 years, etc. The interest rate you pay won't change over your "term." So, if you can get a good rate, and think rates may go higher, go for a longer term.

You may make your mortgage payments monthly, bi-weekly, bimonthly, or weekly. Pay as frequently as you can. You can save a great deal of money by paying on a weekly or biweekly basis rather than monthly

When you buy a home there are a number of costs to pay at the time you "close the deal." These can include: fees to the real estate agent, lawyers' fees, surveyor's cost if a survey is needed, cost for a house inspection, and so on. If you get to where you are going to look to buy a house, learn about all the other costs involved.

Smartphones And Plans Today, many, if not most, young people have smartphones or something similar to use for texting, gaming, going online, etc. Many young people may start out with someone else paying the bill. Or you may pay for yours right from the start – or take over payments at some point. In any case, decisions you make about smartphones, rate plans, data packages, etc. can have a big impact on cost. You'll want to make a careful decision. A good suggestion when you are exploring all smartphone options is to use the six decisionmaking steps discussed earlier. It can help guide your decision. In making your decision, you will need to consider things such as: • how much can you afford to spend – a key part of any decision? • what features do you want? or do you really need? • how many minutes a month will you use? • what areas will you be in when you use it? • what rate plan should you choose – if any?

Do you have a smartphone? Do you pay for it yourself? Do you know what can affect the monthly cost? Do you feel confident you have the right plan for you?

There will be many different features offered to you. Think about the ones you really need – and will use. Don't waste money on features you may never – or seldom – use. You may be offered a free phone – or a large discount on the price of a phone – if you sign up and sign a contract with a "provider" for a period of time – e.g. 3 years. This can help you get a phone at low or no cost – but you will be committing to using that provider for that period of time. This may be okay for you. You may find that the provider has a plan that works for you. And you can usually change the kind of plan you have, if you wish, during the contract if things should change. On the other hand, you may not need a contract with a provider. You may just want to pay month to month and keep things flexible. That is one decision you will have to make – to commit to a plan or not. When making your phone decision, think about how you will use the phone – talk with friends and family; send text messages; download music; play games; go online and so on. In addition, think about whether you will be using the phone in different locations – in the place where you live – in the place where you go to school – when you travel? Will you usually have access to free Wi-Fi or will you be relying on cellular service a great deal? See where service is provided for your phone without extra costs. If you use the phone outside of those areas, you can be charged "roaming fees" – and these can really add up! Look into and compare available data packages to see which would be most economical for you.

Getting out of a phone contract before it ends can be expensive. You may have to pay hundreds of dollars to do so. So think carefully about the decision you make with a service provider. $ Tip Phone plans and providers are changing all the time. Keep in touch with the changes and the deals and terms offered. You may be able to reduce your costs – even after you sign the contract. If you are looking to sign a contract for a phone plan, there are some things you should know or consider before you sign a contract: 1. What is included for the monthly fee you will pay? 2. What is your total monthly fee going to be – including taxes? 3. What is the charge if you use more minutes in a month than the plan covers? 4. What are the rates for long distance charges – and what are the areas where I can use the phone without paying long-distance charges? 5. What are the charges for text messaging and web browsing and downloading data? 6. Are there any special options such as free calling to a certain number of friends and family? 7. Are there ways to avoid or lower long-distance charges if you will be making long distance calls? 8. What would be the cost if, at some point, you wanted to get out of the contract? 9. Can you change the terms of your plan, at any time, without cost, during the contract? 10. What would be the best plan for you based on the amount you will use the phone – and how you will use it? Most providers will try and help you select the best plan for you – if you know how you will be using the phone. 11. See if a family member has a corporate phone plan that may allow you to join and reduce your costs. 12. Consider a family plan if more than one member of the family is getting a phone.

Phones can end up being very costly. Use them wisely. You don't want to find that a high cost each month is using up a lot of your monthly budget – or causing tension between you and a family member who may be paying your phone costs. We have now looked at a number of major purchases that many people make – and on which they spend their money. But spending is only one thing we do with our money. You will also hope to be able to "save" and "invest" some of your money to try to earn a return and increase the purchasing power of the funds saved. Let's turn our attention now to the topics of borrowing money and using credit.

BORROWING MONEY AND USING CREDIT

BORROWING MONEY

Most Canadians will have to borrow money at some point in their lives. It may be using a credit card to borrow money for a short time (hopefully a short period!). It may be a mortgage for a house that may take 25 years to repay. Borrowing money, and using debt, does not have to be a bad thing. It can help you in times of need or trouble – help you with large purchases – help you manage your monthly cash flow (consolidation loan) – and so on.

Borrowing money becomes a problem if you borrow too much – that is, more than you can afford. It's a problem if you borrow to where you can't do other things – or if you need to borrow to pay your regular monthly expenses. Just like your own money, you have to stay in control of the money you borrow from others. Let's begin by covering a few terms. A debtor is someone who borrows money from others. A creditor is someone who lends money to others. A debt is a liability – something that you owe. A credit is an asset – it is money that has been loaned to someone else to be paid back.

What is your attitude towards borrowing money? There is an old saying "never a borrower or lender be." Some people work to avoid debt. Some take on way too much. Where do you fall?

Borrowing Money Today Today, in general, more people are borrowing money than people did 30 or 40 years ago. Why is that? One reason people borrow more money today is that, by and large, incomes are higher than they used to be. With higher incomes, people can often afford to carry more debt. For example, if you earn an income of $80,000 a year and want to borrow $3,000 for three years, you probably won't have much of a problem (if you have a good "credit rating" and are seen as "credit worthy" – more on that shortly.) Why? Because your income is such that you probably won't have trouble paying back what you borrowed. The amount you borrow is called the "principal." The cost you pay for using someone else's money is called "interest." When you take out a loan, you will have to pay back both the principal and interest.

However, if you have an income of $10,000 a year, you might be less willing, and less able, to borrow $3,000. You will have a lower "ability to pay" or "ability to carry the debt." People often refer to money that is borrowed as "carrying a debt" or a "debt load." That is because debt is usually seen as a financial burden. A person's ability to pay and "carry debt" will change, then, with their income. As your income rises, you may be able to afford more debt. You certainly don't have to borrow more. Just because you may earn more, think carefully before taking on more debt. Another reason for more borrowing today is due to higher prices. As prices rise, the need to borrow may increase – especially if prices rise at rates faster than incomes. Housing is an example. House prices have, on average, risen over the years to the point where very few people can buy a house today without taking on a mortgage – often quite a sizeable mortgage. A mortgage is a loan taken out to buy a house or other property. More people likely have bigger mortgages today than was the case 30-40 years ago because the cost of housing is now so high. Another reason people are borrowing more today is because, overall, people are spending more of their income – and saving less. Back in the early 1980s, Canadians, on average, were saving over 20% of their income. In recent times, the average has fallen to much lower levels, Canadians, overall, were spending as much as was earned in income. Recently, the savings rate has risen to about 4% – but that is still pretty low. The result – without much in savings, Canadians are finding they have to take on more debt to cover expenses as they come up. So borrowing increases. That brings us to another reason why there is more borrowing today – the cost of borrowing has been so low. Like it is for other things, if the cost to borrow money goes down, people will probably borrow more of it. And that is what people have done – borrowed more as the cost of borrowing – interest rates – fell. There is little doubt that, overall, we have likely borrowed too much. Many people are under financial stress. Many live paycheque to paycheque and many would be in difficulty if they lost their job, got ill, or had an unexpected expense arise. People such as the Governor of the Bank of Canada have spoken about the concern that Canadian "household debt" is too high. Why? If we struggle with debt as many do, what happens when the cost of that debt (interest rates) rises? Any struggle Canadians have carrying debt will be harder when the cost of debt goes up.

Why do you think we are spending so much of their income and saving so little?

Why Borrow Money? • Unexpected expenditures: Maybe your car has broken down – or your air conditioner dies during the hottest days of the year. It is important to try and save to be prepared for these unpleasant surprises. But, if they happen, and you don't have the funds available, borrowing money may be an option. • The "big buys": Some items cost so much most people can't pay for them out of current income and savings

– for example, cars, boats, houses, and cottages or cabins. To be able to buy them you will likely have to tap into your future income by borrowing money that will be paid back over time – sometimes many years with money you will make in the future. • Investments: Some people borrow money to invest. They try to pick good investments to increase the value of that money in the future. People will do this if they believe they can earn more from the investment than it costs them to borrow. That is, they think the "rate of return" will be higher than the rate of interest to borrow. There is always risk in this kind of borrowing. • Education and training: This is actually another type of investment – an investment in the improvement of a person's knowledge and skills. You can look upon it simply as an investment in you.

People will often borrow to improve their How About You? education and training because this can help them to get the job or career they want – or to get a better paying job. The benefits of this kind of investment can last a lifetime. But, if you borrow money for education or training, make it a good decision. You don't want to find you are $25,000 in debt after university and feel that you are not where you hoped to be. Make wise choices about how you use borrowed money to invest in you. • Opportunities: Sometimes opportunities come up – opportunities too good to pass up. For example, suppose you love to play the piano and one of your goals is to get your own piano some day. Suppose you come across the deal of a lifetime – just the piano you want at a price better than you are likely to see again. You may decide that borrowing money is worth the cost of the debt to get something you've always wanted. Remember – an important part of managing money is to be happy. Having debt troubles won't make you happy. You will want to do all you can to avoid them. But, if the piano will help you with your "happiness" goal, and if you can afford the debt, that may be a good decision for you. • Rainy days: Some day you may suddenly lose your job and find it necessary to borrow money to get through a difficult time. You or a family member may also become ill or disabled and not be able to earn an income for a while. Once again, borrowing money may help. • Start a business: If you are, or hope to be, an entrepreneur, you may need to borrow money to help start up, launch, and run your business. Very few entrepreneurs are able to get started without getting some financial help. You may also need to borrow money to help the business grow if it is successful.

Travel: There are some people for whom travel is very important. They may have a dream of taking a certain trip or travelling for a period of time. It is not uncommon today for some students to want to do some travel before moving on to post-secondary education or training – or before settling into a job. Such travel may require debt. Therefore, some people may be willing to borrow money, and give up some other things in the future, to be able to travel today. • Simplify purchases: Carrying cash today is becoming less and less common. People seem to be carrying less money and using cards to simplify purchases. This may mean using a debit card – which takes money out of your bank account right away. Or it may mean using a credit card, borrowing money, and paying it back later. So some short-term borrowing by using credit cards can help with purchases.

These are some of the reasons why you may decide to borrow money. But, if you want to borrow money, who lends money – and why? Parents, other family members, and friends may lend you money to help you out. Be careful though, about borrowing from friends and family. You don't want "money issues" to affect your relationships. For the most part, though, people borrow money from sources other than friends and family. These other sources will charge interest to you for the money you borrow (some friends and family members may too.) There will be a number of things that will affect the interest rate they charge. We will look at the "cost of credit" shortly. First, let's look at the different kinds of borrowing you can do.

GETTING AND MANAGING CREDIT

Your Credit Worthiness If you want or need to borrow money, you will have to make sure the possible lender is confident that you are able to pay back the loan.

When might someone need a loan? When might a person want a loan? What's the difference? Be aware that it may be harder to get a loan when you need it than when you don't.

Anyone thinking of lending you money will be interested in your "credit worthiness." Your credit worthiness is simply a lender's check on your ability to take on, carry, and pay back debt. To check your credit worthiness, a lender will consider the "3 Cs" – your capital, character, and capacity. These aren't the only things that will be of interest to the lender. Your "credit rating" will also be very important. More on that shortly. But let's look at the 3Cs so that you know about some of the things that might affect your chances of getting a loan.

Try and arrange to have some credit available to you – even when you don't need it. Don't use it – just have it available in case you do need it. You may do this by the credit limit you have on a credit card or through a "line of credit" you set up with your financial institution.

Capital This refers to things you own. They have value and could possibly be sold if money was needed to pay back the loan. As you may know, things you own that have value are called "assets." Your assets can include any "equity" you have in a house (that part of the house that you own – the value of the house minus the mortgage), stocks, bonds, cars, savings, and so on. As a borrower, you would probably not have any intention of selling these assets or cashing them in to pay back the loan. However, if for some reason you were unable to make the payments or pay back the loan in full, then the lender wants some protection. The lender would like to know what assets you own that could be cashed in or sold ("liquidated") to get the money needed. Assets that you use to "secure" a loan – show you could find a way to pay back a loan if need be – are called "collateral." The problem some people face is that they may not have much collateral to back a loan. In that case, the lender may ask for someone to "co-sign" the loan. A co-signer is someone who will agree to pay back the loan if the borrower, for some reason, is not able to repay. Asking someone to cosign a loan is asking them to take on a serious responsibility. And being a co-signer is taking on considerable responsibility. Any co-signer should be careful before co-signing a loan – a loan he or she may have to help repay. So your "capital" is the assets that you have, to provide some possible "collateral" if needed. If you don't have capital, the lender may ask for a co-signer – another person who will take on some responsibility for the loan. Now, how about your character?

Character When you apply for a loan, the loans officer will also be interested in your "character" – how responsible you seem to be and how reliable you are likely to be in repaying the loan. Some of the questions that you have to answer on a loan application may surprise you. You may be asked how long you have worked at your current job; how long you have lived at your current address; and whether you have incurred any other debts; whether you are married; and if you have any dependents. Why such questions? The lender (creditor) will be looking for signs of "stability," "responsibility," "reliability," and so on. Being with an employer for quite a while, living at the same address for some time, being married, or having children or other dependents tend to be signs of stability and that you have taken on responsibility. This doesn't mean that you can't get a loan if you aren't married with two kids and haven't worked and lived at the same place for ten years. It also doesn't mean that you will get a loan if you have. It does mean that if you have changed jobs frequently, are unemployed, or have moved from place to place, or have been married three times you may encounter some hesitation from loans officers when you apply for a loan. The lender will be looking to learn something about you – and the kind of person you are. You would probably want to know something about a person who asked you for a loan too. We've looked at your capital (what you own) and your character (indications of the kind of person you are). Now how about whether you can afford the loan? That's your capacity

Do you have any "assets" at the moment? You may not use them to get a loan – but many young people sell things they own to get money, e.g. computer games, used sports equipment, used musical instruments, used bikes, etc. These arc things of value – assets – since they can possibly be turned into money be selling them.

Capacity The creditor will also want to know if you can afford the payments on the loan. Do you have enough income to pay the monthly cost? Do you have other expenses that may make it hard for you to make the monthly payments? Do you have other debts? What you own, what you owe, and what you earn will be of interest to the possible lender. These, then, are "the 3 Cs" that help to show your credit worthiness – and whether you are a credit risk. However, your credit rating will probably be as, or more important, to the lender if you are looking for a loan.

If someone asked you for a loan, what might you want to know about them before making your decision? Would you lend money to you at this point? Would you be a good "credit risk?" What changes are likely to happen in your life that may change your credit risk?

Of people you know well, who would you be willing to lend money to if asked –and if you had the money to lend? Are there others to whom you wouldn't lend money? If so, why not? What differences are you thinking about when you consider whether you would lend them money or not?

Many people don't know a credit rating system exists. But it does. Those who are in the business of lending money share information. They share information about people to whom they have loaned money. They share information about those who have been good in repaying their debts – and making payments on time. They also share information on those who have not been so good – or who regularly make payments late – or who have not paid their debts.

For example, suppose you purchased something from a store on a credit card. Then, for some reason you did not pay the charges on the card. If that happens, the credit card company will probably first try and get you to pay the charge. If you still don't pay, the credit card company may notify the "credit bureau." And that can go on your record and may affect your ability to borrow money. There are a number of "credit rating agencies" that keep this information. For example, two large agencies in Canada are "Equifax" and "TransUnion Canada." They keep records on people who borrow money – who they borrow from, how much they have borrowed, how good they are at repaying their debts, and so on. They also have information on bills you may not have paid – and should have. Based on all the information they have, they will calculate a credit score. The credit bureaus will make the information they have available to other lenders. Therefore, before making a loan, lenders will usually check with the rating agencies and check out your credit score. Now here is a very important point. You can go to these companies to check out your credit rating – and you should. You may find things there you didn't know about – or you may find things that are wrong. A lender may have sent in notice that you didn't pay a debt – but you did, only late. But it may show on your credit rating that you never paid the debt – and that won't help your credit score. Most creditors will work with a borrower to try and help the borrower repay the loan before providing any information to the credit bureau that would hurt a person's credit rating. After all, their goal is to get their loan back or have the bill paid. They may work out new terms with you to help you. That is why it is always important to contact the creditor if you are having problems repaying a debt or paying a bill that is overdue. You can often work out a payment plan. However, if a creditor does not hear from you, they may simply assume you aren't going to pay what is owed and send that information to the credit bureau. Before information is sent to the credit bureau, people who are having trouble paying their debts or bills will often be contacted by a "collection agency." A collection agency will work for those to whom you owe money. Their job is to try and get you to pay. It is best to get in touch with anyone to whom you owe money – and haven't paid – before they get a collection agency to get in touch with you. If you are contacted by a collection agency about a debt, take this as a warning and deal with the matter right away so that you don't end up with a negative report going to the credit agency. Even if you don't have any intention of borrowing money, you never know when the need may arise. It is always wise to be able to borrow money just in case you have to some day. That means having a good credit rating.

The following are some tips for maintaining a good credit rating

Repay your debts and make payments on time • Don't borrow more than you can afford • Set a borrowing limit and stick to it. This sounds easier than it is. Most people don't know how to set a credit limit – that is, the maximum amount you can afford to borrow. Here is one suggestion. Set up a budget. (See the Module on budgeting.) As you do, see how much you could afford each month for debt payments. That amount should help set your debt limit. If you borrow money, don't borrow more than could be covered by the limit you have set. The cost of a loan will vary with how much you borrow, how long you will take to pay it back, and the interest rate. Therefore, the maximum amount of debt that you can comfortably afford to carry will change as these things change. Try to stay in your "comfort zone" and borrow only what you can afford. • Don't sign any kind of loan agreement until you have read it thoroughly, understand it, and know what you are etting into. Sometimes you may feel a little awkward doing this. It may be a person you know. The following are some tips for maintaining a good credit rating: Or the person may make it seem like time is short and you should hurry – or that this is just standard stuff and you shouldn't worry about it. Or it may be that the document is quite lengthy and may take some time to read over. Don't let that stop you. Most people will understand that you want to read what you are signing. If they don't, it may be because they really don't want you to read it. Even if you feel awkward, take the time. It is a small price to pay to be comfortable with what you are signing. • Never sign a blank form of any kind where information could be filled in or added after you sign • Always try to pay your monthly bills on time (like phone, electricity, etc.) • Contact your creditors if you are having trouble making payments on your debts • Deal with reputable creditors (they should have a good credit rating too) • Be cautious about co-signing for a loan

Don't just wait for your credit rating to be built up by others – try and build a good credit rating for yourself. If you can borrow some money without paying interest – like with some credit cards – and pay it back promptly and in full – consider doing this to build a good rating. Also, if you rent an apartment and pay electricity bills (on time), and phone bills, (on time), etc., this will show on your credit rating. So don't just let your credit rating happen. Try and do some things, as you can, to build a good credit rating.

As we noted, co-signing a loan is a serious responsibility. A parent may co-sign a loan for a child if the child is still relatively young and needs help with borrowing money. That is quite common until there has been time for the child to build up a credit rating. But always think carefully if you are asked to cosign for a loan. It may affect your own credit rating if things go wrong. It's also a good idea to start to develop a good credit rating as early as possible. To do this, some young people decide to get a credit card from a retailer or credit card company, make purchases, and pay off the bills promptly and fully each month. In this way, a good credit rating can begin to be established even at a relatively young age. Many people borrow money by using a credit card or taking out loans to buy things. How you use a credit card or manage a loan can affect your credit rating. Let's take a look at some of the advantages and disadvantages of using credit through credit cards and loans.

The Advantages and Disadvantages of Credit

Advantages • You can use something and enjoy it now (for example, a car, a house, a vacation, education, new clothes) and pay for it out of future income. • You can buy things you could not buy from your current income. You can use some of your future income to pay for it. • Credit enables you to handle emergencies and unexpected costs due to an illness, accident, losing a job, car repairs, and so on. • Credit can enable you to pay more to buy goods of higher quality that you otherwise could not afford now. Buying better quality can mean it will last longer. That may make it a wise consumer choice. • You can take advantage of sales and deals – if a really good one comes along. (Just make sure that the amount you save through the sale is more than it may cost you in interest.) • Using a credit card provides you with a record of your expenses. Credit card issuers provide a monthly statement which lists all of the spending you did with the credit card. • Credit can make it easier to deal with a number of debts you have if you are having difficulty repaying. By taking out a "consolidation loan" you can borrow one amount to pay all or most of your bills and then make a single payment each month rather than many.

Disadvantages • Credit can encourage you to live beyond your means and get you into financial difficulty. • Credit can mean that your future income will be tied up in paying past debts. You may not be able to buy things in the future that you wish you could. • Using credit can increase your total cost for a product or service since the interest you will pay must be added to the price. • Credit can lead to more impulse buying, which may lead to buying things you don't really need – and wish you hadn't. • If you get and use a credit card for a particular store, you may just shop there and do less comparison shopping. You may lose out on cheaper prices or better deals elsewhere. • Tapping into credit now will mean that you will have less available if unforeseen emergencies arise.

One way to keep a good credit rating is to avoid getting into debt trouble. When you "get in over your head" and have more debt than you can afford, you can start missing payments, paying late, or not repaying your debts. That can lead to problems with your credit rating. So avoiding debt trouble in the first place is the wise thing to do. But how do you know if you are heading toward debt trouble? Let's take a look at some of the signs that you may be headed in the wrong direction. Signs That You May Be in Debt Trouble You may be heading for debt trouble if you find you are: • finding it difficult to save anything; • continually short of money; • using your savings to pay debt costs; • near your credit limit on all or most of your credit cards and accounts; • missing payments or due dates for your bills; • always making only the minimum payments on your credit cards and accounts. Each month you will likely see a "minimum" monthly payment on your credit card statement. This is the minimum amount that the lender is willing to take as payment for that month. It is not the minimum you would be best to pay. The best thing is to pay off the full amount. If you can't, pay off as much as you can. If you just make the minimum monthly payment it can take a long time to pay back the money – and you end up paying a great deal of interest; • unaware of how much you owe; • worrying a lot about money – your debts are always on your mind – you are having trouble sleeping; • borrowing money to pay off past debt costs; and • having to borrow money to meet your week-to-week or month-to-month living expenses.

What To Do If You Have a Debt Problem Do all that you can to avoid debt problems. Know how much debt you can afford and don't go over that limit. Set up a budget so you know how much debt you can afford. Don't borrow to that limit – leave yourself some room in case something comes up. Think about the trade-offs you are making when you borrow money – and borrow only when it is a good decision for you. But in the end, some people will get into debt trouble. What can you do if that happens? • Perhaps the most important advice for you if you are having debt troubles is to face up to your problems and start to do something about them. Don't try to handle it all alone. If you have close personal friends or family, seek their help and advice. They can also help you deal with what may be a bad situation. You will probably be surprised at how many people will understand and will try to help see you over a rough period. • Contact your creditors. Don't simply start missing payments. Most of those who have loaned you money will try to help you get out of the hole you are in. After all, they have an interest in helping you – they hope to get their money back. Work out a new payment schedulewith them. You will probably be surprised at how co-operative most creditors will be. • Put all of your credit cards away to avoid getting into worse trouble. In fact, stop all further borrowing. No sense digging a deeper hole. • Consider a consolidation loan for your debts. A consolidation loan is one loan you take out to pay back your other loans. In this way you can turn a number of payments for a number of different loans into a single payment for one loan. The monthly cost may be less than the total monthly cost of all other payments combined. If you are carrying debt on credit cards, the interest you will pay on a regular loan will usually be much lower than that on a credit card balance. • Consider a second job, if you can, to see you over the hurdle and tough times. • Cash in some investments or savings to lower your debt position. The costs you pay on your debt will usually be greater than the interest you earn on your investments. It may make sense to give up the investment to do away with the debt. • Seek some professional advice and counselling if you can get it – or if someone will help you get it. • Review your lifestyle and past decisions. What got you into trouble? What could you change to get out of trouble? What can you give up to get money to help you pay your debts? When it comes to handling money, and making good money decisions, few things are more important than getting and keeping a good credit rating. Right from the outset, make that one of your priorities. Debt can help you – or debt can hurt you. Borrow wisely. And always stay within a limit you can afford.

SAVING AND INVESTING MONEY

W hen it comes to saving and investing, there is no "chicken and egg" dilemma. You don't have to wonder which comes first. You can't invest if you don't have savings. Once you have savings, you can make decisions about how to invest them. With any money you get, you will have some basic choices in how it is used. You can spend it, save it, pay taxes, or give some away .

Do you keep your money in a bank? If so, how did you come to pick that bank? What kind of account(s) do you have?

Basic Banking Do you keep your money in a bank? If so, how did you come to pick that bank? What kind of account(s) do you have? How About You? Most people will use a bank to help manage their money. Banks provide chequing accounts, savings accounts, chequing-savings accounts and so on. Money is deposited into these accounts and the bank will usually pay some interest on that money. Why? Because the bank will lend out a good portion of the money deposited to others as loans. The banks hold on to enough money to do their day to day business – but will lend out money to businesses and to borrowers as car loans, mortgages, etc. The banks will make money on "the spread" – the difference between the interest rate paid to savers and the interest rate charged to borrowers. The banks also make money from fees, investments, etc. Overall, Canada's banks do pretty well and are some of the safest in the world.

If you have one or more bank accounts, check and see if there are monthly fees on the account. If so, see what the fees cover. See if you can make changes to lower your monthly fee.

If you deposit money in a bank, you can usually get your money, as you need it, by withdrawing it at a branch or using an ATM. You can usually make payments by using cash, writing a cheque (less common these days), using a debit card, making an online transfer, etc. So there are different ways to get and use your money. You can use banks to hold your money that you will spend as you need. And, you can use banks to hold on to money you aren't using today for spending – and that you will save for the future. In the end you will make decisions, probably every day, about how you will use your money – spend it, save it, give some away, etc.

Be careful and use only ATMs that you can trust – preferably those of your bank. You may pay a fee if you use an ATM from another bank or a generic ATM that is not associated with any of the major banks. ATMs can also be "compromised" by people who are trying to steal your PIN and account number. Again, try and use only ATMs you trust and that are in a well secured and protected area.

How do you use your money? Do you know where it's going? How much are you spending? Paying in tax? Saving? Giving to help others?

You won't have much choice in how you use some of your money. There will be monthly expenses and taxes that you will have to pay. But what about the money left over – if there is any? You may be spending all your money – and paying some taxes as you do your spending (remember GST, HST, gas taxes, etc.) That may be your choice. But saving is important and can help you in a number of ways, such as helping you: • Save up over time to help you achieve your goals and to afford some of the more expensive things you might hope for – car, home, etc. • Be prepared if unexpected things come up – both good and bad. • Choose things you could do when opportunities come up – travel, help others, buy something you want or need without using debt, etc. • Feel better knowing you have money available – so you may worry less about money matters. You can have more "peace of mind."

The "Magic of Compounding" You may hear someone talk about "the magic of compounding." This refers to how savings and investments can grow in value more quickly because of "compound interest." Here's a brief example of how it works. Suppose you were able to save $1,000 for a year and was paid 5% interest. That means you would make $50 in interest to add to your savings. If you leave the money that you earned in interest with your $1,000, you now have $1,050. Over the next year, your $1,050 will earn 5% – or another $52.50. If you leave that money in, you now have $1,102.50. Your $1,000 has grown – and is now growing faster because you are earning "interest on your interest." If you continued to leave the money to grow for another year, you would earn 5% on $1,102.50 = $55.12. Your money grew $50 the first year, $52.50 the second, and $55.12 the third – and this has happened without you having to add any new money. That's the magic of compounding. And that's the magic of saving and investing. If you start saving at a young age, you can have many years for your money to grow through compound interest. And if you can add more to it each year, your savings will grow that much faster. Use the "magic of compounding" to help your savings grow wherever you can. Although saving pays off, a recent survey found that almost 50% of Canadians are living paycheque to paycheque. This means half of Canadians have expenses and debts that are taking up most of their income. They aren't saving anything. That's not the best way to handle your financial affairs. In some ways, though, it's not surprising. Until recently, little effort was made to help teach Canadians about how to handle money. People weren't taught about budgeting, managing debt and credit cards, setting their own debt limits, saving for education and retirement, and so on. Therefore, many Canadians were not well prepared for their money decisions and challenges. We're trying to change that for young people today.

The following are some things to do to start – and continue to save. 1. Make saving a priority. Save some money – even a little – before you do anything else with your money. As we have shown, compound interest can help your money grow. 2. Set a savings goal. Have a target. Give yourself something to work towards and reach for. Try and set a time period to get there. 3. Reward yourself if you succeed in reaching a savings goal. You'll deserve it. 4. Track your spending. Know where your money is going. This will help you look for ways to save more if you need to. 5. Try and use a budget and stick to it. This will help you better control how you use your money.

Did any of your family members get a financial education of any kind? Are any of them able to help you? Are you able to help any of them with what you are in this book?

Saving is not easy for many people. But it's important to save if you can. If you currently aren't saving – or aren't saving as much as you would like – what can you do to try and save more?

Investing Money Saving is holding on to some of your money to use it in the future. Investing is what you do with your savings to try and: • protect the value of your savings – the purchasing power – over time against the effects of inflation. • increase value of your savings – and acquire greater purchasing power – by earning a return greater than inflation. • save enough, and earn enough from investments, to be able to achieve your goals. Investing, therefore, is not only for those with lots of money. Anyone who has savings can make decisions about how to invest those savings – and put them to work. Protecting the value of your savings is "job one." You don't want money you hold for the future to buy less later than you could buy today. Lately, the rate of inflation (the increase in the average level of prices in the economy) has been about 2% a year. The Bank of Canada has done a pretty good job keeping inflation in that range.

That means to protect your savings from losing value to inflation, you want to make at least 2% on your savings if you can. That may sound easy but, if interest rates are very low, as they have been, regular savings accounts may not pay 2% interest. A regular savings account is one of the safest places to put your savings. banks are very sound and you don't take on a lot of risk by putting your money in a savings account. So a savings account is very low risk – but also gives you a very low return. That is one of the most important lessons to learn about investing – low risk will mean a low return. Let's look more closely at this key point about investing.

Do you have savings in the bank? If so, do you know the interest rate you are earning? If you don't have savings, check out the interest rate banks are paying for money in savings accounts. Do the rates surprise you?

Suppose you decide that you would like to buy and sell stocks as one of your investments. Let's suppose that you haven't had a lot of experience with investing in the stock market. Therefore, you decide to work with a "broker." Suppose you tell your broker that you have some savings and you would like to achieve the following: • You want your investments to hopefully make you a 20% return each year, and • You don't want to run the risk of losing any more than 5% of the value of your savings.

If you were making an investment, what rate of return would you look for – considering how comfortable you are with risk? What might lead you to take on more risk? Less risk?

A broker is someone who is trained, and has a license, to buy and sell stocks. Be aware that all stocks must be bought and sold through a licensed "broker." This may be a broker to whom you pay a fee to get help and advice. Or it may be an "online brokerage" company that lets you make your own buying and selling decisions. You will pay a lower fee if you make your own decisions – but you won't get any advice.

Is this a reasonable thing to ask on your part? The answer, unfortunately, is no. Your broker would likely tell you "No can do." Why not, you might ask? The reason is that your potential return on an investment, and your potential risk, have to be in balance. If you want your investment to provide a possible 20% return, you have to accept the risk that your investment may fall 20% in value. The higher your target return, the more risk you have to take. If possibly losing 20% of your savings is more than you are comfortable with, then you will have to lower the target for your potential return. You will have to find your "risk/return" balance point.

There are many reasons why one person's comfort with risk may be different than another's. But it will be important for you to have a sense of your attitude to risk when it comes to investing. What level of risk are you comfortable with? What level of risk will let you sleep at night without worrying? And what level of risk do you need to take, or are you willing to take, to reach your goals? Your risk/return balance point will be affected by many factors, such as: • Your age. For example, younger people tend to be better able to accept higher risk than older people since they have a longer time to recoup losses if the value of an investment falls or if they lose on an investment. • How much you have to invest. Those with more money to invest are usually in a position to accept more risk since it is easier for them to afford a loss. • Your goals and how much you are hoping to earn from your investments in order to realize your goals. If you set a certain goal and find that you will need an average return of 10% on your investments to reach your goal, are you comfortable with that level of risk? If not, you might have to change the goal – or set a longer date to give yourself more time. • Your time horizon, that is, how long before you need to use the money from your investments. If you need the money from your investments in two years for education, you won't want to take on much risk. Someone who doesn't need their money until their retirement in 35 years will likely be willing to take more risk.

The role of investing is to put the money that you don't need today to work for you to help you achieve your goals in the future. Before we explore investing in more detail, let's just take a moment to look at the role of investment in the economy. It can help you better understand why investing is important. Our economy has a number of jobs. A key one, though, is to produce goods and services to satisfy people's needs and wants. Entrepreneurs and businesses combine resources such as labour, capital equipment, natural resources, and technology to produce goods and services that Canadians need and want. They also produce some goods and services to sell in other countries – exports. We distribute goods and services in our economy through a price system. That is, every good or service has a price. If you are willing and able to pay that price, then you can acquire it. People work to get income to be able to pay the prices and get the things they want.

Are you aware of any investments that have been made in your community to make things better? For example, a new business, a new school, a renovated business, etc. If so, who made those investments – and why do you think they made them?

Overall, the well-being of people living in our societywill depend on the wealth that we create in our economy – and the degree to which people are able to acquire the wealth that is produced. As more products and services are produced by our economy, more wealth is generated. This growth in output usually means with it more jobs, higher incomes, and an improved standard of living. One of our economic goals, then, is to create more goods and services to create more jobs and incomes for everyone. At the same time, over the years, we have become much more conscious of the environment – and to look for ways to achieve growth in our economy without harming the environment. We even look for ways that economic activity can help the environment. This has also become one of our priority economic goals. But how do we get funds working to improve our economy – achieve growth – create new jobs and incomes – improve the well-being of all – and improve the environment? That takes money. That takes investment. And the funds for investment to fuel growth and improvement in our economy come from people's savings. How does that happen? It starts with people putting some of their savings in banks. Banks then lend money to companies that are looking to invest – improve – and grow. People may also use some of their savings to buy "bonds." In this way, with "corporate bonds," they are lending money to companies that are looking to invest – improve – and grow.

And some people use some of their savings to buy shares in companies. This also provides money to companies to invest – improve – and grow. People's savings, then, are put to work – through savings, buying bonds, buying shares, etc. Savings find their way through loans and investments to businesses. By using savings for investment, new resources are discovered, businesses are expanded, new techniques are devised, new technology is developed, new training programs are provided, and so on. In essence, the money saved by savers in our economy is placed into investments that allow the productive capacity of the economy to grow. In this way, our economy is able to develop and grow over time, create jobs, create incomes, and increase the overall level of well-being in our society

Research ways in which efforts are being made to produce goods and services in a way that can help sustain or improve the environment. Do you see business activity in your community that may be doing harm to the environment? Do you see businesses that are working to help the environment – or taking steps to make sure their activities do not do any environmental damage?

What are some of the major businesses in your community? Have you noticed any changes lately – any improvements? Have any been doing better and helping to create jobs for others?

If you understand how investments lead to growth and improvements in our economy, you will then understand why investingyour funds can lead to an increase in the value of your savings. If your savings are put to use in investment – and that investment helps to make things better – and helps increase the level of wealth that is produced – then those funds have helped to create value and become more valuable. That is why an investment may bring you a return of 10%. If it was a good investment and helped a company to become better and earn a 10% higher return, then your savings may earn a 10% return through that investment. On the other hand, if you invested in a company that didn't make good decisions and ended up worse off, your investment may lose money. It is also why you have to make good investment decisions. Make sure you have good information before making an investment decision. Make sure you understand any investment you are considering. And get help and advice if needed. Let's take a minute to look at some of the criteria you may want to consider when making investments.

Investment Criteria The following are important things to think about when investing. They are: • Safety/risk • Liquidity • Return on the investment • Time management involved • Growth potential • Knowledge of the investment Let's take a quick look at each. As we noted, the safety, or the level of risk, involved in an investment is a key factor to consider. Don't get involved in risky investments if they make you anxious – or if you can't accept the loss if the investment should lose value. You will have to know your risk tolerance – your level of comfort with risk – and know if an investment you are considering "fits" with you and your comfort level. Time horizon refers to when you will need the money from an investment. Do you need it in six months, one year, three years, five years, ten years, twenty years, twenty-five years, or more? The time horizon – and when you need the money – will depend on your goals and how you plan to use the money. For example, will you need the money for education, training, a house, children, travel, retirement, or .....? Your "time horizon" is important since it may affect the kind of investments you can consider. Investments can differ in their "variability" – that is, how much they can change in value. Some invest-ments are more "volatile" than others. They may rise 35% in value and then, over time, fall 40% in value – and then rise again, and so on. Other investments may be much more stable and vary a lot less in value. If your time horizon is quite soon, even 2, 3, or 4 years, you probably won't want an investment that swings a lot in value. Why? Because if it happens to be down when you need your money, you might not be able to wait for it to bounce back up. You may have to take a loss. Better to avoid those kinds of investments if you need your money soon. The "growth potential" of an investment is another thing to consider. Will the return you get from the investment possibly change and improve over time? An investment that pays a "fixed rate of return" obviously has little growth potential in its value. For example, if you invest in a Canada Savings Bond that pays a 4% return, that is what your return will be – 4%. However, an investment in a stock or a house may be another matter. The value of this type of investment may rise, or fall, over time. These investments would have greater "growth potential" than "fixed income" investments like a Canada Savings Bond. Of course, it also has a greater risk of a loss in value. There's the old "risk/return balance" again. The "liquidity" of an investment should also be considered. Liquidity refers to how easily and quickly an investment or asset can be turned back into cash – and how certain you can be of its value. A savings account is an example of a "highly liquid asset" – it can be turned into cash quickly, easily, and you know what its value is. A five-year term deposit – where you lock your savings away for five years at a certain rate of return – is not a very liquid asset. Your investment is locked up for five years. Your money isn't easy to get if you need it. A house is also not a liquid asset. You can't turn a house into cash quickly. Its value may also be quite uncertain. Until you sell it, you may not know what it is worth. The "time management" involved in looking after an investment is also something to consider. If you invest in a savings account or a term deposit, little of your time is needed to watch over the investment. An investment in stocks, or a business, or in a house, for example, may require a good deal of your time. You need to decide how much time you have available and are willing to spend looking after your investments. You may decide to use the services of an advisor who can invest the time and expertise to manage your investments for you (for a fee). Lastly, your "knowledge of the investment" is also important. It is never a good idea to invest in any investment that you don't understand. As a rule of thumb, understand what you are investing in, and don't invest in something simply because others have. Be a knowledgeable investor – or work with someone who has the knowledge you need.

Do you have any investments? Has anyone made any investments for you? If you don't have investments yet, and find you are able to save, what kinds of investments would be of interest to you?

These, then, are things to think about when you are investing – and deciding among different investment options. But what kinds of investments are there that you can consider. There are three general types of investments: • Cash (and "cash equivalent") • Fixed income • Equity Cash, or close-to-cash, or "cash equivalent" investments are those that are very "liquid,“ are low risk, and provide a relativelylow return. Examples of cash, or close-to-cash, investments, are those such as cash, bank deposits, term deposits, and Guaranteed Investment Certificates (GICs). "Money market funds" are another example. More on "funds" shortly. Fixed income investments are those like bonds. Bonds are basically a loan that you make to a government or company. For example, you might buy a $5,000 10-year corporate bond at 6%. In doing so, you are lending the company $5,000 for 10 years. In return, you will be paid 6% per year for as long as you own the bond. You may choose to hold and own the bond for 10 years – or you may choose to sell it. You can buy and sell bonds in the "bond market" the same way that you can buy and sell stocks in the "stock market." The price of a bond will change in the bond market over time. For example, if you hold a 6% bond, and the interest rate generally offered on new bonds is 4%, then your bond becomes more valuable. Someone looking to buy a bond will be able to get a higher return from your bond than a new one. You may choose to sell your bond in the bond market for more than the $5,000 that you paid – if someone is willing to pay more to get the higher interest rate. In this way, even though bonds provide "fixed income" – a fixed rate of return – they can be bought and sold in the bond marketat different prices. Based on what happens to interest rates, its "market value" may rise or fall. In the end, though, after 10 years, whoever owns the bond will be paid back the $5,000 by the company that issued the bond and borrowed the money.

So "fixed income investments" provide a fixed rate of return for a particular period of time. The most common types are bonds – corporate and government – and "bond funds" – once again, more on "funds" in a moment. Another kind of investment is equity – that is, buying a share of ownership in a company. Companies may sell stock to raise money for expansion and improvement. Money raised by selling stock is raised through "stock brokers." That is, a company will provide shares to one or more brokers who sell the stock to clients. The stock brokerage company will earn a fee for selling the stock. The company receives the money from the stock sale to invest in the company.

If the investments are good and pay off, and the company does well, the value of the shares of stock should rise. The higher stock price indicates that the value of the company is higher. If you buy stocks on the stock exchange, you are not buying new stock. You are buying stock from someone else that owned it. That is why it is called a "stock exchange" – it is where shares of stocks in companies are bought and sold – exchanged. The company doesn't receive the money when you buy stocks on the stock exchange. The company get its money when the stock was originally sold. In the "old days" all stock exchanges had a "trading floor" where brokers met to do deals and buy and sell stocks for their clients. Today, some exchanges do not have trading floors. For example, at the Toronto Stock Exchange all trades are done electronically.Some exchanges, however, still have trading floors. Equity investments, like stocks, are riskier than fixed income investments. Their value is more volatile and less predictable. A stock's value may rise – or fall – sometimes by a great deal. The possible return on an "equity" investment is higher – but so is the risk of loss. You want to know what you are doing if you buy and sell stocks – or get some help and advice. There are also "equity funds" – in the same way we noted that there are "money market funds" and "bond funds," etc. We will discuss such "funds" in just a minute.

So those are the three general types of investments. You can also invest in other things such as real estate, collectibles (art, cars, etc.), directly in a business as an owner/partner, etc. Having looked at the three general types of investments, this is a good point at which to talk about an investor's "portfolio." When a person invests, he/she will build up a "portfolio of investments" – a term used to refer to the collection of investments a person has. When you start investing, you will start to build a portfolio of investments. When you do, you will need to think about your "investor profile." If you choose to work with an advisor, your advisor will ask you questions to learn about your investor profile. Your investor profile basically looks at the kind of investor you are – and what you want to achieve. For example, your investor profile would include things such as: • What are your goals? What are you hoping to achieve from your investments? • What is your target rate of return – that is, what are you hoping to earn from your investments? • What is your level of investor knowledge and experience with investing? • What is your "risk tolerance?" What level of risk are your comfortable with? • How much do you have to invest? • What is your "time horizon" – at what points will you need money – and how much will you need?

If you have a chance, visit a stock exchange. Take a tour. Learn a little about how they work – how trades take place – the different fees that are paid, and so on.

These are the kinds of questions that you will be asked – or that you should ask yourself – to get an idea of your "investorprofile." Once this is known, you can start building your "portfolio" – putting together a collection of different kinds of investments that fit with your needs and goals. The mix of investments that is best for you will often be different than for others. Why? Because your profiles will be different. There is a certain mix of investments that may be best for you – but which will be different for someone else. Regardless of your "investor profile" you will want to "diversify" your investments. In a nutshell, this means not "putting all your eggs in one basket." You will want to have a good mix of different kinds of investments. Why? Because that provides you with some protection. If some of your investments fall in value, others may rise. If some are quite volatile, others may be pretty stable. By diversifying your portfolio you lower your risk. One of the primary rules of investing is to diversify! In real estate, it's location, location, location! In investing, its diversify, diversify, diversify!

Are there any risks in life that you have faced – or face today? Not just money – but any kind of risk? If so, have you done anything to reduce the amount of risk? Is there anything you could do?

Before wrapping up this section on investing, there are a couple more things to cover. First, we have mentioned "funds" on a number of occasions. This refers to "mutual funds." Let's see what these are. A mutual fund is when investors pool their money in a fund and the fund is then invested, and managed, by a professional. You don't have to get together with others to pool your funds. There are "fund companies" that will do this for you. You will have to decide which fund companies, and which funds, to invest in. Investors will buy "units" of a fund they want to invest in. The value of the units can change according to how well the investments in the fund perform. If the unit value rises, the value of your investment in the fund rises. If it falls, then the value of your investment falls. You will also pay a fee to the professional, and the professional's company, for managing the fund. Another thing to think about – probably when you have some savings built up and you are looking to build an investment portfolio – is the possibility of working with an advisor. It is possible to do your own investing with help from banks and online brokerages. However, although you will pay a fee to work with an advisor, it may be worth it. This is especially true if you don't know a lot about investing. They may be able to help you get the return you are looking for – even taking into account the fee you pay for the help and advice. An advisor can help you set your goals, work through your profile and your comfort with risk, help you pick investments, diversify, and put together a financial plan.

Whenever you invest, today or in the future, you can diversify in terms of the type of investments you make (stocks, bonds, GICs, etc.). You can diversify in terms of the location of your investments, for example, in Canada, the U.S., Asia, etc. You can diversify in terms of the level of risk of your investments. And so on. However you may choose to do so, make sure to diversify your investments.

As with all kinds of services, there are those that are good and those that aren't so good. If you are looking for financial help (advisor, broker, insurance agent, etc.), talk with others who use their services. Find out who is happy with the service they are getting and set up a meeting to see if the same person would work well for you. If you don't know anyone getting financial help, check out respected companies that provide financial services and help. Meet with one – or a few – people to see if there is a good fit and one you would like to work with. A few final quick tips and reminders on investing: • Tip number one is to be very cautious about investing on the basis of a "tip" from someone. Tips are highly unreliableand probably lead to losses more often than gains. • Check out every investment carefully and fully understand it before investing in it. • Don't panic if things don't go well; keep calm and avoid irrational decisions. When the market fell sharply in2008-2009 it recovered most of its losses in the year or twoafter. Those who sold their investments when things went bad, lost money. Those who held on, and didn't panic,in many cases, got their money back. So avoid panic.Be careful about making quick decisions if things startto go a little crazy. That is also when an advisor can help. • Keep inflation in mind when making your investment decisions. You'll want to earn a rate of return that is at least equal to the rate of inflation. • Invest even small amounts; you will be surprised how they can add up over time. • Diversify your investments. • Never make investments that you don't understand. • Keep in mind what J.P. Morgan said: "Sell down to your sleeping point," which basically means, avoid investmentsthat cause you too much anxiety; invest so you can sleep at night. Find your risk/return balance point. In summary, investing is something that should be considered by everyone, not only those with lots of money or great wealth. Investing is not only good for the individual investor; it also provides the fuel for the growth and development of our whole economy. So, be prepared to be an investor at whatever level is possible for you – and at whatever age you are. As an example, suppose you had saved $100 at age 15. Suppose further that you were able to save an additional $100 each year. And suppose you were able to earn an average return of 5% a year for 40 years. After 40 years, your $100 a year in savings, well invested, would be worth almost $13,000. Investing can work to your advantage, bring benefits, and help you to achieve your goals. Invest when you can, and what you can – but do so wisely and make investments that are comfortable for you.

PROTECTING ASSETS AND PLANNING FOR THE FUTURE

N othing is more frustrating than working very hard to achieve something and then losing it. The same is true in the world of money. It can be very sad (sometimes tragic) if all of a sudden things for which we have worked so hard are destroyed or taken away. Part of good financial planning is to plan for things that may go wrong – and to protect the things you care about most. This includes the relationships in your life and your family members. And it can include the material things – a home, cottage, car, boat, etc

What are the things that you care about most in your life at this time? Has any item you have ever owned, and that you really cared about, been lost, damaged, or stolen? If so, were you able to do anything about it?

That is the role of insurance. Insurance is a way to reduce or eliminate risk. What kinds of risk? • The risk that, when you have a family, a life partner, children,etc., that you may die or become injured or disabled – and not be able to earn an income; • The risk that another member of your family, on whom you may rely for support or assistance, may die or become unable to provide support; • The risk that something you have worked hard to get – a computer, bike, cell phone, home, cottage, car, etc. – may become damaged, destroyed, or stolen; • The risk that, while driving a car, you hit and hurt, or kill, someone.

And so on. There is a somewhat crude saying about what can happen in life – and it's true. Bad things will happen. We wish they didn't, but they do – and, if they do, you'll want to be prepared – and protected if you can. Insurance can help. For a fee, you can buy a "policy" that can help you be prepared for such possibilities. Even at a young age, insurance will be important – for those who drive a car, or travel out of the country, or rent a house or apartment, etc. Bad things can happen – car accident, injury or sickness while in another country, a fire starts in your apartment – and you'll want to be protected if this happens.

What are some of the common risks that young people face? What, if anything, can they do to reduce those risks?

Have you thought about possible "risks" in your life? Are there risks that you face? If so, are you protected? If so, how? If not, could you be?

The challenge, in some cases, is to think about things that could happen that you don't really want to think about. But it is necessary if you are going to be prepared. In addition to insurance and trying to reduce or eliminate risks, another key part of financial planning is to look ahead to a goal that most people have – to be "financially independent" some day. Sometimes this is referred to as "planning for retirement." But what is "retirement?" Sounds like "getting old." But, in reality, to be able to retire, most people are trying to get to where they no longer have to work for a living. It is when they have saved, or acquired, enough money that they can live off the money they have – or can get from "non-working" sources – so they don't have to work anymore. The money they live off may come from government or company pensions, savings and investments they have made, "assets" – like a home – that they have acquired that could be sold, etc. It is a great moment in life when a person can be "financially independent" and not have to work.

I encourage you to look ahead to your financial future not so much as "planning to retire" but rather planning to build up "non-working" sources of income so that you can decide whether you want to work or not. If you want to get to where you can work or not work at some target point in your life, early planning is crucial. Let's take a quick look at these two important areas of managing money – (1) how to protect the things in life you care about (or will care about) and (2) how to plan ahead for financial independence.

You are just starting your working life. But do you hope to not have to work to make a living some day? If so, when – when you are 45, 55, 65, 75, ever?

If you hope to get to a point some day in your life when you can choose to work or not work – and stop work if you want to do other things – try and start planning for that as soon as you can. Many people leave it too late and struggle to ever get to that point. Pick an age when you would like to have that freedom to choose – and see what it will take to get there.

Protecting You And Your Assets: Insurance Insurance is a way to reduce, eliminate, or share risk. You buy insurance from insurance companies. These are companies that pool the money they receive from "policy-holders" (those who buy insurance) and then use that money to make payments to those who make "claims" when things happen. The payments made to insurance companies by policy-holders are called "premiums." Insurance companies will also put some of that money to work by making investments. The insurance companies stay in business, and earn a profit, if they can take in more money through premiums and their investments than they have to pay out in claims. The premium that you will pay for an insurance "policy" will depend on how much risk you represent for the insurance company. Insurance companies have very detailed records, and use "probability tables," to help them decide how much risk they would take on by providing possible clients with insurance "coverage." For example, and as you may know, past statistics show that young males tend to get more speeding tickets – and get in more car accidents – than young females. Because of this, young male drivers represent a higher risk. Therefore, if you are a young male, you are probably going to find that your monthly premium payments for car insurance are going to be higher than if you are a young female. That's how insurance works. The higher the risk, the more you will have to pay to get insurance coverage. That may not seem fair if you are a young male and a good and careful driver. Unfortunately, the "odds" work against you. Because the odds show that young males are more likely to have a car accident, young males usually pay more than young females for insurance.

It is also the case that some people may be, or may become, such a high risk that companies won't insure them at all – or the costs of getting insurance are so high that the person may not be able to afford the insurance. In the same way that you want to keep a good credit rating, you also want to try and keep your "risk factor" as low as possible. What does that mean? If you drive a car, the better driver you are, the longer you have been driving, the fewer tickets you have, the fewer accidents you have, etc. the lower risk you are – or the lower risk you will become and the cheaper your car insurance. You may not get a break at the beginning (although insurance is often reduced if you can prove you have had "driver training") but, over time, as you drive more, and time passes, your driving, speeding, and accident record will affect your insurance rates. The same is true for life and health insurance. The healthier you are, the younger you are, if you don't smoke, if you don't take drugs, the safer your job, the better the health of your parents and others in your family, etc. the lower will be your "health risk" – and risk of dying. Therefore, you will likely be able to get insurance on your life and health at a lower cost.

There are basically two types of insurance – (1) general insurance and (2) life and health insurance. General insurance refers to insurance policies that cover property and physical assets – house, boat, car, jewellery, etc.

Life and health insurance policies, not surprisingly, cover your life and your health. The cost of a general insurance policy (how much your premium is monthly, semi-annually, or annually) will depend on a number of things including: • the value of the asset you are protecting (e.g. a house at $350,000 or a car at $35,000) – the more valuable the asset, the more costly the insurance. • the risk of something happening to the asset or how frequently it is used (e.g. do you drive your car 30,000 kms. a year or do you drive your car 10,000 kms. a year?) The more it is used, the more likely an accident will happen– and the higher will be the cost of insurance. • your personal record with respect to your assets, their loss, and previous insurance claim you may have made (e.g. you may have claimed for lost jewellery and also claimed twice for house insurance – a break-in and theft and a flooded basement). The more you claim the more things seem to happen to you – the higher the risk – and the higher the cost of insurance. • the type or style of the asset being insured (for example, insurance for a sports car will probably cost more than insurance for a conservative sedan because past history has shown that sports cars are involved in more accidents). • the area you live in (for example, insuring a house and its contents in a high crime rate area may cost more than in a house in a low crime rate area).

Life and health insurance is what you will acquire to (a) provide for others in the event you should die (life insurance) and (b) provide for yourself and others in the event you become sick or disabled and you are unable to earn an income (disability insurance). With respect to life insurance, there are two general types – "term" insurance and "permanent" insurance. Term insurance is cheaper. It provides protection for those things for which the financial need for protection is more temporary. For example, suppose some day you have children. Suppose you want to be sure that, should you die, their post-secondary education costs would be covered. That would be a temporary need for insurance. Why? Once the children are beyond post-secondary school age, the insurance protection would no longer be needed. Therefore, you may arrange for term life insurance that would end when the children reached that age. The life insurance would be temporary and would only be paid if you died before the policy ended. If the children complete their education, and the policy ends, and you didn't die – first, celebrate! But you don't get anything from the policy. You were buying protection in case anything happened to you. If nothing did, the insurance company keeps the money. Their risk was that you might die. If you did – they pay. If you didn't – they don't. The payments you made would have been temporary. And the cost of term insurance is often relatively low compared with other kinds of insurance. Permanent insurance (such as "whole life" policies) are different. They are just that – permanent. They last for life. Whereas term insurance might be paid (for example, if you die), permanent insurance will be paid when you die. Permanent insurance is for permanent protection. For example, suppose you want to ensure that estate taxes are covered when you die. (The government receives taxes levied on the estate of a person when he or she dies). Or maybe you want to leave money for a life partner, children, etc. after you die. That means you want insurance to provide money when you die – not if you die. You want permanent protection. That is when you would consider permanent insurance, which is more expensive than term insurance. Why? With permanent insurance, the company knows they eventually will pay. They pay when you die. That is why it costs more than a policy where they might not pay – in fact, the odds may be pretty good that they won't pay. So remember, insure things that are important to you – and insure them with the right kind of insurance. But don't take on more insurance than you need. Most people will work with an insurance agent to help provide advice on how much insurance to buy. But insurance, and deciding on the right amount, and the right kind, can be complicated. Do your homework.Read about insurance before making insurance decisions. And work with an agent who is able to explain things in a way you can understand. Try to make sure you have enough insurance – but not too much and more than you need.

Have you done anything to date that might affect your "risk factor" – either positively or negatively? Are there others in your life who may have an influence on your "risk factor" – either today or in the future?

At a young age, you will most likely have your first dealings with insurance when you drive a car, or when you travel (and need out-of-country) life and health insurance, or possibly "renter's insurance" if you move out and rent a house, condo, or apartment. You will probably need advice – and maybe help – from family members to make insurance decisions and cover the costs. Now, let's turn our attention to the goal of financial independence.

If you move out and rent a place – or if you have already – look into "renter's insurance.“ You might want some to protect you in case anything happens to the place you are renting – and it's your fault. Don't put off thinking about life insurance too long. No one wants to think about dying – but life insurance policies can be a lot cheaper if they are started at a young age. As soon as you start thinking about forming a household with someone, or having a family, start to think about – and look into – health and life insurance.

Pablo Casals, the famous Spanish cellist, once said that: "To retire is to begin to die." Casals obviously saw retirement as an unwanted change in life. To him, it meant shifting your focus from preparing to live to preparing to die. That would not inspire many people to think about retirement. However, here is a suggestion. Don't think about "retiring." Think about getting to where you are "financially independent" – and don't have to work for an income. Perhaps society made a mistake in creating the concept of "retirement" in the first place. In early civilizations, many privileges came with age. There was no fixed date after which you suddenly became "retired." Elders were highly respected – and often seen as having the most to offer based on their wisdom and experience. Setting A Target For Financial Independence Things have changed over time. The world changes so fast these days that older people are often seen more today as "out of touch" or "not up on things" or "behind the times." That is probably an unfortunate change since there is still a great deal that can be gained from the wisdom and experience of those who are "older" in our society. Regardless of whether it was a good or bad thing, the concept of "retiring" came into being rather recently in our society. For a long time, the common target date to retire was age 65. At that age, it was assumed most people would stop working for an income. In some cases, they even had to stop working because retirement was "compulsory" at age 65. This is becoming less common today. Why?

Many people are not prepared financially to retire at age 65; • More and more people are not getting a pension from their employer to help them in retirement; • More people are in good health and don't want to retire; and • In some cases, we don't have enough skilled, trained, or experienced workers in an area of work and we need people – so they are being encouraged not to retire.

At your age "retirement" is way off in the distant future. You probably feel that life, over the next few years, holds out enough challenges that deserve your attention without thinking about retirement. But your attitude and interest might be different if, instead of "retirement" you set a goal for your "financial independence."Would you be interested in thinking about a “financial independence point” – and getting to where you could decide whether to work or not? That may be a more interesting goal, at this point in your life, than retirement – something to think about for your future. And there is another thing to think about in terms of your future – and that is how long you may live. Statistics show that if you are like most people today, you may live 20% to 30% or more of your life after you stop working. That’s a lot of your lifetime. It could be 30 years – or more. With the advances that are taking place in health care and medicine,- maybe the portion of your life spent in years after work will be even higher. That makes it even more important to plan ahead – and start to plan early. If you can set a goal of financial independence, and reach it – then you can be much better prepared Do you know people who are working well past age 65? Do you see people over age 65 working at jobs in your community? If so, do you think it is because they need to work, or does the employer need or want their services? How About You? for those later years. In looking into your future, and thinking about financial independence, a question comes up. How much money will you need to earn from “non-work sources” of income to be “financially independent” – and be able to choose to work or not work? To live the kind of life you want to live – without working from an income – will you need to have an annual income of $25,000 – $40,000 – $60,000 – $80,000 or more? What lifestyle are you aiming for? This will determine how much you will need to have in savings, investments, pensions, etc. to hit your financial independence goal if you would be content living on an annual income of $25,000 a year, you won’t need to build up as much if you hope to be able to get $75,000 a year.

Without thinking about inflation, what level of income do you think you would need to make from nonwork sources to be able to choose not to work?

Let’s look at some of the more common “nonworking” sources of income that may allow you to reach financial independence. Savings And Investments Over the course of your life, you will hopefully set aside, and put to work, savings and investments. Hopefully, these will build up over time so that, in the future, they can help to provide an income for you. As an example, suppose that from age 25 you saved and invested $1,000 a year and that you were able to earn an average of 4% interest or return a year. At age 60, those savings would be worth almost $80,000. As another example, if from age 30 to 65, you saved $2,500 a year, that would end up as almost $200,000! Starting to save and invest early will be very important to you later in life.

Pensions How does a pension plan work? Payments from employees and the employer are pooled together. The pooled funds are invested and hopefully grow in value as a result. These are "pension funds" that are then invested and managed by professionals and professional companies. This creates a pool of money that employees will draw from as they retire and leave work with the company. As we have noted, fewer companies are offering pensions today – but many still do. For those that do, you will likely make payments into the pension plan and the employer will likely also contribute a certain amount. The longer you work with the company, and the more payments you make into the plan, the higher will be the benefits that you can receive when you leave. If you work with a company that provides a pension plan, make sure that you become familiar with the pension program. Know your benefits, how they can change, and how you can maximize your benefits from the plan. If you do get a company pension, it will most likely be a "defined contribution" pension rather than a "defined benefit" pension. What does that mean? In the past, companies would often offer a "defined benefit" pension plan. That means, you were told the amount you would receive each year as pension when you retired. That is now seldom the case. Today, if the company provides a pension, it will likely be a "defined contribution" pension. That means the company will contribute a certain amount each year to your pension. The money contributed will then have to be invested and managed. How well it is invested and managed will determine how much pension money you will receive when you retire. Why does that matter? A defined contribution pension plan means it will be less certain how much pension money you will have when you leave work. It also means when economic times are difficult – as in the years 2008 and those that followed – the value of pension investments can take a real hit. If they lose value, people may not be able to retire when they had hoped – or may have to live on less in retirement than they planned. It makes future income from pensions more uncertain. And how the pension money is managed becomes very important. In the end, a defined contribution pension plan, rather than a defined benefit pension plan, makes planning for the future – and reaching a goal of financial independence – more challenging. On the other hand, many people may not receive a company pension at all.

For many people, at some point in their lives they may inherit some money or some assets from others. It's not always something you want to think about or plan for – but it is something many people will receive. Interestingly, though, people are living longer and longer these days – many into to their late 80's and 90's and beyond. Some people may receive inheritances – but won't receive them until they have actually stopped working themselves. That may mean that the inheritance may not be received by the "beneficiary," (person who received an inheritance according to a will) until he/she is 65 or older. In addition, more and more people have to draw upon their money in their later years of life to help get the care they need. This can often use up much, if not all, of the money that might have otherwise been passed on to others as inheritance. The cost of caring for elders – especially if they need constant care, sometimes for many years – can be very expensive. Therefore, as much as some money or assets might be inherited some day, this is a difficult source of income to include in future planning. In addition, as times and needs change, as people live longer, as the cost of "elder care" rises, people may actually have to start planning for how they will care for aging parents more than receiving an inheritance. That is unfortunate,but, as people live longer and longer – and often in ill-health – it becomes more of a possibility. These, then, are possible "non-work" sources of income that you may be able to get or plan for. Although the present has lots of challenges and takes a lot of your attention, try and give some thought to your later years. You (hopefully) may live a long time. A great many of those years will be in the latter period of your life. You may not want to work. You may not be able to work. If you start planning and preparing in your 20's, you may be very glad you did when you reach your 60's, 70's, 80's, 90's, or..... Set a goal for financial independence so that you can take care of you – and your loved ones – whether you work or not. It will be an important goal to reach in life.

CHAPTER THREE

RULES OF MONEY

There's an old saying "Money, money, money—it's all they can think about." Unlikely to be true of course, given that hardly anybody thinks about money itself (unless they happen to be a coin collector). The reason we all pursue and desire and fiercely protect money is because of what we can do with it. And no, of course money can't buy you love or happiness. Although it can buy a good deal of pleasure—and remove a lot of unhappiness. But it can buy you plenty of other things. Over the years I've identified the ten things which people most seem to want to spend their money on: 1 Security: A home of your own and enough money in the bank to support you in the way you want, plus a bit in hand for emergencies, and a big enough pension to ensure a comfortable retirement. 2 Comfort: A warm and spacious house, a big car, someone to clean or mow the lawns or do the laundry or mind the kids, and good quality medical care whenever you want it. 3 Luxuries: Exotic vacationss, fine wines, meals at top-class restaurants, expensive clothes, the best seats at sports events or opera or whatever you enjoy. 4 Mobility: First-class train seats and plane tickets, trips on cruise ships, chauffeur-driven cars wherever you are in the world. 5 Status: Prestigious invitations, access to important people and exclusive clubs, and perhaps even gratifying deference from others.

6 Influence: As a generous donor of substantial sums, you can make sure that your views and wishes are listened to and taken seriously. 7 Freedom: Not being dependent on employers, bosses, creditors, clients, customers. Not being a slave to the calendar, diary, or clock. Knowing you won't have to be a burden on your children. 8 Leisure: Time to do the things you want, go where you want, meet who you want, when you want. 9 Popularity: Being able to entertain friends, acquaintances, and contacts frequently and generously does wonders for your social life. 10 Philanthropy: Being able to make regular and substantial donations gives you the satisfaction of

helping people, supporting organizations, and furthering causes you believe in. Seems a reasonable enough list to me. And whether it's some or all those things that you'd like more of, you need to know how to go about generating greater wealth—which means you need to know what it is that separates the wealthy from the not-so-wealthy. So, what you need to know is what principles, and what behaviors the rich have, that you don't (yet). Some of them you will realize that you know, but don't do. None of this is actually rocket science; it's about understanding and then doing. I've studied a lot of wealthy people, and it's clear to me that there are some fundamental common principles followed by almost all. The bulk of the Rules in this book fall into that category. Then there are also some principles which some rich people swear by, but not all. I've included some of those too for good measure, just in case you too are one of the people they do the trick for. Security, comfort, luxuries, mobility, status, influence, freedom, leisure, popularity, philanthropy—that's all some people think about. They may not be everything; they may not even guarantee a happy life, but they're a pretty good basis to build happiness on.

Money is a concept. You can't really see or touch it (unless you are holding a gold bar in your hand). You can only do that with some physical symbol of it like stock certificates or a check. Bits of paper, yes, but bits of paper with enormous power. The concept of money comes with a lot of baggage to most of us. We have an inherent belief that it is good or bad and that wanting it is good or bad. That loving it is good or bad. That spending it is good or bad. What I am going to suggest in the first few Rules is that maybe, just maybe, how we think about wealth might be holding us back from having wealth. If, in our heart, we believe (even subconsciously) that money is a bad thing and having lots and lots of it is a really bad thing, then chances are we might be undermining our own efforts, unwittingly, to get lots of it. I am also going to get you to look at how much effort you are prepared to put into making money. It's a bit like a sport—the more you practice, the better you become. Likewise you can't make money while being lazy. You've got to put in some work here, you know. You've also got to know pretty intimately what you want, why you want it, how you think you are going to get it, what you are going to do with it after you've got it—stuff like that. No one said this was going to be easy...

The lovely thing about money is that it really doesn't discriminate. It doesn't care what color or race you are, what class you are, what your parents did, or even who you think you are. Each and every day starts with a clean slate so that no matter what you did yesterday, today begins anew, and you have the same rights and opportunities as everyone else to take as much as you want. The only thing that can hold you back is yourself and your own money myths (see Rule 7). Of the wealth of the world, each has as much as they take. What else could make sense? There is no way money can know who is handling it, what their qualifications are, what ambitions they have, or what class they belong to. Money has no ears or eyes or senses. It is inert, inanimate, impassive. It hasn't a clue. It is there to be used and spent, saved and invested, fought over, seduced with, and worked for. It has no discriminatory apparatus so it can't judge whether you are "worthy." I have watched a lot of extremely wealthy people, and the one thing they all have in common is that they have nothing in common—apart from all being Rules Players, of course. The wealthy are a diverse band of people—the least likely can be loaded. They vary from the genteel to the uncouth, the savvy to the plain stupid, the deserving to the undeserving. But each and every one of them has stepped up and said, "Yes please, I want some of that." And the poor are the ones saying, "No thank you, not for me, I am not worthy. I am not deserving enough. I couldn't. I shouldn't."

That's what this book is about, challenging your perceptions of money and the wealthy. We all assume the poor are poor because of circumstances, their background, their upbringing, their nurture. But if you have the means to buy a book such as this and live in comparative security and comfort in the world, then you too have the power to be wealthy. It may be hard. It may be tough but it is doable. And that is Rule 1—anyone can be wealthy, you just have to apply yourself. All the other Rules are about that application. YOU HAVE THE SAME RIGHTS AND OPPORTUNITIES AS EVERYONE ELSE TO TAKE AS MUCH AS YOU WANT.

So, what, to you, is wealth? This is one you have to sit down and work out in advance if you are going to get wealthy. My observation is that wealthy people invariably have worked this one out. They know exactly what, to them, wealth means. I have a wealthy and extremely generous friend who says that he knew long ago when he was starting out in business that he would consider he had made enough when he wasn't living off the money he had amassed (which we will call his capital). Nor would he be living off the interest on his capital. No, he would consider himself wealthy when he was living on the interest on the interest on his capital. Sounds good to me. Now, this friend knows how much his interest on the interest is making him, pretty much by the hour. Thus if we all go out for a meal in the evening he knows (a) how much the meal has cost and (b) how much he has made while eating the meal. He says that as long as (b) is more than (a), then he is happy. This is setting the definition of wealth pretty high you might think. Maybe you wouldn't want to set it this high. And that's fine of course. Then again, maybe you'd want to put some kind of figure on it. In the old days everyone wanted to be a millionaire. That was an easy one to judge if you'd got there or not. Today there are a lot of people who have houses worth more than that and they wouldn't consider themselves wealthy at all and yet haven't quite got around to upping the ante to wishing themselves billionaires.

My own definition, for comparison, is having enough so that I don't have to worry about having enough. How much is that? I never know. There always seems to be more to worry about—and less coming in. But seriously, I feel that I have been "comfortable" since I started counting in thousands rather than in dollars. I know to the nearest thousand how much I've got, how much I need and how much I can spend. For some people, not worrying might mean having enough to pay for any emergency that might arise in your family or home. So how will you define it? By the number of cars you own? Servants? Cash in the bank? Value of your house? Portfolio of investments? There are, of course, no right or wrong answers, but I do feel that until you've worked this one out you shouldn't read on. If we don't have a target, we can't take aim. If we don't have a destination, we can't leave home or we'll be driving around in circles for hours. If we don't have a definition, how can we monitor or judge success? If we don't do this, how will you know if this book has been helpful to you?

By defining what you mean by wealth, you now have a destination. Setting your objectives is establishing a timetable to reach that destination. It's quite simple. If you know you are going to drive to a certain place, it makes sense to know r What time you are leaving home r What time you expect to arrive r What route you are going to take r What you will be doing when you get there Getting rich is exactly the same. You will want to know in advance what rich means to you, how you intend getting there, how long you expect it to take, and what you are going to be able to do or want to do with your money when you get it. So, having defined what wealth means to you, can you now see the importance of setting your objective? Think about how you intend getting rich and how long it is going to take you, and then set your objective. It might be simple: "I am going to be a millionaire by my fortieth birthday, and I shall make my money by running my own property development company." That was easy. Well it was for me because I'm only making up an example for you. For you I wager it's going to be pretty hard. This is because you won't have thought about this before. Oh, I daresay you might have had a casual dream—I want to be very, very rich and/or famous and/or successful. But few people—only the rich, famous, and successful ones in my observation—actually decide what and when and how. You have to if you too want to be wealthy. And I assume you do or you wouldn't be reading this far. Good for you. Now set your objective. I can wait. Back already? How did it go? Your objective has to be realistic, honest, and achievable. By realistic I mean that setting an objective of being the richest person in the world might happen, but it isn't going to, it isn't realistic. Honest means you have to be true to yourself and set an objective that you can live with and work with. Lying to yourself means it will fail. Lying to others means it will fail. Achievable? Yes—that, too. If you know nothing about property and aren't interested in learning, have no capital and can't get a mortgage, then setting an objective to be a property developer isn't realistic, honest, or achievable. Happy with what you've got? Good. If not, try again and let's get a move on; we want to get you up and running as soon as possible.Now that you have embarked on a new journey, a new direction, it might be worth keeping it under your hat. There may come a time when you will need to discuss what you are doing with money mentors (see Rule 71) but for the moment don't broadcast what you are doing. There are several reasons for this: r Other people's opinions can often be negative, and this can discourage you. r If everyone is doing it, there may be less room for you. r There's no need to give away all your best ideas. r Having other people discussing your business among themselves is never good for you. r You don't want to be seen as preaching or trying to convert people to your way of thinking. r No one else really wants to know what you're up to—if they ask how you are, reply with a simple "Fine" rather than a lengthy explanation of what you are doing. r It's nice having a secret—gives you a warm, smug, glowing feeling. If you go round broadcasting what you're doing, there will be people around you who will get jealous and will do pretty well anything to discourage you. After all, you are saying goodbye to them in a way. You are proclaiming that the old you, the old lifestyle, isn't good enough any more and you are off to greener pastures. Of course, they are going to be unhappy about that. So keep it under your hat. That doesn't cost anything or require you to do anything. Let this be our little secret. Carry on learning and practicing the Rules, but just don't go telling everyone—no matter how much you think they might benefit from reading this book. Leave a copy around by all means, of course. The interesting bit is that even if you did go telling everyone, they're unlikely to do anything about it. Most people would rather watch television than drag themselves out of their pit of poverty. I am only thinking of you when I say keep it under your hat. Anyone who gets religion of any sort needs to keep a tight lip on it. People really hate being preached at, lectured at, encouraged to think about their lifestyle, or told that what they are doing isn't good enough. Gaining prosperity is one of those things you do privately, clandestinely, surreptitiously. Not that there is anything wrong, just that it's best done alone.

You have to get up early, work hard all day, and go to bed still working on your objective. Yes, money does sometimes grow on trees—or so it seems. Yes, people do win the lottery, the jackpot, the big prize. People do get sudden inheritances from long-lost relatives. Yes, people do suddenly find fame and fortune where they sought for none. But it isn't going to happen to you. Well, the odds are that it won't. If you set your objective as Win the lottery and live in the lap of luxury forever, then read no further. Put this book down and go and buy lottery tickets. If your objective is a little more realistic then read on. Most people are too lazy to be rich. They may say they want to be, but they don't. They may buy a lottery ticket as a sort of half-hearted gesture of wanting to be rich, but they aren't prepared to put in the work. They aren't prepared to make sacrifices, study, learn, work their socks off, put in the effort, and make it a determined and concentrated focus of their life. And for a lot of them—not you—it is because they believe that if you do so you are somehow tainted with evil (see Rule 7). But is it OK to work hard to make money? Is it a worthwhile thing to want? It depends on why and what you are going to do with it I guess. Most people don't want to do the work. Yes, they want the money but only if it comes to them by accident, by luck, by chance. Then it's OK. Then it's not tainted with sweat and work and passion and focus. I think if you look at anyone rich enough to be a role model— Bill Gates, Richard Branson, Warren Buffett, Simon Cowell,James Dyson, Petr Kellner*—you'll notice only one thing in common...they work their socks off. They might make their money from computers, sales, business, the film industry, vacuum cleaners, pop music, radio stations, whatever. But the one thing they all share is the ability to do more in a day than most of us do in a month. And that's the wonderful thing about wealth—it's lying around waiting to be claimed (remember Rule 1). And those who claim it are the ones who get up early, work hard, and put in the hours. And you are going to have to as well. I don't have slackers or freeloaders on my team. I want hard-working, dedicated, focused, ambitious, driven money makers. With a sense of fun of course.

MOST PEOPLE ARE TOO LAZY TO BE RICH. THEY MAY SAY THEY WANT TO BE, BUT THEY DON'T.

CHAPTER FOUR

Raju & skyladder

Raju was living happily with his mother in his village. He had a garden full of trees which bore delicious fruits and he made a good living by selling them at a good price.Raju used his money wisely. After purchasing the monthly grocery and household goods.........Raju saved the rest in his bank account

Time passed smoothly for Raju. Lying on his cot under the star studded sky at night, Raju often dreamt about using some money and his experience to help others prosper in life like Gopi Chacha had helped him.One night Raju had a new dream. He dreamt that he was climbing a skyladder and was amazed to find himself amidst the stars and the moon and the skyladder was branching out like a bridge leading to various stars.

Why can't we have a sky ladder like that leading to success and prosperity?

I will ask Gopi Chacha. He will definitely tell me how this can be made possible.

Raju eagerly waited for Gopi Chacha's visit.

Thank God, you have come! I was anxiously waiting for you.

What's the matter? Can we get a skyladder which will also act as a bridge to prosperity for all the people in our village?

Gopi Chacha was amazed at Raju's imagination.

What? A skyladder? A bridge to prosperity? Hmmm... Yes, I get the idea

Here goes Raju with one more of his dreams.

Let me see if I can make his dream come true.

Listen Raju, making a skyladder and starbridges requires a great effort. But even the longest journey starts with a small step!

See how you learnt to save money and have come to lead a comfortable life. You can teach your friends also to do that. This is the first step and it will put all of you on the road to prosperity.

How and where shall we start, Gopi Chacha?

On the way to bank....

Well, I am sure, a person like you will soon find an opportunity to do this.

Meanwhile, Raju started visiting the bank and discussing with the bank manager. He gathered a lot of information.

One day Raju and Gopi Chacha were passing by Shamu's house. Shamu was sitting with his father Bhola and sister Tara. They were excitedly discussing something. Raju and Gopi Chacha joined them.

Tara, what's that paper you are holding in your hand?

My school has given me a scholarship of Rs. 1000 per month and this is the first time I have ever seen a cheque.

And we don't know what to do with it.

Raju took the cheque and examined it closely.

Simple.

Open a bank account. Once the money gets deposited in your bank account...

....You can withdraw the money from your account as and when you need it.

But I have heard that anyone can directly give the cheque to a bank and exchange it for cash?

Yes, but you can't do that with this cheque.

Well, see this cheque? It is an account payee cheque. Do you see the two diagonal lines at the top left hand side corner?

This is called the 'crossing' of the cheque. When the cheque is crossed and made account payee, you can not directly receive the payment in cash at the bank counter.

The amount mentioned in a crossed or an account payee cheque can only be credited to the bank account of the person whose name is written in the first line of the cheque

Had the cheque been a bearer cheque meaning if it had not been crossed at the top

Anyone could have exchanged it for cash by producing it at the bank counter. It's not very safe.

How can you be so sure?

I also receive some payments for my fruits by cheque when the buyers come from the city. That is how I know about it.

Yes. Raju is right.

Raju, you know so much. Please tell us something more about a bank account.

There are different kinds of bank accounts. The Savings Bank (S/B) account is the most popular.

The main advantage of such an account is that you can easily deposit and withdraw your money from the bank and you also earn interest on the money lying in your account.

You can issue cheques against the amount in your account.

You can withdraw money from this account for a fixed number of times during a month.

What are the other types of bank accounts?

Well, the other types of accounts are Current Account and Fixed Deposit Account.

Current Accounts are mainly used by business people who need to frequently deposit and make payments from their accounts. You can withdraw money from your current account any number of times during a month but you don't earn interest.

And what about the Fixed Deposit accounts?

The Fixed Deposit or Term Deposit Accounts are deposits accepted by a bank for a fixed period.

Such an account earns a higher rate of interest than the savings bank account. Your money however, gets blocked for a fixed period of time .

In case you wish to withdraw the money before the end of the fixed period, you may have to accept a lower rate of interest as a penalty for not having retained the deposit with the bank for the specified period.

A variation of the Fixed Deposit is the Recurring Deposit Account where you need to deposit a fixed amount of money at fixed intervals (every week/ month) for a particular period of time, say, a year or two as per your convenience.You cannot withdraw money from this account before the fixed period. You can withdraw the money only at the end of that period.

This account also earns a higher rate of interest than the Savings Bank account. You can keep money in such deposit accounts if you plan to meet large expenditure like marriage, college admission or house construction at some fix time in the future.

Then I think the Savings Bank account is best suited for Tara's needs.

Yes. This account is most suited for managing household expenditure, paying periodical bills, etc.

Yes, I will open a savings account. Every month I can save some money and put it in the recurring deposit account. At the end of two years I have some lumpsum for my college entrance expenditure.

That's a very wise way of saving money, Tara.

You can also instruct your bank to transfer a fixed amount every month from your Savings Bank account to your Recurring Deposit account.

This way you will not have to go to the bank every month just to deposit some money. This is called a standing instruction and it saves you the trouble of going to the bank every month just to withdraw from one account and put it in another.

You can also give standing instruction to your bank to do other routine chores like paying your regular bills, insurance premium, etc.,

I also get my pension payment through my Savings Bank account and have given instruction for payment of my telephone, electricity bills, etc., from the balance in the account.

That's great!

Let us all go to the bank branch so that we can learn about the process while opening the account

Yes. But do not forget to take your photographs, an identity proof and a proof of your address.

Any document that has your photo and address will be accepted as proof of identity and proof of residence. So you can take documents like voter's identity card, ration card, PAN (permanent account number) card, driving licence, passport, etc..

We will need to give these to the bank alongwith our application for opening the account. And remember to carry the minimum amount of money too to open the account!

But do not worry too much. If you do not have much money , you can open a 'no-frills' account and still meet your basic banking needs.

All leave for the bank.

Good, Raju. See how you are setting your friend's feet on the journey to prosperity?

My skyladder and star bridge!!

Hello ! Can I help you?

We all have come to open a bank account.

This is the account opening form. Please fill up all the details in the form like your name, address, operational instructions, nominee, etc.

After filling up the form give it to me along with a copy of the documents of proof of your identity and address that you have brought.

In case you have any problem in filling up the forms, I will help you.

What is the meaning of operational instructions?

Your bank must know how you would operate your account.

You can either operate your account by yourself or with someone like your mother, father, brother....that is, in single name or in joint names with somebody else.

Joint names?

Yes. A joint account is an account in the names of two or more persons.

Two or more persons? You mean Tara and I can open an account jointly?

Yes

Can Shamu withdraw the money lying in my account without my knowledge?

That you will have to choose and indicate in this form. If you choose to operate singly, you can indicate that. If you want to operate the account jointly with your brother then both of you will have to sign. You can also choose for either one of you to operate the account at a time.

If you choose 'either or survivor' option, the money can be withdrawn by any of the account holders on their own without taking the signature of the other account holder.

This option is really useful in case one of the account holders dies or cannot operate the account for some reason.

The other holder can continue to operate the account without any difficulty. This is actually very useful for elderly people and for officials who travel a lot as their family members can operate the account for meeting expenses in their absence.

If you opt for joint operation, the money can be withdrawn only when all the account holders sign.

Such an option ensures that none of the other account holders can withdraw the money without the consent of the others.

In other words, if you take this option then Shamu cannot withdraw money from your account without your knowledge!

This is also useful for groups and organisations who maintain accounts which are required to be operated by two or more officials together.

There is still one more option - 'former or survivor'. When you choose this option, only the person whose name appears first can operate the account.

The other account holder can operate the account only after the death of the 'former' person.

You can always choose to operate your account.

You have to make this choice at the time of opening the account. You can change the choice later if you want to. But you must give clear instructions to your bank.

Gopi Chacha takes them to the bank manager who is very happy to see new customers.

Namaste Ramansa'b. Namaste Gopi Chacha.

Hello, Raju. I am happy to see that today you have brought your friends to the bank for opening accounts.

Yes Sir. We know that our money will be safe in the bank and will also earn interest.

Will you please help us?

Oh sure, Raju. Please give me a few minutes to verify the documents.

A few minutes later..... Can I deposit my cheque now? Congratulations. We have opened an account in your nameA few minutes later..... Can I deposit my cheque now? Congratulations. We have opened an account in your name

Yes, you can.

And the money will actually get deposited in my account?

Yes, it will. Only since you are depositing a cheque, the money will show up in your account after a couple of days

Tara and Shamu fill up the deposit slips for the money (minimum balance required to be kept) as they were opening a normal Savings Bank account and not a 'no frill' account.

Tara and Shamu fill up their deposit slips with Gopi Chacha's help.

The Bank Manager gives them their passbooks.

But Sir, how will I know, the money has actually come into my account?

Here is your passbook.

We will record all the transactions you have done in your bank account in any given period of time in the passbook.

It also tells you at any point of time how much money you have in your account. See the cash that Shamu has deposited in his account is already shown in the pass book.

Bring the passbook to the branch day after tomorrow for updating and you will see the amount of the cheque credited in your account.

You should get your passbook updated regularly

Yes, and if you find any mistake in it, you must tell us immediately.

Suppose I find a mistake and tell you about it, will you correct it immediately?Yes. Of course.

Although, some times, we may take some days to correct it, if we need to check something. And in case we do not correct our mistake in reasonable time, you must bring it to my notice.

In fact, if you have any complaint with your bank you must first give it in writing to the bank

If the bank does not resolve it in one month...

...you can send your complaint to the Banking Ombudsman, who has been appointed by the Reserve Bank of India to take care of such customer complaints.

omb... What?

Banking Ombudsman. There is one Banking Ombudsman for each State who is located in the Office of the Reserve Bank of India .

The address of this Banking Ombudsman should be available in the bank branch itself. If the bank does not give a satisfactory response to your complaints, the Banking Ombudsman will.

Gopi Chacha, is there a possibility that the bank will close down? And if that happens, will I get my money back?

All individual bank deposits upto Rs 1 lakh are compulsorily insured, which means that if any bank fails, these individual depositors get back their deposits upto Rs. one lakh.

I would really like to know more about this. But I can see the Manager uncle is very busy so may be some other time

That night, Raju was lying on his bed looking very satisfied and very happy. He went to sleep peacefully and dreamt of Gopi Chacha's words.

Raju, this is the real skyladder - the ladder of knowledge. This is just the beginning, Raju. As the knowledge spreads, every person in the village will prosper and the whole village will have wealth. And that will be the skyladder to success and prosperity !

Yes Gopi Chacha! Knowledge is the real skyladder and a starbridge. There is no end to what we can learn in life.

CHAPTER FIVE

MAKE THE MOST IMPORTANT FINANCIAL DECISION OF YOUR LIFE

My wealth has come from a combination of living in America, some lucky genes, and compound interest. —WARREN BUFFETT Let's kick it in gear now. It's time to begin our journey by tapping the power that can create real wealth for anyone. It's not some get-rich-quick scheme, and it's not what most people think will make them financially free or wealthy. Most people are looking to make some "big score"—a financial windfall—and then they think they'll be set. But let's face it, we're not about to earn our way to wealth. That's a mistake millions of Americans make. We think that if we work harder, smarter, longer, we'll achieve our financial dreams, but our paycheck alone— no matter how big—isn't the answer. I was reminded of this fundamental truth on a recent visit with the noted economist Burton Malkiel, author of one of the classic books on finance, A Random Walk Down Wall Street. I went to see Malkiel in his office at Princeton University because I admired not just his track record but also his no-nonsense style. In his books and interviews, he comes across as a straight shooter—and the day I met him was no exception. I wanted to get his insights on some of the pitfalls facing people at all stages of their investment lives. After all, this was the guy who helped create and develop the concept of index funds—a way for the average investor to match, or mimic, the markets; a way that anyone, even with a small amount of money, can own a piece of the entire stock market and have true portfolio diversity instead of being stuck with the ability to buy only a small number of shares of stock in one or two companies. Today this category of investments accounts for over $7 trillion in assets! Of all the people I'd planned to interview for this book, he was one of the best-qualified to help me cut through the clutter and doublespeak of Wall Street and assess our current investment landscape. What's the biggest misstep most of us make right from the start? Malkiel didn't even hesitate when I asked him. He said the majority of investors fail to take full advantage of the incredible power of compounding—the multiplying power of growth times growth. Compound interest is such a powerful tool that Albert Einstein once called it the most important invention in all of human history. But if it's so awesome, I wondered, why do so few of us take full advantage of it? To illustrate the exponential power of compounding, Malkiel shared with me the story of twin brothers William and James, with investment strategies that couldn't have been more different. He gives this example in one of his books, so I was familiar with it, but to hear him tell it live was an incredible experience—a little like hearing an 81-year old Bruce Springsteen play an acoustic version of "Born to Run" in his living room. The story supposes that William and James have just turned 65—the traditional retirement age. William got a jump-start on his brother, opening a retirement account at the age of 20 and investing $4,000 annually for the next 20 years. At 40, he stopped funding the account but left the money to grow in a tax-free environment at the rate of 10% each year. James didn't start saving for retirement until the ripe old age of 40, just as his brother William stopped making his own contributions. Like his brother, James invested $4,000 annually, also with a 10% return, tax free, but he kept at it until he was 65—25 years in all. In sum, William, the early starter, invested a total of $80,000 ($4,000 per year × 20 years at 10%), while James, the late bloomer, invested $100,000 ($4,000 per year × 25 years at 10%). So which brother had more money in his account at the age of retirement? I knew where Malkiel was going with this, but he told the story with such joy and passion that it's like he was sharing it for the very first time. The answer, of course, was the brother who'd started sooner and invested the least money. How much more did he have in his account? Get this: 600% more! Now, step back for a moment and put these numbers in context. If you're a millennial, a Gen Xer, or even a baby boomer, pay close attention to this message—and know that this advice applies to you, no matter where you are on your personal timeline. If you're 35 years old and you suddenly grasp the power of compounding, you'll wish you got started on it at 25. If you're 45, you'll wish you were 35. If you're in your 60s or 70s, you'll think back to the pile of money you could have built and saved if only you'd gotten started on all that building and saving when you were in your

50s and 60s. And on and on. In Malkiel's example, it was William, the brother who'd gotten the early start and stopped saving before his brother had even begun, who ended up with almost $2.5 million. And it was James, who'd saved all the way until the age of 65, who had less than $400,000. That's a gap of over $2 million! All because William was able to tap into the awesome power of compounding for an additional 20 years, giving him an insurmountable edge—and saddling him with the family dinner checks for the rest of his life. The man on top of the mountain didn't fall there. —VINCE LOMBARDI Not convinced that compound interest, over time, is the only sure way to grow your seed of money into the bumper crop of financial security you'll need to meet your future needs? Malkiel shared another favorite story to bring home his point—and this one's from our history books. When Benjamin Franklin died in 1790, he left about $1,000 each to the cities of Boston and Philadelphia. His bequests came with some strings attached: specifically, the money was to be invested and could not be touched for 100 years. At that point, each city could withdraw up to $500,000 for designated public works projects. Any remaining money in the account could not be touched for another 100 years. Finally, 200 years after Franklin's death, a period of time that had seen stocks grow at an average compounded rate of 8%, each city would receive the balance—which in 1990 amounted to approximately $6.5 million. Imagine that $1,000 grows to $6.5 million, with no money added over all those years. How did it grow? Through the power of compounding! Yes, 200 years is a long, long time—but a 3,000% rate of return can be worth the wait. Malkiel's examples show us what we already know in our hearts to be true: that for most of us, our earned income will never bridge the gap between where we are and where we really want to be. Because earned income can never compare to the power of compounding! Money is better than poverty, if only for financial reasons. —WOODY ALLEN Still think you can earn your way to financial freedom? Let's take a quick look at how it's worked out for some of the highest-paid people in the world: Legendary baseball pitcher Curt Schilling earned more than $100 million in an incredible career that included not one but two World Series championships for the Boston Red Sox. But then he poured his savings into a videogame startup that went bankrupt—and brought Schilling down with it. "I never believed that you could beat me," Schilling told ESPN. "I lost." Now he's $50 million in debt. Kim Basinger was one of the most sought-after actresses of her generation, torching the big screen with indelible roles in such films as 91/2 Weeks,

Batman, and L.A. Confidential, which earned her an Academy Award as best supporting actress. At the height of her A-list popularity, she earned more than $10 million per picture —enough to spend $20 million to buy a whole town in Georgia. Basinger ended up bankrupt. Marvin Gaye, Willie Nelson, M.C. Hammer, Meat Loaf—they sold millions of albums and filled stadiums with adoring fans. Francis Ford Coppola? He packed theaters as the director of The Godfather, one of the greatest American films, which—at least for a while— held the all-time box office record with gross ticket sales of $129 million. All had near-brushes with bankruptcy—Coppola, three times! Even Michael Jackson, the "King of Pop," who reportedly signed a recording contract worth almost $1 billion and sold more than 750 million records, was forced to the brink of bankruptcy in 2007, when he was unable to pay back a $25 million loan on his Neverland Ranch. Jackson spent money like he would never run out —until he finally did. At his death two years later, he reportedly owed more than $300 million. Do you think any of these ultra-megastars imagined a day when the money would stop flowing? Do you think they even considered preparing for such a day? Have you ever noticed that no matter how much you earn, you find a way to spend it? By these examples, it's clear to see that you and I are not alone. We all seem to have a way of living up to our means—and some of us, I'm afraid, find a way to live beyond our means. We see this most of all in the stars who take the biggest falls—like the rich-beyond-theirdreams prizefighters who hit the canvas with a thud. Just look at the up-and-down-and-out career of former heavyweight champ Mike Tyson, who made more money in his time than any other boxer in history —nearly a half billion dollars—and went bankrupt. But five-division world champion Floyd "Money" Mayweather Jr. is about to beat Iron Mike's earning record. Like Tyson, Mayweather fought his way up from hardscrabble beginnings. In September 2013 he scored a guaranteed purse of $41.5 million for his bout against Saúl "Canelo" Álvarez—a record amount that grew to more than $80 million based on pay-per-view totals. And that was just for one fight! Before this giant payday, he'd already topped the Sports Illustrated "Fortunate 50" list ranking the richest athletes in the United States. I love Mayweather personally. He's an extraordinarily gifted athlete—with a work ethic like few alive. He's also incredibly generous with his friends. There is a lot to appreciate in this man! But Mayweather had fought his way to the top of this list before, only to lose his fortune to wild spending sprees and bad investments. He is reported to spend so recklessly, he's known to carry around a backpack filled with

$1 million in cash—just in case he needs to make an emergency donation to Louis Vuitton. Like so many achievers, the champ is smart as a whip, and my hope is that he is following better investment practices today, but according to no less an authority on money than 50 Cent, Mayweather's former business partner, the champ has no income outside of fighting. The rapper summed up the boxer's financial strategy in plain terms: "It's fight, get the money, spend the money, fight. Fight, get the money, spend the money, fight." Sound like a ridiculous strategy? Unfortunately, we can all relate at some level. Work, get the money, spend the money, work—it's the American way! Before you speak, listen. Before you write, think. Before you spend, earn. Before you invest, investigate. Before you criticize, wait. Before you pray, forgive. Before you quit, try. Before you retire, save. Before you die, give. —WILLIAM A. WARD Here's the $41.5 million question: If these individuals couldn't build on their talents and blessings and earn their way to financial freedom, how can you expect to earn your way? You can't. But what you can do is make a simple change in strategy and embrace a whole new mind-set. You have to take control and harness the exponential power of compounding. It will change your life! You have to move from just working for money to a world where money works for you. It's time to get off the sidelines and get into the game —because, ultimately, we must all become investors if we want to be financially free. You're already a financial trader. You might not think of it in just this way, but if you work for a living, you're trading your time for money. Frankly, it's just about the worst trade you can make. Why? You can always get more money, but you can't get more time. I don't want to sound like one of those tearjerker MasterCard commercials, but we all know that life is made up of priceless moments. Moments that you'll miss if you're trading your time for money. Sure, from time to time, we all need to miss a dance recital or a date night when duty calls, but our precious memories aren't always there for the taking. Miss too many of them, and you might start to wonder what it is you're really working for, after all. THE ULTIMATE ATM So where do you go if you need money and you're not a world champion fighter with a backpack of large bills? What kind of ATM do you need to complete that transaction? Right now, I'm betting, the primary "money machine" in your life is you. You might have some investments, but let's say you haven't set them up with income in mind. If you stop working, the machine stops, the cash flow stops, your income stops—basically, your financial world comes to a grinding halt. It's a zero-sum game, meaning that you get back just what you put into it.

Look at it this way: you're an ATM of another kind— only in your case, the acronym might remind you of that lousy "time-for-money" trade. You've become an Anti– Time Machine. It might sound like the stuff of science fiction, but for many of you, it's reality. You've set things up so that you give away what you value most (time) in exchange for what you need most (income)—and if you recognize yourself in this description, trust me, you're getting the short end of the deal. Are we clear on this? If you stop working, you stop making money. So let's take you out of the equation and look for an alternative approach. Let's build a money machine to take your place—and, let's set it up in such a way that it makes money while you sleep. Think of it like a second business, with no employees, no payroll, no overhead. Its only "inventory" is the money you put into it. Its only product? A lifetime income stream that will never run dry—even if you live to be 100. Its mission? To provide a life of financial freedom for you and your family—or future family, if you don't have one yet. Sounds pretty great, doesn't it? If you set up this metaphorical machine and maintain it properly, it will hold the power of a thousand generators. It will run around the clock, 365 days a year, with an extra day during leap years—and on the Fourth of July, too. Take a look at the accompanying graphic, and you'll get a better idea how it works. As you can see, the "machine" can't start working until you make the most important financial decision of your life. The decision? What portion of your paycheck you get to keep. How much will you pay yourself—of the top, before you spend a single dollar on your day-to-day living expenses? How much of your paycheck can you (or, more importantly, will you) leave untouched, no matter what else is going on in your life? I really want you to think about this number, because the rest of your life will be determined by your decision to keep a percentage of your income today in order to always have money for yourself in your future. The goal here is to enable you to step off the nine-tofive conveyor belt and walk the path to financial freedom. The way to start off on that path is to make this simple decision and begin to tap into the unmatched power of compounding. And the great thing about this decision is that you get to make it. You! No one else! I can't afford to waste my time making money. —JEAN LOUIS AGASSIZ Let's spend some time on this idea, because the money you set aside for savings will become the core of your entire financial plan. Don't even think of it as savings! I call it your Freedom Fund, because freedom is what it's going to buy you, now and in the future. Understand, this money represents just a portion of what you earn. It's for you and your family. Save a fixed percentage each pay period, and then invest it intelligently, and over time you'll start living a life where your money works for you instead of you working for your money. And you don't have to wait for the process to start working its magic. You might say, "But Tony, where do I come up with the money to save? I'm already spending all the money I have." We'll talk about a simple yet extraordinary technique to make saving money painless. But in the meantime, let me remind you of my friend Angela, the one who realized she could drive a new car for half the money she was spending on her old car. Well, guess what she did with 50% of the money she was paying out? She put it toward her Freedom Fund—her investment for life. When we started, she thought she couldn't save anything; the next thing you know she was saving 10%. Then she even added an additional 8% from her savings on the cost of the car for short-term goals as well! But she never touches the 10% of her income that is locked in for her future! In the end, it doesn't matter how much money you earn. As we have seen, if you don't set aside some of it, you can lose it all. But here you won't just set it aside stuffed under your mattress. You'll accumulate it in an environment you feel certain is safe but still offers the opportunity for it to grow. You'll invest it—and, if you follow the Money Power Principles covered in these pages, you'll watch it grow to a kind of tipping point, where it can begin to generate enough in interest to provide the income you need for the rest of your life. You might have heard some financial advisors call this pile of money a nest egg. It is a nest egg, but I call it your money machine because if you continue to feed it and manage it carefully, it will grow into a critical mass: a safe, secure pile of assets invested in a risk-protected, taxefficient environment that earns enough money to meet your day-to-day expenses, your rainy-day emergency needs, and your sunset days of retirement spending. Sound complicated? It's actually pretty simple. Here's an easy way to picture it: imagine a box you'll fill with your investment savings. You'll put money into it every pay period—a set percentage that you get to determine. Whatever that number is, you've got to stick to it. In good times and bad. No matter what. Why? Because the laws of compounding punish even one missed contribution. Don't think of it in terms of what you can afford to set aside—that's a sure way to sell yourself short. And don't put yourself in a position where you can suspend (or even invade) your savings if your income slows to a trickle some months and money is tight. What percentage works for you? Is it 10%? Or 15%? Maybe 20%? There's no right answer here —only your answer. What does your gut tell you? What about your heart? If you're looking for guidance on this, experts say you should plan to save at least a minimum of 10% of your income, although in today's economy many agree 15% is a far better number, especially if you're over the age of 40. (You'll find out why in section 3!) Can anybody remember when the times were not hard and money not scarce? —RALPH WALDO EMERSON By now you might be saying, "This all sounds great in theory, Tony, but I'm spread thin enough as it is! Every penny is accounted for." And you wouldn't be alone. Most people don't think they can afford to save. But frankly, we can't afford not to save. Believe me, all of us can find that extra money if we really have to have it right now for a real emergency! The problem is in coming up with money for our future selves, because our future selves just don't seem real. Which is why it's still so hard to save even when we know that saving can make the difference between retiring comfortably in our own homes or dying broke with a tiny bit of financial support from the government. We've already learned how behavioral economists have studied the way we fool ourselves about money, and later in this chapter I'll share some of the ways we can trick ourselves into doing the right thing automatically! But here's the key to success: you have to make your savings automatic. As Burton Malkiel told me during our visit, "The best way to save is when you don't see the money in the first place." It's true. Once you don't even see that money coming in, you'll be surprised how many ways you find to adjust your spending. In a few moments I'll show you some great, easy ways to automate your savings so that the money gets redirected before it even reaches your wallet or your checking account. But first, let's look at some real examples of people living from paycheck to paycheck who managed to save and build real wealth even when the odds were against them. DELIVERING MILLIONS Theodore Johnson, whose first job was with the newly formed United Parcel Service in 1924, worked hard and moved his way up in the company. He never made more than $14,000 a year, but here's the magic formula: he set aside 20% of every paycheck he received and every Christmas bonus, and put it into company stock. He had a number in his head, a percentage of income he believed he needed to save for his family—just as you will by the end of this chapter— and he committed to it. Through stock splits and good old-fashioned patience, Theodore Johnson eventually saw the value of his UPS stock soar to over $70 million by the time he was 90 years old. Pretty incredible, don't you think? And the most incredible part is that he wasn't a gifted athlete like Mike Tyson or a brilliant director like Francis

Ford Coppola— or even a lofty corporate executive. He ran the personnel department. But he understood the power of compounding at such an early age that it made a profound impact in his life—and, as it turned out, in the lives of countless others. He had a family to support, and monthly expenses to meet, but to Theodore Johnson, no bill in his mailbox was more important than the promise of his future. He always paid his Freedom Fund first. At the end of his life, Johnson was able to do some beautiful, meaningful things with all that money. He donated over $36 million to a variety of educational causes, including $3.6 million in grants to two schools for the deaf, because he'd been hard of hearing since the 1940s. He also set up a college scholarship fund at UPS for the children of employees. — Have you heard the story of Oseola McCarty from Hattiesburg, Mississippi—a hardworking woman with just a sixth-grade education who toiled for 75 years washing and ironing clothes? She lived simply and was always careful to set aside a portion of her earnings. "I put it in savings," she explained of her investment philosophy. "I never would take any of it out. I just put it in. It just accumulated." Oh, boy, did this woman's money accumulate. At 87 years old, McCarty made national news when she donated $150,000 to the University of Southern Mississippi to start a scholarship fund. This woman didn't have the compelling screen presence of a Kim Basinger or the distinctive musical talent of a Willie Nelson, but she worked hard and knew enough to see that her money worked hard, too. "I want to help somebody's child go to college," she said—and she was able to do just that, on the back of her good diligence. There was even a little left over for a small luxury item: she bought an air conditioner for her house. All the way at the other end of the spectrum, we see the rousing example of Sir John Templeton, one of my personal role models and one of the greatest investors of all time. I had the privilege of meeting John and interviewing him several times over the years, and I'm including our last interview in our "Billionaire's Playbook." Here's a little background. He didn't start out as "Sir John." He came from humble beginnings in Tennessee. John had to drop out of college because he couldn't afford the tuition, but even as a young man, he recognized the incremental power of compounded savings. He committed to setting aside 50% of what he earned, and then he took his savings and put it to work in a big way. He studied history and noticed a clear pattern. "Tony, you find the bargains at the point of maximum pessimism, " he told me. "There's nothing —nothing—that will make the price of a share go down except the pressure of selling." Think about it. When things are going well in the economy, you might get multiple offers on your house and you'll hold out for the highest price. In bull markets, it's hard for investors to get a good deal. Why? When things are going well, it's human nature to think they're going to continue going well forever! But when there's a meltdown, people run for the hills. They'll give away their homes, their stocks, their businesses for next to nothing. By going against the grain, John, a man who started with practically nothing, became a multibillionaire. How did he do it? Just when Germany was invading Poland in 1939, plunging Europe into World War II and paralyzing the world with fear and despair, he scraped together $10,000 to invest in the New York stock market. He bought 100 shares of every company trading under $1, including those considered nearly bankrupt. But he knew what so many people forget: that night is not forever. Financial winter is a season, and it's followed by spring. After WWII ended in 1945, the US economy surged, and Templeton's shares exploded into a multibillion- dollar portfolio! We saw the same kind of growth happen as the stock market soared from the lows of March 2009 to more than 142% growth by the end of 2013. But most people missed it. Why? When things are going down, we think they're going to go down forever—pessimism takes over. I'll show you in chapter 4.4, "Timing Is Everything?," a system that can help you keep your head and continue to invest when everyone else is afraid. It's in these short, volatile periods that astronomical returns really become available. I took those insights to my Platinum Partners, an exclusive mastermind group I'd started to support my foundation, and shared with them some of the potential opportunities in front of them. Take the Las Vegas Sands Corp. listed on the New York Stock Exchange. On March 9, 2009, its stock price had dropped to $2.28 a share. And today it's $67.41— a 3,000% return on your money! That's the power of learning to invest when everyone else is afraid. So what can we learn from Sir John Templeton? It's amazing what research, faith, and action can do if you don't let everybody else's fears paralyze you. This is a good lesson to remember if, as you're reading these pages, we're going through more tough financial times. History proves that those "down and scary times" are the times of greatest opportunities to invest and win. He knew if he could set aside half of his meager earnings, he'd stake himself to where he could take full advantage of any investment opportunities. But even more important, he became one of the world's leading philanthropists, and after he became a British citizen, the Queen of England knighted him for his efforts. Even in death, his legacy of giving continues: each year, the John Templeton

Foundation gives away more money in grants "to advance human progress through breakthrough discoveries"—about $70 million—than the Nobel Prize Commission awards in a decade. And what's the great takeaway of Theodore Johnson's story? You don't have to be a financial genius to be financially free. The lesson of Oseola McCarty's life? Even a day laborer can pinch enough pennies to make a meaningful difference. The lesson of these three wise investors? By committing to a simple but steady code of savings, by drawing down on your income each pay period and paying yourself first, there's a way to tap the power of compound savings and let it take you to unimaginable heights. The most difficult thing is the decision to act, the rest is merely tenacity. –AMELIA EARHART So how much will you commit to set aside? For Theodore Johnson, that number was 20%. For John Templeton, it was 50%. For Oseola McCarty, it was simply a case of penny wisdom: putting those pennies in an interest-bearing account and letting them grow. What about you? Got a number in mind? Great! It's time to decide, it's time to commit. It's time to take the first of the 7 Simple Steps to your Financial Freedom! The most important financial decision of your life needs to be made right now! It's time for you to decide to become an investor, not just a consumer. To do this, you simply have to decide what percentage of your income you will set aside for you and your family and no one else. Once again, this money is for you. For your family. For your future. It doesn't go to the Gap or to Kate Spade. It doesn't go to expensive restaurants or a new car to replace the one that's still got 50,000 miles to go on the odometer. Try not to think of it in terms of the purchases you're not making today. Focus instead on the returns you'll reap tomorrow. Instead of going out for dinner with friends—at a cost, say, of $50—why not order in a couple pizzas and beers and split the cost among your group? Trade one good time for another, save yourself about $40 each time out, and you'll be way ahead of the game.What's that, you say? Forty dollars doesn't sound like much? Well, you're right about that, but do this once a week, and put those savings to work, and you could take years off your retirement time horizon. Do the math: you're not just saving $40 a week, but this one small shift in your spending can save you approximately $2,000 each year—and with what you now know, that $2,000 can help to harness the power of compounding and help you to realize big, big gains over time. How big? How about $500,000 big? That's right: a half million dollars! How? If you had Benjamin Franklin's advisors, they'd tell you to put your money in the market, and if you too generate an 8% compounded return over 40 years, that $40 weekly savings ($2,080 per year) will net you $581,944! More than enough to order an extra pizza— with everything on it! Are you starting to see how the power of compounding can work for you, even with just a few small, consistent actions? And what if you found some more aggressive savings than $40 a week? Even $100 could mean a $1 million difference at the time you would need it most!It's a great way to begin your journey by setting in place automatic reminders to capture your commitments and make sure you implement your new plan! If you haven't done it yet, do it now! It will help guide you through the following easy steps: • If you get a regular paycheck, you'll most likely be able to set up an automated plan with a call to the human resources department, instructing it to send a specific percentage of your paycheck—that you and you alone choose—directly to your retirement account. • If you already have automatic deductions going into your 401(k), you can increase the amount to the percentage you've chosen. (And in the following sections of this book, I'll show you how to make sure your retirement plan is set up in such a way that you can actually "win" this game, to make sure you're not paying hidden fees and that your money is free to grow in a compounded environment—ideally, tax-deferred or tax free for maximum growth.) Got that taken care of? Outstanding! • But what about if you're self-employed, or if you own your own business or work on commission? No problem. Just set up an automatic transfer from your checking account.

Execution is mastery. Execution will trump knowledge every day of the week. I hate losing more than I even want to win. —BRAD PITT as Oakland A's general manager Billy Beane in Moneyball What if, after everything you've just learned, you still haven't taken that first step to set aside a percentage of your earnings to save for compounded interest? Is there something holding you back? What's really going on? Could it be that you're not systematically saving money because it feels like a sacrifice—a loss—instead of a gift to yourself today and in the future? In my search for answers, I met with Shlomo Benartzi of the UCLA Anderson School of Management. He said, "Tony, the problem is people feel like the future is not real. So it's hard to save for the future." Benartzi and his colleague, Richard Thaler of the University of Chicago, came up with an amazing solution called Save More Tomorrow (SMarT) with a simple but powerful premise: if it hurts too much to save more money now—just wait until your next pay raise. How did they come up with it? First, Shlomo told me, they had to address the challenge of immediate gratification, or what scientists call "present bias." He gave me an example: when he asked a group of students whether they wanted a banana or some chocolate for a snack when they met again in two weeks, a full 75% said they wanted a banana. But two weeks later, with the choices in front of them, 80% picked the chocolate! "Self-control in the future is not a problem, " said Shlomo. It's the same with saving, he told me. "We know we should be saving. We know we'll do it next year. But today we go and spend." As a species, we're not only wired to choose today over tomorrow, but also we hate to feel like we're losing out on something. To illustrate the point, Shlomo told me about a study in which monkeys—our not-so-distant cousins—were given an apple while scientists measured their physiological responses. Enormous excitement! Then another group of monkeys was given two apples. They also displayed enormous excitement. And then one change was made: the monkeys that were given two apples had one taken away from them. They still had one apple, but what do you think happened? You guessed it. They were angry as hell! (Scientifically speaking.) Think this happens with people, too? In fact, how often does this happen with the average person? We forget what we already have, don't we? Remember this study when I tell you the story of a billionaire named Adolf Merckle in the next chapter. You'll have a flash of insight. The bottom line is, if we feel like we're losing something, we avoid it; we won't do it. That's why so many people don't save and invest. Saving sounds like you're giving something up, you're losing something today. But you're not. It's giving yourself a gift today of peace of mind, of certainty, of the large fortune in your future. So how did Benartzi and Thaler get around these challenges? They came up with a simple system to make saving feel painless. It aligns with our natures. As Shlomo said in a TED Talk, "Save More Tomorrow invites employees to save more maybe next year—sometime in the future when we can imagine ourselves eating bananas, volunteering more in the community, exercising more, and doing all the right things on the planet." Here's how it works: you agree to automatically save a small amount of your salary—10%, 5%, or even as little as 3%. (This is a number so small you won't even notice the difference!) Then you commit to saving more in the future—but only when you get an increase in pay. With each pay raise, the percentage saved would automatically get a little larger, but you wouldn't feel it as a loss, because you never had it in the first place! Benartzi and Thaler first tested the Save More Tomorrow plan almost 20 years ago at a company in the Midwest where the blue-collar workers said they couldn't afford to squeeze another dime out of their paychecks. But the researchers persuaded them to let their employer automatically divert 3% of their salaries into a retirement account, and then add 3% more every time they got a pay raise. The results were amazing! After just five years and three pay raises, those employees who thought they couldn't afford to save were setting aside just under a whopping 14% of their paychecks! And 65% of them were actually saving an average of 19% of their salaries. When you get to 19%, you're approaching the kinds of numbers that made Theodore Johnson, the UPS man, incredibly wealthy. It's painless, and it works. It's been proven time and again. Let me show you the chart that Shlomo uses to illustrate the impact that each increase in savings will have on an employee's lifestyle. At 3%, there's an image of a pair of sneakers— because that's all you'll be able to afford if you save only 3%! At 4%, there's a bicycle. It goes all the way up to 14%, where there's a luxury car and the clear message that life is great! That's a big difference! Now 60% of larger companies are offering plans like Save More Tomorrow. Find out if yours does, and if not, show this book to the HR department and see if you can get one put in place. Of course, you'll still need to go out and actually "earn" your raise—your boss isn't likely to hand it to you just because you've asked nicely. But once you do, you're free to earmark the full amount of the raise, or just a portion, depending on your circumstances. In some cases, if you work for a matching company, your employer will help to effectively double your contribution—and you'll be well on your way soon enough.

If your employer doesn't offer the plan, you can set one up with America's Best 401k, and many other 401(k) systems. You could start out with 5% (although I would encourage you to start with no less than 10%, if at all feasible) automatically going into your Freedom Fund, and then commit to 3% more every time you get a raise. Go online or make one phone call, and it will be happening for you. You could do this today and lock in your future in the most painless way possible. There's no excuse for you not to do it! You can even go to our app, where we've prewritten an email that you can send to your boss or head of HR so you can put this process to work for you right away. How's that for easy? Do it right now! But what if you're self-employed? What if you own your own business, and you feel like you need to put every cent into it? Believe me, you'll find a way. What if there was a new tax that came out, and you had to pay 10% more, or even 15% more to the government? You'd hate it! You'd scream bloody murder! But you'd find a way to pay it. So think of this percentage as a tax you "get to pay"—because the money doesn't go to Uncle Sam but to your family and future self! Or think of yourself as a vendor who's got to be paid first. If it has to be done, you'll do it. But in this case, it's something you're setting aside that is yours and your family's to keep forever, right? And remember, you want to automate it. That's the whole secret: earn more, spend less, and automate it. LIKE LETTERS OF FIRE ACROSS THE SKY As a young man, I came across George Samuel Clason's classic 1926 book The Richest Man in Babylon, which offered commonsense financial advice told through ancient parables. I recommend it to everyone. Over the years, one passage has stayed with me: " 'A part of all I earn is mine to keep.' Say it in the morning when you first arise. Say it at noon. Say it at night. Say it each hour of every day. Say it to yourself until the words stand out like letters of fire across the sky. Impress yourself with the idea. Fill yourself with the thought. Then take whatever portion seems wise. Let it be not less than onetenth and lay it by. Arrange your other expenditures to do this if necessary. But lay that portion first." No one would have remembered the Good Samaritan if he'd only had good intentions. He had money as well. —MARGARET THATCHER Lay that portion first, my friend. And then act on it! It doesn't matter what the number is, just get started. Ideally, it shouldn't be less than 10%. But as time goes by, make the number mean something. THE NEXT STEP Now that you've set up an automated investment plan— your Freedom Fund, your new money machine—there may be two questions burning in your mind: First, where do I put this money? And second, how much am I going to need to achieve financial security or freedom? We're going to answer both of those questions clearly. And the answers are going to come from the best financial achievers in the world. But first we need to understand what you're really investing for. What's behind your personal desire for financial freedom? And what does wealth really mean to you? What are you really after? So let's take a quick moment—just a few pages—to look at how you are going to master money

MONEY MASTERY: IT'S TIME TO BREAK THROUGH Gratitude is the sign of noble souls. —AESOP Money is one of the ways we can turn the dreams we have into the reality we live. Without enough money, or a true scarcity of it, life can feel miserable. But when you have money in your pocket, does everything automatically get better? I think we all know the answer. Money can't change who we are. All it does is magnify our true natures. If you're mean and selfish, you have more to be mean and selfish with. If you're grateful and loving, you have more to appreciate and give. Take a moment and think back to the financial meltdown of 2008. Trillions of dollars of stock and home values evaporated into thin air. Millions of jobs were lost in a matter of months. What did you experience? How did it hit you? How did it affect your family? How about your friends? Some of us reacted with fear, some with anger, some with resignation, some with resolve. All these responses were not about money but about us. These events shined a light on what money really means to us. What power we give it. Whether we let money control us, or whether we take control of it. YOUR MONEY OR YOUR LIFE One of the most powerful examples I know from that time is a gentleman named Adolf Merckle. In 2007 he was the 94th richest man in the world, and the richest man in Germany, with a net worth of $12 billion. He owned the largest pharmaceutical company in Europe, and then he expanded his empire into manufacturing and construction. He was proud of what he'd accomplished. He was also something of a speculator. In 2008 he decided to make a bet in the stock market. He was so certain that Volkswagen was going down, he decided to short the company. Just one problem: Porsche made a move to buy Volkswagen, and the stock price shot up, not down. Almost overnight, Merckle lost nearly three-quarters of a billion dollars on that single gamble. To make matters worse, he desperately needed some cash to pay off a huge loan. But in 2008, banks weren't loaning money to anyone: not you, not me, not billionaires—not even other banks. So what did Merckle do? Search for new financing? Cut his expenses? Sell some companies at a loss? No. When he realized he'd lost a total of $3 billion and was no longer the richest man in Germany, that he had failed his family, he wrote a suicide note and walked in front of a speeding train. That's right. He killed himself. In a tragic irony, his family discovered only a few days later that the loans he sought had come through, and his companies were saved. Did Adolf Merckle die because of money? Or did he die because of what money meant to him? For Merckle, money was an identity. It was a source of significance. The loss of his status as the richest man in Germany was too much to bear, and he felt like a failure—even though there was still $9 billion left in his pocket! You might be thinking, "What a waste." But it may be a little too easy for us to judge this man. How often have we attached our identity—or our future prospects—to money at some level? Probably more than we'd all like to admit. THE BILLIONAIRE WHO WANTS TO DIE BROKE On the other hand, there are people like Chuck Feeney, an Irish-American from Elizabeth, New Jersey, and a self-made billionaire. Have you ever tried to get through an airport, anywhere in the world, and found yourself lured into a room full of shiny bottles of liquor and perfume and other tax-free luxury items? Duty Free Shopping (DFS). That's Chuck Feeney's idea. He started with nothing in 1960 and ended up with a sales empire worth $7.5 billion. At one point, Forbes had listed him, like Merckle, as one of the richest men in the world. But Feeney was so humble, you would never have known it. Most of his life, he didn't own a car or a home. He flew coach and wore a plastic watch. Like Merckle, his bank account was dwindling—right now he's in his 80s, and Feeney has just over $1 million left to his name. But the big difference between him and Merckle is that instead of trying to hold on to every last penny, Chuck Feeney gave away all his money. This is a guy who, for the last 30 years, has made it his mission to take this vehicle called money and use it to change lives everywhere. His philanthropy reaches all over the world, from helping to create peace in Northern Ireland, to fighting AIDS in South Africa, to educating kids in Chicago. The most amazing thing about Feeney is that he did it all anonymously. Feeney wanted no credit. In fact, only recently has word gotten out that he's the man behind all these incredible projects. And he's still going! Chuck Feeney says his goal is to bounce the last check he writes. Obviously money meant very different things for Adolf Merckle and Chuck Feeney. What does money really mean to you? Do you use money, or does money use you? Like I've said from the beginning: if you don't master money, at some level, it's going to master you. THE ULTIMATE GOAL: GIVING BACK For me, money was always out of reach as a child. It was always a source of stress because there was never enough of it. I remember having to knock on the neighbor's door to ask for food for my brother and sister and me. Then, on Thanksgiving Day when I was 11 years old, something happened that changed my life forever. As usual, there was no food in the house, and my parents were fighting. Then I heard someone knocking at the front door. I opened it a crack and saw a man standing on the steps with grocery bags filled with enough food for a big Thanksgiving dinner. I could hardly believe it. My father always said that nobody gave a damn about anybody. But all of a sudden someone I didn't know, who wasn't asking for anything in return, was looking out for us. It made me think, "Does this mean that strangers care?" And I decided that if strangers care about me and my family, I care about them! "What am I going to do?" I promised myself that day, I was going to find a way, somehow, someday, to give back and pay it forward. So, when I was 17, I saved my money from working nights as a janitor and went out on Thanksgiving and fed two families. It was one of the most moving experiences of my life.

It lifted my spirit to see faces turned from despair to joy. Truly, it was as much a gift to me as it was to them. I didn't tell anybody what I was doing, but the next year, I fed four families. Then eight. I wasn't doing it for Brownie points, but after eight, I thought, "Man, I could use some help." So I enlisted some friends, and they got into it too. It grew and grew. Now my foundation feeds 2 million people every year in 36 countries, through our International Basket Brigades. Would I have known the joy of giving if it wasn't for that terrible Thanksgiving when I was 11? Who knows? Some would call it luck or fate or plain old good fortune. I see the hand of God in it; I call it grace. Here's what I know: I learned the joy of giving, and it had nothing to do with money. Money is simply a vehicle for trying to meet our needs, and not just our financial needs. Much of our life is guided by the beliefs we develop over the course of time; the story we create about what life's about, how we're supposed to be, what we're supposed to do or give. Ultimately, what's going to make us happy or fulfilled. Everyone has a different "happy." Some people find happiness pleasing others, while others find happiness in power and domination. Others define their happy as a billion dollars. Some think the way to happiness and a meaningful life is to get closer to God and give up everything material. Still others think the ultimate idea of happiness is freedom. Whatever emotion you're after, whatever vehicle you pursue—building a business, getting married, raising a family, traveling the world— whatever you think your nirvana is, I have found it's only an attempt by your brain to meet one or more of six human needs. These six basic needs make us tick. They drive all human behavior and are universal. They are the force behind the crazy things (other) people do and the great things we do. We all have the same six needs, but how we value those needs, and in what order, determines the direction of our life. Why are the six human needs so important to understand? Well, if you're going to build wealth, you've got to know what you're really after—what you're building it for. Are you looking for wealth to feel certain and secure? Are you chasing wealth to feel special and unique? Or are you looking to have a sense of contribution—you want to do things for others in a way you've never been able to do before? Or maybe all of the above? If you value certainty as the most important need in your life, you're going to move in a very different direction, act differently in relationships, in business and finance, than if love is your number one need. If we get underneath what you're really after, it's not money at all. What you're really after is what you think money is going to give you.

Ultimately, it's a set of feelings. And beneath those feelings are needs. NEED 1: CERTAINTY/COMFORT The first human need is the need for Certainty. It's our need to feel in control and to know what's coming next so we can feel secure. It's the need for basic comfort, the need to avoid pain and stress, and also to create pleasure. Does this make sense? Our need for certainty is a survival mechanism. It affects how much risk we're willing to take in life—in our jobs, in our investments, and in our relationships. The higher the need for certainty, the less risk you'll be willing to take or emotionally bear. By the way, this is where your real "risk tolerance" comes from. But what if you're totally certain all the time? If you knew what was going to happen, when it was going to happen, how it was going to happen. You knew what people were going to say before they said it. How would you feel? At first you'd feel extraordinary, but eventually you'd be what? Bored out of your mind! NEED 2: UNCERTAINTY/VARIETY So, God, in Her infinite wisdom, gave us a second human need, which is Uncertainty. We need variety. We need surprise. Let me ask you a question: Do you like surprises? If you answered "yes," you're kidding yourself! You like the surprises you want. The ones you don't want you call problems! But you still need them to put some muscle in your life. You can't grow muscle—or character—unless you have something to push back against. NEED 3: SIGNIFICANCE The third is Significance, that basic human need that drove Adolf Merckle. We all need to feel important, special, unique, or needed. So how do some of us get significance? You can get it by earning billions of dollars or collecting academic degrees—distinguishing yourself with a master's or a PhD. You can build a giant Twitter following. Or you can go on The Bachelor or become one of the next Real Housewives of Orange County. Some do it by putting tattoos and piercings all over themselves and in places we don't want to know about. You can get significance by having more or bigger problems than anybody else. "You think your husband's a dirtbag? Take mine for a day!" Of course, you can also get it by being more spiritual (or pretending to be). Unfortunately, one of the fastest ways to get significance—that costs no money and requires no education—is through violence. If someone puts a gun to your head, in that instant he becomes the most significant thing in your life, right? Spending a lot of money can make you feel significant, and so can spending very little. We all know people who constantly brag about their bargains, or who feel special because they heat their homes with cow manure and sunlight. Some very wealthy people gain significance by hiding their wealth. Like the late Sam

Walton, the founder of Wal-Mart and for a time the richest man in America, who drove around Bentonville, Arkansas, in his old pickup, demonstrating he didn't need a Bentley—but, of course, he did have his own private fleet of jets standing by. Significance is also a moneymaker—that's where my dear friend Steve Wynn has made his fortune. The man who made Las Vegas what it is today knows people will pay for anything they believe is "the best"—anything that makes them feel special, unique, or important; anything that makes them stand out from the crowd. He provides the most exclusive, luxurious experiences imaginable in his casinos and hotels—they are truly magnificent and unmatched in the world. He's got a nightclub called XS (what else?) that is the hottest spot in Las Vegas. Even on a weeknight, it has a line out the door. Once you're in, you have the privilege of purchasing an ordinary bottle of champagne for $700, or if you want to step up and show everyone you're a player, you can spend $10,000 for a special "Ono cocktail" of rare vintage cognac and fresh orange juice that comes with a white-gold necklace. Hey, it comes to your table with a sparkler, just so everybody knows you're significant (and out of your mind). NEED 4: LOVE AND CONNECTION The fourth basic need is Love and Connection. Love is the oxygen of life; it's what we all want and need most. When we love completely, we feel alive, but when we lose love, the pain is so great that most people settle on connection, the crumbs of love. You can get that sense of connection or love through intimacy, or friendship, or prayer, or walking in nature. If nothing else works, you can get a dog. These first four needs are what I call the needs of the personality. We all find ways to meet these: whether by working harder, coming up with a big problem, or creating stories to rationalize them. The last two are the needs of the spirit. These are more rare—not everyone meets these. When these needs are met, we truly feel fulfilled. NEED 5: GROWTH Number five is Growth. If you're not growing, you're what? You're dying. If a relationship is not growing, if a business is not growing, if you're not growing, it doesn't matter how much money you have in the bank, how many friends you have, how many people love you— you're not going to experience real fulfillment. And the reason we grow, I believe, is so we have something of value to give. NEED 6: CONTRIBUTION That's because the sixth need is Contribution. Corny as it may sound, the secret to living is giving. Life's not about me; it's about we. Think about it: What's the first thing you do when you get good or exciting news? You call somebody you love and share it. Sharing enhances everything you experience. Life is really about creating meaning.

And meaning does not come from what you get, it comes from what you give. Ultimately, what you get will never make you happy long term. But who you become and what you contribute will. Now, since this is a book about your money, think about how money can fulfill the six human needs. Can money give us certainty? You bet. Variety? Check. Obviously it can make us feel important or significant. But what about connection and love? In the immortal words of the Beatles, money can't buy you love. But it can buy you that dog! And it can, unfortunately, give you a false sense of connection because it attracts relationships, although not always the most fulfilling kind. How about growth? Money can fuel growth in business and in learning. And the more money you have, the more you can contribute financially. But here's what I truly believe: if you value Significance above all else, money will always leave you empty unless it comes from a contribution you've made. And if you're looking for significance from money, it's a high price to pay. You're looking for big numbers, but it's unlikely you'll find big fulfillment. The ultimate significance in life comes not from something external but from something internal. It comes from a sense of esteem for ourselves, which is not something we can ever get from someone else. People can tell you you're beautiful, smart, intelligent, the best, or they can tell you that you are the most horrible human being on earth—but what matters is what you think about yourself. Whether or not you believe that deep inside you are continuing to grow and push yourself, to do and give more than was comfortable or you even thought possible. There is nothing more significant than growing and giving. So while money is an extraordinary vehicle to meet many of our six needs, it's not the only one. When you are pursuing money, don't forget why you are pursuing it. You're trying to meet some emotional and psychological desires. Underneath those emotions are the needs that must be fulfilled for your life to be extraordinary. When the astronauts went to walk on the moon, imagine the journey they went on. From being a small child dreaming of someday flying to outer space, to the day when Buzz Aldrin and Neil Armstrong stood on the moon, looking back at that extraordinary view of planet Earth that we've all seen only in pictures. They were the first human beings to do it in the entire history of the species—how incredibly significant. What happened next? Ticker-tape parades. Shaking the president's hand. They were heroes. And then what? What do you do after you've walked on the moon, and you're only 39 years old? If you've studied the history of the astronauts, or read their biographies, you'll know that many of them became extremely depressed. Why? Because the only way they could find adventure was by traveling into space or all the way to the moon. They forgot how to find adventure in a simple smile. I'm not going to preach to you anymore, but I wanted to take this short time to say that while it's time to master your money, don't wait to master yourself. The fastest way to feel connection, a sense of how significant your life is, a deep sense of certainty and variety, and put yourself in a state where you can give to others, is to find a way each day to appreciate more and expect less. The wealthiest person on earth is one who appreciates. I interviewed Sir John Templeton for the first time when I was 33 years old. Remember, he was the multibillionaire who started with nothing and made all of his money when everyone else was afraid, during the worst times in history: WWII, Japan after the war, and in the late 1980s and early 1990s when massive inflation hit parts of South America. When others were fearful, he went out and invested. I asked him, "What's the secret to wealth?" And he said, "Tony, you know it, and you know it well. You teach it to everyone. It's gratitude." When you're grateful, there is no fear; when you're grateful, there is no anger. Sir John was one of the happiest and most fulfilled human beings I have ever known. Even though he passed in 2008, all these years later his life continues to inspire others. If you want to be rich, start rich. What can you be grateful for today? Who can you be grateful for today? Could you even be grateful for some of the problems and the pain that you've been through in your life? What if you took on the new belief that everything in life happens for a reason and a purpose, and it serves you? What if you believed in your heart of hearts that life doesn't happen to you, it happens for you? That every step along the way is helping strengthen you so that you can become more, enjoy more, and give more. If you'll start from that place, money won't be the source of your pleasure or your pain. Making money will just be a fun journey of mastery, and wealth a great vehicle to achieve what matters most in life. But as long as money is such a part of our lives, let's get right back on the money track. As heartfelt as this chapter has been, not all the people you'll meet along the financial path will be operating from the benevolent place of Growth and Contribution! You're going to be entering a world that is filled with people and organizations that too often will be looking to take advantage of your lack of experience and understanding. So I want to prepare you for what's ahead. Before we discuss where to put your money and what to look for, I have to show you what to look out for. There's a reason why most investors do not make money over time. I want to arm you with the knowledge that will both protect you and allow you to maximize the growth of your investments so you can achieve true Financial Freedom faster than you can imagine.I know that you want to jump right in and learn where to put your money to obtain financial freedom. And I want to dive in and show you! I absolutely light up when I see someone really "get it" and come to understand and embrace that the game is truly winnable. But it's not enough to just save your money, get a great return, and reduce your risk. You have to know that there are a lot of people looking to take a piece of your wealth. The system is riddled with loopholes—what I would call landmines—that can blow up your financial future. So in this section, we're going to go through 9 Myths—you might call them lies—that have been marketed to you over the years. And if you aren't aware of them—if you don't see them coming—they will systematically destroy your financial future. This next section is where this book starts to pay off! In fact, if you have the average American salary of $50,000 per year, and currently save 10% of your income and invest that money over time, you'll save $250,000 over your investment lifetime by just part of what you will learn in this section. That's five years of your current lifestyle, at your current income, without having to work a single day! And that is statistically proven, not a number I'm pulling out of a hat. If you make only $30,000 per year and save just 5% of your income each year, you'll still save $150,000 over your investment lifetime. That's a half decade's worth of your current income without having to work for it. If you're in the $100,000-plus category, this section could put $500,000 to $1 million back in your pocket over your lifetime. Sounds like a massive promise, huh!? I will let the numbers do the talking in the pages ahead. It's a short section, so pay attention because you're going to want to take immediate action. By shattering these myths, you will be able to immediately "stop the bleeding" in areas where you never thought you needed to. Knowing these 9 Myths will protect you and insure that you get to the level of financial freedom that you're truly committed to. Let's begin! WELCOME TO THE JUNGLE Whether you are a seasoned investor or just beginning to see yourself as an investor, the jungle that Ray Dalio so vividly described holds the same dangers for all of us. But most of the danger lies in the fact that what you don't know can hurt you. THE OFFER I want you to imagine that someone comes to you with the following investment opportunity: he wants you to put up 100% of the capital and take 100% of the risk, and if it makes money, he wants 60% or more of the upside to come to him in fees. Oh, and by the way, if it loses money, you lose, and he still gets paid! Are you in? I'm sure you don't need any time to think this through. It's a no-brainer. Your gut response has to be, "There's no way I'm doing this. How absurd!" The only problem is that if you're like 90% of American investors, you've invested in a typical mutual fund, and, believe it or not, these are the terms to which you've already agreed. That's right, there is $13 trillion in actively managed mutual funds3 with 265 million account holders around the world. How in the world do you convince 92 million Americans to participate in a strategy where they willingly give up 60% or more of their potential lifetime investment upside with no guaranteed return? To solve this riddle, I sat down with the 85-year-old investment guru Jack Bogle, the founder of Vanguard, whose 64 years on Wall Street have made him uniquely qualified to shed light on this financial phenomenon. His answer? "Marketing! "Tony, it's simple. Most people don't do the math, and the fees are hidden. Try this: if you made a onetime investment of $10,000 at age twenty, and, assuming 7% annual growth over time, you would have $574,464 by the time you're nearly my age [eighty]. But, if you paid 2.5% in total management fees and other expenses, your ending account balance would only be $140,274 over the same period." "Let's see if we've got this straight: you provided all the capital, you took all the risk, you got to keep $140,274, but you gave up $439,190 to an active manager!? They take 77% of your potential returns? For what?" "Exactly." Money Power Principle 1. Don't get in the game unless you know the rules! Millions of investors worldwide are systematically marketed a set of myths— investment lies—that guide their decision making. This "conventional wisdom" is often designed to keep you in the dark. When it comes to your money, what you don't know can—and likely will—hurt you. Ignorance is not bliss. Ignorance is pain, ignorance is struggle, ignorance is giving your fortune away to someone who hasn't earned it. A FAILED EXPERIMENT It's not just high-cost mutual funds that are the problem. The example above is just a peek under the sheets at a system designed to separate you from your money. Without exception, every expert I have interviewed for this book (from the top hedge funds managers to Nobel Prize winners) agrees that the game has changed. Our parents didn't have a fraction of the complexity or dangers to deal with that we have today. Why? They had a pension—a guaranteed income for life! They had CDs that paid conservative but reasonable rates—not the 0.22% you would be paid at the time of this writing, which won't even keep up with inflation. And some had the privilege of putting small investments into blue-chip stocks that paid steady dividends. That ship has sailed. The new system, which really got rolling in the early '80s with the introduction of the 401(k), is an experiment that's now been conducted for the most part on the single largest generation in US history: the baby boomers. How is this experiment working? "This do-it-yourself pension system has failed," said Teresa Ghilarducci, a nationally recognized expert in retirement security at the New School for Social Research and an outspoken critic of the system as we know it. "It has failed because it expects individuals without investment expertise to reap the same results as professional investors and money managers. What results would you expect if you were asked to pull your own teeth or do your own electrical wiring?" What's changed? We exchanged our guaranteed retirement pensions with an intentionally complex and often extremely dangerous system, filled with hidden fees, which gave us "freedom of choice." And somehow, in the midst of working your tail off, providing for your family, staying in shape, and taking care of the important relationships in your life, you are supposed to become an investment professional? You're supposed to be able to navigate this labyrinth of products, services, and unending risk of your hard-earned money? It's near impossible. That's why most people give their money to a "professional," often a broker. A broker who by definition works for a company that is not required by law to do what's in your best interest (more on this baffling concept in Myth 4). A broker who gets paid to funnel your money to the products that may be the most profitable for him and/or his firm. Now, let me be clear: this is not another bash-WallStreet-book. Many of the large financial institutions have pioneered some extraordinary products that we will explore and advocate throughout this book. And the vast majority of people in the financial services industry care intensely for their clients, and more often than not, they are doing what they believe to be the best thing. Unfortunately, many don't also understand how the "house" reaps profits whether the client wins or not. They are doing the best they can for their clients with the knowledge (training) and the tools (products) they have been provided. But the system isn't set up for your broker to have endless options and complete autonomy in finding what's best for you. And this could prove costly. Giving up a disproportionate amount of your potential returns to fees is just one of the pitfalls you must avoid if you plan on winning the game. And here is the best news yet: THE GAME IS STILL WINNABLE! In fact, it's more than winnable—it's exciting as hell! Yes, there are major challenges and more pitfalls you must avoid, but consider how far we have come. Today, with the click of a button and a minimal charge, you can invest in just about anything you want anywhere in the world you want. “It’s easier than it’s ever been to do pretty well,” said James Cloonan in a recent Wall Street Journal article. Cloonan is founder of the nonprofit American Association of Individual Investors. “You just have to decide to do the right thing.” Heck, just 35 years ago “you had to spend hours in a public library or write away to a company just to see its financial statements. Brokerage costs and mutual-fund fees were outlandish; tax rates were larcenous,” wrote Jason Zweig in his Wall Street Journal article “Even When Stocks Make You Nervous, Count Your Blessings.” Aside from high-frequency traders, technology has made the world of investing a much more efficient space for all of us. And this fits perfectly with the millennial generation, which wouldn’t accept anything less. “For us, it’s all about convenience!” exclaimed Emily, my personal assistant, who is a “straight-down-the-fairway” millennial. “There is no tolerance for slow or inefficient. We truly want everything to be at the touch of a button. We order everything on Amazon; we lift one finger, and it’s done. I can stream a movie on Netflix. I can get a car registration online. I can buy stocks online. I can do my presentation online. This morning I took a picture of my check and had it in my bank account by six—I didn’t even have to get out of my pajamas.” THE HOUSE HAS THE EDGE Steve Wynn, the billionaire gambling mogul credited with transforming Las Vegas into the entertainment capital of the world, is one of my dearest friends. The casinos he’s built are considered to be some of the most magnificent playgrounds in the world. Through it all, he’s made his fortune from one simple truth: the house has the edge. But by no means does he have a guaranteed victory! On any given night, a high-rolling gambler can take millions out of Steve’s pocket. And they can also leave if his “house” doesn’t completely captivate them. On the other hand, nearly all mutual fund companies have a stacked deck. They are the ultimate casino. They’ve captured you, you’re going nowhere, and they are guaranteed revenue whether you win or not. TWICE BURNED After 2008, when the US stock market lost more than 37%, the financial world was completely changed for most Americans. Even five years later, a survey from Prudential Financial showed that 44% of American investors still say they would never put their money in the stock market again, while 58% say they lost faith in the market. But the insiders are still in the game. Why? Because they know better. They know the “right” way to play the game. They know that today there are powerful tools and strategies that have never existed before. Get this: Today you can use a tool, issued and backed by one of the largest banks in the world, that will give you 100% principal protection guaranteed by its balance sheet and allow you to participate in 75% to 90% of the upside of the market (the S&P 500) without being capped! That is not a misprint. You can participate in up to 90% of the upside, but if the market collapses, you still get back 100% of your money! Sounds too good to be true? And if a product like this did exist, you would have already heard of it, right? Wrong. The reason? In the past, to even hear about this, you had to be in the top 1% of the 1%. These are not "retail" solutions, where they sit on the shelf. These are custom designed for those with enough money to partake. This is just one example of how, as an insider, you'll soon know the new rules of how to achieve wealth with minimal risk. Risk comes from not knowing what you're doing. —WARREN BUFFETT THE ROAD LESS TRAVELED The journey ahead is one that requires your full participation. Together we are going to climb this mountain called Financial Freedom. It's your personal Mount Everest. It won't be easy, and it will require preparation. You don't head up Everest without a very clear understanding of the dangers that lie ahead. Some are known, and some could sneak up on you like a violent storm. So before we set foot on the mountain, we must fully grasp what's on the path before us. One false step could mean the difference between wondering how you will pay next month's mortgage and an abundant life, free of financial stress. We can't ask someone to climb it for us, but we also can't do it alone. We need a guide who has our best interests at heart. THE PINNACLE The core concept of successful investing is simple: Grow your savings to a point at which the interest from your investments will generate enough income to support your lifestyle without having to work. Eventually you reach a "tipping point" at which your savings will hit a critical mass. This simply means that you don't have to work anymore—unless you choose to—because the interest and growth being generated by your account gives you the income you need for your life. This is the pinnacle we are climbing toward. The great news is that if you become an insider, today there are new and unique solutions and strategies that will accelerate your climb and even protect you from sliding backward. But before we explore these solutions in more depth, let's map out our journey with more clarity. There are two phases to your investing game: the accumulation phase, in which you are socking away money for growth, and the decumulation, during which you are withdrawing income. The journey up the mountain will represent our accumulation phase with the goal of reaching the pinnacle, or critical mass. The goal is to stay on top of the mountain as long as we can. To take in the views and breathe in the fresh air of freedom and accomplishment. There will be many hurdles, obstacles, and, if you're not alert, even lies, that will prevent you from reaching the peak. To ensure our best chance of success, we will flush these out in the pages to come. And when we enter the second act of our life, when it's time to enjoy what we made, we will have the freedom to work only if we want to. At this stage we will ski down the mountain and enjoy ourselves. Spending time with the ones we love, building our legacy, and making a difference. It's during this phase that we will eliminate the number one fear of baby boomers: the fear of outliving our money. This second phase is rarely discussed by the asset management industry, which is focused on keeping money invested. "It's not about having some arbitrary amount of money in your account on some given day," exclaimed Dr. Jeffrey Brown, professor of finance at the University of Illinois and consultant to the US Treasury and the World Bank. "I think a lot of people are going to get to retirement and suddenly wake up and realize, 'You know what? I did a fairly good job. I have all this money sitting here, but I don't know how long I am going to live, and I don't know what my investment returns are going to be, and I don't know what inflation is going to be. What do I do?' " After I read one of his recent Forbes columns, I called Dr. Brown to see if he would be willing to sit down and share specific solutions for investors of all shapes and sizes. (We'll hear from Dr. Brown on how to create income for life and even how to make it tax free in his interview in section 5, "Upside Without the Downside: Create a Lifetime Income Plan.") And who better to outline the solution than the man who is not only a top academic expert but was also one of only seven people appointed by the president of the United States to the Social Security Advisory Board.When you turn on the financial news today, you can see that it is less "news" and more sensationalism. Talking heads debate with zeal. Stock pickers scream their hot picks of the day while sound effects smash, crash, and "kaching!" through our living room speakers. Reporters film "live on the scene" directly from the trenches of the exchange floor. The system, paid for by advertisers, breeds the feeling that maybe we are missing out! If only we had a hot tip. If only we knew the next "must-own" mutual fund that would surely be the "5 star" comet. (Mutual funds are rated between 1 and 5 stars by rating authority Morningstar.) Chasing returns is big business. Personal finance writer Jane Bryant Quinn once referred to this sensational hype as "financial porn." Luring us into glossy pages where the centerfolds are swapped with fivestar ratings and promises of carefree walks on the beach and fishing off the dock with our grandkids. The bottom line is that advertisers are fighting to get a grasp on our money. The war for your assets rages on! So where do you put your money? Who can you trust? Who will protect you and get you the best return on your investment? These are the immediate questions that are sure to come to mind now that you've committed to becoming an investor—now that you've committed to socking away a percentage of your income. So where do most people put their money for the long haul? Usually the stock market. And the stock market has indeed been the best longterm investment over the past 100 years. As Steve Forbes pointed out at one of my financial events in Sun Valley, Idaho, in 2014, "$1 million invested in stocks in 1935 is worth $2.4 billion today (if you held on)." But the moment you open an IRA or participate in your 401(k) plan at work, there will be a jolly salesman (or sales process) telling you to park your money in a mutual fund. And by buying an actively managed mutual fund, what exactly are you buying? You are buying into the fund manager in hopes that his or her stock-picking abilities will be better than yours. A completely natural assumption, since we have insanely busy lives, and our method of picking stocks would be the equivalent of throwing darts! So we hand over our money to a "five-star" actively managed mutual fund manager who by definition is "actively" trying to beat the market by being a better stock picker than the next guy. But few firms will discuss what is sometimes called the $13 trillion lie. (That's how much money is in mutual funds.) Are you ready for this? An incredible 96% of actively managed mutual funds fail to beat the market over any sustained period of time! So let's be clear. When we say "beat the market" as a whole, we are generally referring to a stock index. What's an index, you ask? Some of you might know, but I don't want to risk leaving anyone in the dark, so let's shed a little light. An index is simply a basket or list of stocks. The S&P 500 is an index. It's a list of the top companies (by market capitalization) in the United States, as selected by Standard & Poor's. Companies like Apple, Exxon, and Amazon make up the list. Each day, they measure how all 500 stocks performed, as an aggregate, and when you turn on the news at night, you hear if the market (all the stocks on the list collectively) was either up or down. So instead of buying all the stocks individually, or trying to pick the next highflyer, you can diversify and own a piece of all 500 top stocks simply by investing in a low-cost index fund that tracks or mimics the index. One single investment buys you a piece of the strength of "American capitalism." In a way, you are buying into the fact that over the past 100 years, the top-tier companies have always shown incredible resiliency. Even through depressions, recessions, and world wars, they have continued to find ways to add value, grow, and drive increasing revenues. And if a company fails to keep making the grade, it falls off the list and is replaced with another top performer. The point here is that by investing in the index, you don't have to pay a professional to try picking which stocks in the index you should own. It's effectively been done for you because Standard & Poor's has selected the top 500 already. By the way, there are number of different indexes out there. Many of us have heard of the Dow Jones index, for example, and we will explore others soon. TEN THOUSAND OPTIONS There are 7,707 different mutual funds in the United States (but only 4,900 individual stocks), all vying for a chance to help you beat the market. But the statistic is worth repeating: 96% will fail to match or beat the market over any extended period. Is this groundbreaking news? No, not to insiders. Not to the smart money. As Ray Dalio told me emphatically, "You're not going to beat the market. No one does! Only a few gold medalists." He just happens to be one of those medalists honest enough to issue the warning "Don't try this at home." Even Warren Buffett, known for his incredibly unique ability to find undervalued stocks, says that the average investor should never attempt to pick stocks or time the market. In his famous 2014 letter to his shareholders, he explained that when he passes away, the money in a trust for his wife should be invested only in indexes so that she minimizes her cost and maximizes her upside. Buffett is so sure that professional stock pickers can't win over time that he was more than happy to put his money where his mouth is. In January 2008 Buffett made a $1 million wager against New York–based Protégé Partners, with the winnings going to charity. The bet? Can Protégé pick five top hedge fund managers who will collectively beat the S&P 500 index over a ten-year period? As of February 2014, the S&P 500 is up 43.8%, while the five hedge funds are up 12.5%. There are still a few years left, but the lead looks like the world's fastest man, Usain Bolt, running against a pack of Boy Scouts. (Note: for those unfamiliar with what a hedge fund is, it is essentially a private "closed-door" fund for only highnet-worth investors. The managers can have total flexibility to bet "for" the market and make money when it goes up, or "against" the market, and make money when it goes down.) THE FACTS ARE THE FACTS ARE THE FACTS Industry expert Robert Arnott, founder of Research Affiliates, spent two decades studying the top 200 actively managed mutual funds that had at least $100 million under management. The results are startling: From 1984 to 1998, a full 15 years, only eight out of 200 fund managers beat the Vanguard 500 Index. (The Vanguard 500, put together by founder Jack Bogle, is a mirror image of the S&P 500 index.) That's less than 4% odds that you pick a winner. If you've ever played blackjack, you know the goal is to get as close to 21 without going over, or "busting." According to Dan and Chip Heath in their Fast Company article "Made to Stick: The Myth of Mutual Funds," "by way of comparison, if you get dealt two face cards in blackjack (each face card is worth 10, so now your total is 20), and your inner idiot shouts, 'Hit me!' you have about an 8% chance of winning!" Just how badly does chasing performance hurt us? Over a 20-year period, December 31, 1993, through December 31, 2013, the S&P 500 returned an average annual return of 9.28%. But the average mutual fund investor made just over 2.54%, according to Dalbar, one of the leading industry research firms. Ouch! A nearly 80% difference. In real life, this can mean the difference between financial freedom and financial despair. Said another way, if you were the person who simply owned the S&P 500, you would have turned your $10,000 into $55,916! Whereas the mutual fund investor, who was sold on the illusion that he or she could outperform the market, ended up with only $16,386. Why the huge performance gap? Because we buy high and sell low. We follow our emotions (or our broker's recommendations) and jump from fund to fund. Always looking for an edge. But when the market falls, when we can't take the emotional pain any longer, we sell. And when the market is up, we buy more. As a famous money manager named Barton Biggs observed, "A bull market is like sex. It feels best just before it ends." WISDOM OF AGES At 82 years young, Burt Malkiel has lived through every conceivable market cycle and new marketing fad. When he wrote A Random Walk Down Wall Street in 1973, he had no idea it would become one of the classic investment books in history. The core thesis of his book is that market timing is a loser's game. In section 4, we will sit down and you'll hear from Burt but for now what you need to know is that he was the first guy to come up with the rationale of an index fund, which, again, does not to try to beat the market but simply "mimics," or matches, the market. Among investors, this strategy is called indexing or passive investing. This style is contrary to active investing, in which you pay a mutual fund manger to actively make choices about which stocks to buy or sell. The manager is trading stocks—"actively" working with hopes of beating the market. Jack Bogle, founder of the behemoth Vanguard, subsequently bet the future direction of his company on this idea by creating the first index fund. When I sat down with Jack for this book, he echoed why Vanguard has become the largest index mutual fund manager in the world. His best single rant: "maximum diversification, minimal cost, and maximum tax efficiency, low turnover [trading], and low turnover cost, and no sales loads." How's that for an elevator pitch! SHORTCUT Now, you might be thinking that there must be some people who can beat the market. Why else would there be $13 trillion in actively managed mutual funds? Mutual fund managers certainly have streaks where they do, in fact, beat the market. The question is whether or not they can sustain that advantage over time. But as Jack Bogle said, it all comes down to "marketing!" It's our human nature to strive to be faster, better, smarter than the next guy. And thus, selling a hot fund is not difficult to do. It sells itself. And when it inevitably turns cold, there will be another hot one ready to serve up. As for the 4% that do beat the market, they aren't the same 4% the next time around. Jack shared me with what he says is the funniest way to get this point across. "Tony, if you pack 1,024 gorillas into a gymnasium, and teach them each to flip a coin, one of them will flip heads ten times in a row. Most would call that luck, but when that happens in the fund business we call him a genius!" And what are the odds it's the same gorilla after the next ten flips? To quote a study from Dimensional Fund Advisors, run by 2013 Nobel Prize–winning economist Eugene Fama, "So who still believes markets don't work? Apparently it is only the North Koreans, the Cubans, and the active managers." 4 This part of the book is where anyone reading who works in the financial services industry will either nod in agreement or figure out which door they will prop open with these 600 pages! Some will even be gathering the troops to mount an attack. It's a polarizing issue, without a doubt. We all want to believe that by hiring the smartest and most talented mutual fund manager, we will achieve financial freedom more quickly. After all, who doesn't want a shortcut up the mountain? And here is the crazy thing: As much as everyone is entitled to his own opinion, nobody is entitled to his own facts! Sure, some mutual fund managers will say, "We may not outperform on the upside but when the market goes down, we can take active measures to protect you so you won't lose as much." That might be comforting if it were true. The goal in investing is to get the maximum net return for a given amount of risk (and, ideally, the lowest cost). So let's see how the fund managers did when the market was down. And 2008 is as good a place to start as any. Between 2008 and early 2009, the market had its worst one-year slide since the Great Depression (51% from top to bottom, to be exact). The managers had plenty of time to make "defensive" moves. Maybe when the market was down 15%, or 25%, or 35%, they would have taken "appropriate measures." Once again, the facts speak for themselves. Whether the fund manager was trying to beat the S&P Growth Index, made up of companies such as Microsoft, Qualcomm, and Google, or trying to beat the S&P Small Cap Index, made up of smaller companies such as Yelp, once again, the stock pickers fell short. According to a 2012 report titled S&P Indices Versus Active Funds Scorecard—SPIVA, for short—the S&P 500 Growth Index outperformed 89.9% of large-cap growth mutual funds, while the S&P 500 Small Cap 600 Growth Index outperformed 95.5% of small-cap growth managers. THE UNICORNS Now, having made it clear that almost nobody beats the market over time, I will give one caveat. There is a tiny group of hedge fund managers who do the seemingly impossible by beating the market consistently. But they are the "unicorns," the rarest of the rare. The "magicians." The "market wizards." Like David Einhorn of Greenlight Capital, who is up 2,287% (no, that's not a typo!) since launching his fund in 1996 and has only one negative year on his track record. But unfortunately, it doesn't do the average investor any good to know they are out there, because their doors are closed to new investors. Ray Dalio's fund, Bridgewater, hasn't accepted new investors in over ten years, but when it did, it required a minimum investment of $100 million and $5 billion in investable assets. Gulp. Paul Tudor Jones, who hasn't lost money in over 28 years, called his investors recently and sent back $2 billion. When a hedge fund gets too big, it's harder to get in and get out of the market—harder to buy and sell its investments quickly and easily. And being slow means lower returns. — Before you begin to think this is a glowing report on hedge funds, let me be clear. For the fifth year in a row, ending in 2012, the vast majority of hedge fund managers have underperformed the S&P 500. According to the financial news site Zero Hedge, in 2012 the average fund returned 8% as opposed to 16% for the S&P 500. In 2013 hedge funds returned an average of 7.4%, while the S&P 500 soared 29.6%, its best year since 1997. I am sure their wealthy clients weren't too pleased. And to add insult to injury, they usually charge 2% per year for management, take 20% of the overall profits, and the gains you do receive are often taxed at the highest ordinary income tax rates. Painful. THE BIGGEST BANK IN THE WORLD No matter what aspect of life, I am always looking for the exception to the rule, as that's where outstanding tends to live. Mary Callahan Erdoes fits that bill. In an industry dominated by men, she has risen to the top of the financial world. Wall Street is a place where performance speaks louder than words, and Erdoes's performance has been extraordinary. Her consistent breakthrough results have led her to become the CEO of J.P. Morgan Asset Management, and she now oversees portfolios that total more than $2.5 trillion—yes, trillion with a t! We had a fantastic interview for this book, and she shared some profound wisdom, which we will cover in section 6. But when I brought up the studies that no manager beats the market over time, she was quick to point out that many of J.P. Morgan's fund managers have beaten the market (in their respective classes) over the past ten years. Why? The examples she provided didn't lose as much as the market when the market went down. This difference, she says, is what provided the edge they needed to stay ahead. Erdoes and many industry experts agree that certain less-developed, or emerging, markets provide opportunities for active managers to get "an edge." They have the opportunity to gain an even greater advantage in frontier markets— places such as Kenya and Vietnam—where information isn't as transparent and doesn't travel as fast. Erdoes says this is where a firm such as J.P. Morgan has massive reach and resources, and can use its on-the-ground contacts in the community to give it valuable insights in real time. According to Jack Bogle, there is no empirical basis to show that active management is more effective for all the major asset classes: large-cap growth, value, core, mid-cap growth, and so on. But it does appear that these frontier markets present opportunities for active management to sometimes outperform. Will they continue to outperform going forward? Only time will tell. We do know that every active manager, from Ray Dalio to J.P. Morgan, will be wrong at some point in their attempt to outperform. Therefore, developing a system and a proper asset allocation is crucial. We will address this in Section 4. It will be up to you to evaluate them for yourself, and don't forget to take into account the fees and the taxes (which we will discuss in the next chapter). ALL WEATHER You might be reading this book in a bull market, a bear market, or a sideways market. Who knows? The point is that you need to have your investments set up to stand the test of time. An "All Weather" portfolio. The people I have interviewed have done well in both good times and bad. And we can all count on ups and downs in the future. Life isn't about waiting for the storm to pass; it's about learning to dance in the rain. It's about removing the fear in this area of your life so you can focus on what matters most.

WHEN, WHERE, AND HOW? So what does the All Weather portfolio look like? "Where do I put my money, Tony?!" First, you don't have to waste your time trying to pick stocks yourself or pick the best mutual fund. A portfolio of low-cost index funds is the best approach for a percentage of your investments because we don't know what stocks will be "best" going forward. And how cool to know that by "passively" owning the market, you are beating 96% of the world's "expert" mutual fund managers and nearly as many hedge fund managers. It's time to free yourself from the burden of trying to pick the winner of the race. As Jack Bogle told me, in investing it feels counterintuitive. The secret: "Don't do something, just stand there!" And by becoming the market and not trying to beat it, you are on the side of progress, growth, and expansion. So far we have referred many times to "the market" or the S&P 500. But remember that the S&P 500 is only one of many indexes or markets. Most have heard of the Dow Jones Industrial Average. There are others, such as a commodities index, a real estate index, a short-term bond index, a long-term bond index, a gold index, and so on. How much of each to buy is critical and something we will get to in section 4. In fact, how would you like to have Ray Dalio tell you what his ideal allocation would be? The strategy he shares in the pages ahead has produced just under 10% annually and made money more than 85% of the time in the last 30 years (between 1984 and 2013)! In fact, when the market was down 37% in 2008, his portfolio model was down only 3.93%! I sure wish I had known this back then! Or how about David Swensen, the man who took Yale's endowment from $1 billion to more than $23.9 billion while averaging 14% annually? He too shared his ideal allocation for you in the pages ahead. Priceless information all captured in section 6, "Invest Like the .001%: The Billionaire's Playbook." So if you look at these experts' models without fully understanding asset allocation, it's like building a house on a weak foundation. Or if you focus on asset allocation before knowing your goals, it will be a complete waste of time. And maybe most importantly, if we don't protect you from the people looking to take a good chunk of your wealth, all is lost. That's why we are uncovering the 9 Myths—Step 2 in our 7 Simple Steps to Financial Freedom—so that you become an "insider." So that you will know the truth. And the truth will set you free. IT PAYS TO BE A STAR Even after everything we have showed you about actively managed mutual funds, there are undoubtedly those who will say, "Tony, I have done my research, and not to worry. I only invest in five-star funds, nothing less." Oh, really? According to Morningstar, over the decade ending

December 2009, roughly 72% of all fund deposits (about $2 trillion) flowed to four- and five-star funds. For those who aren't familiar, Morningstar is the most popular and thorough service for evaluating mutual funds, and they apply a five-star ranking system to their past performance. Brokers are starry-eyed as they share with you the next hot fund. David Swensen told me that "the stars are so important that mutual fund companies are quick to eliminate funds which fall below the four-star threshold. For the five-year period ending in 2012, 27% of domestic equity funds and 23% of international equity funds were either merged or liquidated; a common practice to eliminate a poor track record from a family of funds." It's routine for mutual fund companies to set up multiple new funds to see which one is hot and euthanize the others. As Jack Bogle explains, "A firm will go out and start five incubation funds, and they will try and shoot the lights out with all five of them. And of course they don't with four of them, but they do with one. So they drop the other four and take the one that did very well public with a great track record and sell that track record." Imagine we could adopt this practice in our own investing life? What if you could pick 5 stocks and if four went down and only one went up, you could pretend all your losers didn't happen? And then tell your friends that you are the hottest stock picker since Warren Buffett. In addition, the lackluster performance of these fourand five-star supernovas (dying stars) is well researched in a Wall Street Journal article entitled "Investors Caught with Stars in Their Eyes." A study was done in which the researchers went back to 1999 and studied the ten-year subsequent performance of those who bought five-star funds. Their findings? "Of the 248 mutual stock funds with five-star ratings at the start of the period, just four still kept that rank after 10 years." How many times have you picked a shooting star only to watch it burn out? We all have at some point. And here we see that it's because we had less than 2% odds that the shooting star wouldn't fizzle into darkness. We all want the guy with the hot hand, but history tells us that it's the hot hand that will inevitably turn cold. Isn't that why Vegas always wins!? An "insider" knows that chasing the highflyer is chasing the wind. But it's human nature to chase performance. It's almost irresistible. Yet the "herd" mentality quite literally results in financial destruction for millions of families, and I know that if you are reading this book, you are not willing to fall victim any longer. You're becoming an insider now! And what other cool strategies do "insiders" use? Let's find out. UPSIDE WITH PROTECTION In the past 100 years, the market was up approximately 70% of the time. But that leaves

30% of the time that the market was down. So while investing in the indexes is a great solution for a portion of your money, it shouldn't be for all of your money. Markets are volatile at times so it only makes sense that you will want to protect a portion of your portfolio if or when the markets take another big dive. Heck, there have been two 50% hits since 2000. One exciting strategy we will introduce allows us to make money when the market (index) goes up, yet it simultaneously guarantees that we will not lose our original investment if the market goes down. The catch? You don't get to capture or participate in all of the gains. Most are in disbelief when I explain that there are tools out there that can guarantee that you don't lose while still giving you the ability to participate in market "wins." Why haven't you heard of them? Because they are typically reserved for high-net-worth clients. I will show you one of the only places where the average investor can access these. Imagine your friends with their baffled and even suspicious looks when you tell them you make money when the market goes up but don't lose money when it goes down. This strategy alone can completely change the way you feel about investing. It's your safety rope while climbing the mountain when everyone else is "white knuckling" it with hope. Imagine the feeling of certainty, of peace of mind, knowing that you aren't at risk. How would this change your life? How would you feel when you open up your monthly statements? Would you be gritting your teeth or feel calm and collected? We've only scratched the surface of the incredible insights and tools that lay ahead, so you must stay tuned. But for now, we can remember the following: • Stocks have by far been the best place to be for longterm growth over time. • Stocks are volatile. In the pages ahead, you will learn from the "market masters" how to "smooth out the ride" by investing in and diversifying across multiple different indexes. • Don't be sold that someone is going to beat the market. Instead, align yourself with the market! Once you put your indexing plan in place (which we will do step by step), you won't have to spend your time trying to pick which stock to buy because the index will have done it for you. This will save you a tremendous amount of time and angst in trying to pick a winner. • Begin to think like an insider! Never again will you tolerate the "herd" mentality in your own life. FEES ON FEES By tapping into the power of indexing, by passively owning the market, you are also combatting our second myth. Nearly every person I ask doesn't know exactly how much he or she pays in fees. I'll admit, I also didn't know at one stage in my life. The fee factories have become masterful at either hiding the fees or making them appear negligible. "No big deal." Nothing could be further from the truth. When climbing the mountain of financial freedom you will need every bit of forward progress to succeed. You can't afford to take two steps forward and one step back by letting excessive fees drain your account.In 2002 Charles Schwab ran a clever TV ad where a typical Wall Street sales manager is giving a morning pep talk to his boiler room. "Tell your clients it's red hot! En fuego! Just don't mention the fundamentals—they stink." He wraps up his morning sermon by dangling courtside tickets to the Knicks for the winning salesman and gives his final send-off: "Let's put some lipstick on this pig!" GET MY GOOD SIDE In 1954 Darrell Huff authored a book entitled How to Lie with Statistics. He points to the "countless number of dodges which are used to fool rather than to inform." Today the mutual fund industry has been able to use a tricky method to calculate and publish returns that are, as Jack Bogle says, "not actually earned by the investors." But before we explain this masterful "sleight of pencil" magic, let's first understand the illusion of average returns. Below is a chart showing a hypothetical market that is up and down like a roller coaster. Up 50%, down 50%, up 50%, and down 50%. This produces an average return of 0%. And like you, I would expect that a 0% return would mean that I didn't lose any money. And we would both be wrong! As you can see by the chart, if you start with an actual dollar amount (let's use $100,000), at the end of the fouryear period, you are actually down $43,750, or 43.75%! You thought you were even, but instead you're down 43.75%! Would you ever have guessed this? Now that you're an insider, beware! Average returns have a built-in illusion, spinning a performance enhancement that doesn't exist. In a Fox Business article titled "Solving the Myth of Rate of Return," Erik Krom explains how this discrepancy applies to the real world: "Another way to look at it is to review the Dow Jones since 1930. If you add up every number and divide it by 81 years, the return 'averages' 6.31%; however, if you do the math, you get an 'actual' return of 4.31%. Why is this so important? If you invested $1,000 back in 1930 at 6.31%, you would have $142,000, at 4.31% you would only have $30,000." THE SCALES ARE WEIGHTED Now that we see that average returns aren't a true representation of what we earn, sit back and relax because the grand illusion isn't over yet. The math magicians on Wall Street have managed to calculate their returns to look even better. How so? In short, when the mutual fund advertises a specific return, it's not, as Jack Bogle says, "the return you actually earn." Why? Because the returns you see in the brochure are known as time-weighted returns. Sounds complicated, but it's not. (However, feel free to use that to look brilliant at your next cocktail party!) The mutual fund manager says if we have $1 at the beginning of the year and $1.20 at the end of the year, we are up 20%. "Fire up the marketing department and take out those full-page ads!" But in reality, investors rarely have all their money in the fund at the beginning of the year. We typically make contributions throughout the year—that is, out of every paycheck into our 401(k). And if we contribute more during times of the year when the fund is performing well (a common theme, we learned, as investors chase performance) and less during times when it's not performing, we are going to have a much different return from what is advertised. So if we were to sit down at the end of the year and take into account the "real world" of making ongoing contributions and withdrawals, we would find out how much we really made (or lost). And this real-world approach is called the dollar-weighted return. Dollarweighted returns are what we actually get to keep whereas time-weighted returns are what fund managers use to fuel advertising. Jack Bogle has been a continual proponent of changing this rule. He believes that investors should see how much they actually earned (or lost) based on their own personal situation (contributions and withdrawals included). Sounds like common sense, right? But it's no surprise why mutual funds are resistant. Bogle says: "We've compared returns earned by mutual fund investors—dollar-weighted returns—with the returns earned by the fund themselves, or time-weighted returns, and the investors seem to lag the fund themselves by three percent per year." Wow! So if the fund advertises a 6% return, its investors achieved closer to 3%.An investment operation is one which, upon thorough analysis, promises safety of principal and an adequate return. Operations not meeting these requirements are speculative. —BENJAMIN GRAHAM, The Intelligent Investor HAVING YOUR CAKE AND EATING IT TOO Superficially, I think it looks like entrepreneurs have a high tolerance for risk. But one of the most important phrases in my life is "protect the downside." —RICHARD BRANSON, founder of Virgin My friend Richard Branson, the founder of Virgin and its many incredible brands, decided to launch Virgin Airways in 1984. In true David-versus-Goliath fashion, the master of marketing knew that he could "out market" anyone including the behemoth competitor British Airways. To outsiders, it seemed like a huge gamble. But Richard, like most smart investors, was more concerned about hedging his downside than hitting a home run. So in a brilliant move, he bought his first five planes but managed to negotiate the deal of a lifetime: if it didn't work out, he could give back the planes! A money-back guarantee! If he failed, he didn't lose. But if he won, he won big. The rest is history. Not unlike the business world, the investment world will tell you, directly or more subtly, that if you want to win big, you've got to take some serious risk. Or more frighteningly, if you ever want financial freedom, you have to risk your freedom to get there. Nothing could be further from the truth. If there is one common denominator of successful insiders, it's that they don't speculate with their hardearned savings, they strategize. Remember Warren Buffett's top two rules of investing? Rule 1: don't lose money! Rule 2: see rule 1. Whether it's the world's top hedge fund traders like Ray Dalio and Paul Tudor Jones or entrepreneurs like Salesforce founder Marc Benioff and Richard Branson of Virgin, without exception, these billionaire insiders look for opportunities that provide asymmetric risk/reward. This is a fancy way of saying that the reward is drastically disproportionate to the risk. Risk a little, make a lot. The best example of risking very little to make a lot is the high-frequency traders (HFT) who use the latest technologies (yes, even flying robots and microwave towers that are faster than the speed of light) to save 1/1000 of a second! What would you guess is their risk/reward while generating 70% of all trading volume in the stock market? I will give you a clue. Virtu Financial, one of the largest HFT firms, was about to go public, a process that requires it to disclose its business model and profitability. Over the past five years, Virtu has lost money only one day! That's right. One single trading day out of thousands! And what is its risk? Investing in faster computers, I suppose. TWO NICKELS TO RUB TOGETHER My friend and hedge fund guru J. Kyle Bass is best known for turning a $30 million investment into $2 billion in just two short years. Conventional wisdom would say that he must have taken a big risk for returns of that magnitude. Not so. Kyle made a very calculated bet against the housing bubble that was expanding like the kid in Willy Wonka & the Chocolate Factory. It was bound to burst sooner rather than later. Remember those days? When ravenous, unqualified mortgage shoppers were enticed to buy whatever they could get their hands on. And with no money down or so much as any proof they could afford it. Lenders were lining up to provide loans knowing they could package them up and sell them off to investors who really didn't understand them. This bubble was easy to spot so long as you were on the outside looking in. But Kyle's brilliance, which he reveals in his interview in section 6, is that he only risked 3 cents for every dollar of upside. How's that for taking a tiny risk and reaping giant rewards? When I spoke with Kyle recently, he shared the details of another asymmetric risk/reward opportunity he had found for himself and his investors. The terms? He had a 95% guarantee of his investment, but if or when the company went public, he had unlimited upside (and he expected massive returns!). But if it all went south, he lost only 5%. Kyle, like all great investors, takes small risks for big rewards. Taking a swing for the fence with no downside protection is a recipe for disaster. "Kyle, how do I get this point across to my readers?" "Tony, I will tell you how I taught my two boys: we bought nickels." "What was that, Kyle?" Maybe the phone was breaking up. "I could have sworn you just said you bought nickels." "You heard me right. I was literally standing in the shower one day thinking, 'Where can I get a riskless return?' " Most experts wouldn't even dream to think of such a thing. In their mind, "riskless return" is an oxymoron. Insiders like Kyle think differently from the herd. And by defying conventional wisdom, he always looks for small investments to return disproportionate rewards. The famed hedge fund guru, with one of the biggest wins of the last century, used his hard-earned money to buy . . . well, money: $2 million in nickels—enough to fill up a small room. What gives? While a nickel's value fluctuates, at the time of this interview Kyle told me, "Tony, the US nickel is worth about 6.8 cents today in its 'melt value.' That means 5 cents is really worth 6.8 cents [36% more] in its true metal value." Crazy to think we live in a world where the government will spend nearly 9 cents in total (including raw materials and manufacturing costs) to make a 5-cent coin. Is anyone paying attention up there on Capitol Hill? Clearly this isn't sustainable, and one day Congress will wake up and change the "ingredients" that make up the nickel. "Maybe the next one will be tin or steel. They did this identical thing with the penny when copper became too expensive in the early eighties." From 1909 to 1982, the penny was made up of 95% copper. Today it's mostly zinc with only 2.5% copper. Today one of those older pennies is worth 2 cents! (Not in melt value; that's the price coin collectors would pay!) That's 100% more than its face value. If you had invested in pennies way back when, you would have doubled your money with no risk, and you didn't even have to melt the pennies! I admit it sounded gimmicky at first, but Kyle was dead serious. "If I could take my entire cash balance of my net worth and press a button and turn it into nickels, I would do it right this second," he exclaimed. "Because then you don't have to worry about how much money they print. The nickel will always be worth a nickel." And his cash would be worth 36% more—and like pennies, likely 100% more in the future, as soon as the government inevitably cheapens the nickel's recipe. Kyle was more than an enthusiast. "Where else can I get a thirty-six-percent risk-free return! If I am wrong, I still have what I started with." Sure, it's illegal to melt down your nickels (for now), but the point is, "I won't need to melt it down because once they change the way they make the nickel, the old nickels become even more valuable than before because scarcity sets in as they begin to remove them from circulation." Needless to say, his boys got the lesson as well as a good workout moving boxes of coins into their storage unit! Now, you might be thinking, "Well, that's great for Kyle Bass, who has millions or even billions just to throw around, but how does that apply to me?" Surely it can't be possible for normal investors to have upside without the downside—to have a protection of principal with major upside potential. Think again. The same level of financial creativity that has propelled high-frequency trading (HFT) from nonexistent into a dominant force in just ten years has touched other areas of finance as well. Following the 2008 crash, when people didn't have much of an appetite for stocks, some very innovative minds at the world's largest banks figured out a way to do the seemingly impossible: allow you and me to participate in the gains of the stock market without risking any of our principal! Before you write this notion off as crazy, I personally have a note, issued and backed by one of the world's largest banks, that gives me 100% principal protection, and if the market goes up, I get to keep a significant chunk of the gains in the market (without dividends). But if the market collapses, I get all my money back. I don't know about you, but I am more than happy to give up a percentage of the upside in exchange for protecting myself from stomach-wrenching losses on a portion of my investment portfolio. But I am getting ahead of myself. We have come to a point in the United States where most of us feel that the only option for us to grow our wealth involves taking huge risks. That our only available option is to white knuckle it through the rolling waves of the stock market. And we somehow take solace in the fact that everyone is in the same boat. Well, guess what? It's not true! Not everyone is in the same boat! There are much more comfortable boats out on the water that are anchored in the proverbial safe harbor, while others are getting pounded in the waves of volatility and taking on water quick. So who owns the boats in the harbor? The insiders. The wealthy. The 1%. Those not willing to speculate with their hard-earned money. But make no mistake: you don't have to be in the .001% to strategize like the .001%. WHO DOESN'T WANT TO EAT

THE CAKE TOO? In the investment world, having your cake and eating it too would be making money when the market goes up but not losing a dime if the market drops. We get to ride the elevator up but not down. This too-good-to-be-true concept is so important that I have devoted an entire section of this book to it: "Upside Without the Downside: Create a Lifetime Income Plan." But for now, this brief appetizer below is designed to dislodge your preconceived notions that you and all of your money must endure the endless waves of volatility. Below are three proven strategies (explored in more depth in section 5) for achieving strong returns while anchored firmly in calmer waters. 1. Structured Notes. These are perhaps one of the more exciting tools available today, but, unfortunately, they are rarely offered to the general public because the high-net-worth investors gobble them up like pigeon seed in Central Park. Luckily, the right fiduciary is able to grant access for individuals even without large sums of investment capital. So listen up. A structured note is simply a loan to a bank (and typically the largest banks in the world). The bank issues you a note in exchange for lending it your money. At the end of the time period (also called the term), the bank guarantees to pay you the greater of: 100% of your deposit back or a certain percentage of the upside of the market gains (minus the dividends). That's right. I get all my money back if the market is down from the day I bought the note, but if the market goes up during the term, I get to participate in the upside. I call these notes "engineered safety." The catch? I typically don't get to keep all of the upside. So you have to ask yourself if you're willing to give up part of the upside for downside protection. Many people would say yes. These solutions become especially valuable when you come to that point in your life, close to or during retirement, where you can't afford to take any big losses. When you can't afford or even survive another 2008. For those looking to take a bit more risk, some notes will allow for even greater upside if you are willing to take more risk on the downside. For example, a note available today will give you a 25% downside-protection "airbag." So the market has to go down more than 25% for you to lose. And in exchange for taking more risk, it will give you more than 100% of the upside. One note available right now offers 140% of the upside if you are willing to absorb a loss beyond 25%. So if the market was up 10% over the term, you would get 14% in return. So what are the downsides of structured notes? First, a guarantee is only as good as the backer! So it's important to choose one of the strongest/largest banks (issuers) in the world with a very strong balance sheet. (Note: Lehman Brothers was a very strong bank until it wasn't! This is why many experts utilize Canadian banks, since they tend to have the strongest financials.) Next challenge? Your timing could be way off. Let's say you owned a note with a five-year term, and for the first four years, the market was up. You would be feeling pretty good at that point. But if the market collapses in the fifth year, you will still get your money back, but you didn't get to capture any of those gains. You also might have limited liquidity if you need to sell the note before the end of the term. It's also important to note that not all structured notes are created equal. Like all financial products, there are good versions and bad versions. Most big retail firms sell you notes that have substantial commissions, underwriting fees, and distributions fees; all of these will take away from your potential upside. Accessing structured notes through a sophisticated, expert fiduciary (a registered investment advisor) will typically have those fees removed because a fiduciary charges a flat advisory fee. And by stripping out those fees, performance goes up. A fiduciary will also help you make sure you own the note in the most tax-efficient way since the tax ramifications can vary. 2. Market-Linked CDs. First things first: these are not your grandpa's CDs. In today's day and age, with interest rates so low, traditional CDs can't even keep pace with inflation. This has earned them the nickname "certificates of death" because your purchasing power is being slowly killed. As I write this, the average one-year CD pays 0.23% (or 23 basis points). Can you imagine investing $1,000 dollars for a year and getting back $2.30? The average investor walks into a bank and is willing to lay down and accept 23 bps. But the wealthy investor, an insider, would laugh and tell them to go to hell. That's not enough to buy a latte! Oh, and you still have to pay taxes on that $2.30 return—an even higher ordinary income tax rate (as opposed to the investment tax rate), which historically is significantly lower! Traditional CDs are very profitable for the banks because they can turn around and lend your money at 10 to 20 times the interest rate they are paying you. Another version of the insider's game. Market-linked CDs are similar to structured notes, but they include insurance from the Federal Deposit Insurance Corporation (FDIC). Here is how they work. Market-linked CDs, like traditional versions, give you some small guaranteed return (a coupon) if the market goes up, but you also get to participate in the upside. But if the market falls, you get back your investment (plus your small return), and you had FDIC insurance the entire time. Typically, your money is tied up for one or two years (whereas structured notes can be as long as five to seven years). To give you a real-life example, today there is a market-linked CD that pays the exact same interest rate as a traditional CD (0.28%) but also allows you to participate in up to 5% of the market gains. So if the market is up 8% total, you get to keep 5%. In this example, you earned over 20 times the return of a traditional CD with the same FDIC protection! But again, if the market goes down you lose nothing. Keep in mind that rates are constantly changing in this field. Rates may be more attractive at certain times than at others. In 2008, when banks were struggling and looking for deposits, they had a sweetheart deal that my buddy Ajay Gupta, who is also my personal registered investment advisor, couldn't pass up. The note had 100% principal protection with FDIC insurance. The value was linked to a balanced portfolio of stocks and bonds, and when all was said and done, he averaged 8% per year with no risk! I must warn you again, however, that accessing these directly from a bank will often incur a host of charges and fees. Conversely, accessing these solutions through a fiduciary advisor will typically remove all the commissions and fees that a retail firm may charge, and thus the performance/terms will be better for you. 3. Fixed Indexed Annuities. Let me be the first to say that there are a lot of crappy annuity products on the market. But in my research and interviews with some of the top experts in the country, I discovered that other types of annuities are used by insiders as yet another tool to create upside without the downside. Fixed indexed annuities (FIA) are a type of annuity that has been around since the mid-'90s but have only recently exploded in popularity. A properly structured fixed indexed annuity offers the following characteristics: • 100% principal protection, guaranteed by the insurance company. This is why we have to pick an insurance company with a high rating and a long history of making good on its promises—often a century or more! • Upside without downside—like structured notes and market-linked CDs, a fixed indexed annuity allows you to participate when the market goes up but not lose if the market goes down. All gains are tax deferred, or if it's owned within a Roth IRA, you won't pay taxes on the returns. • Lastly, and probably most importantly, some fixed indexed annuities offer the ability to create an income stream that you can't outlive. A paycheck for life! Think of this investment as your own personal pension. For every dollar you deposit, the insurance company guarantees you a certain monthly income payment when you decide to trigger, or turn on, your lifetime income stream. Insurance companies have been doing this work successfully for 200 years. We will explore this strategy in depth in section 5, "Upside Without the Downside: Create a Lifetime Income Plan." A WORD OF WARNING Before we move on, let me be very clear on one point: this does not imply that all versions of these products and strategies are great. Some have high fees, high commissions, hidden charges, and on and on. The last thing I want is some salesman using these few pages to sell you something that's not in your best interest. And when we dive into these solutions in section 5, I will give you a specific list of pitfalls you must avoid as well as a list of things you absolutely want to make sure you receive when utilizing these solutions. YOU GET WHAT YOU TOLERATE The point of this chapter is to begin to show you ways in which you can have your cake and eat it too. Sometimes, when you have endured the choppy waters for so long, you begin to believe that there is no other option. This tendency is called "learned helplessness." But that's not the way insiders think. From Buffett to Branson, they all look for asymmetric risk/reward. Insiders are not helpless, nor are you. In every area of life, you get what you tolerate. And it's time to raise the standard. HOW FAR WE HAVE COME We have made some serious progress! Let's recap the myths we have shattered and the truths we have uncovered thus far: • We have learned that nobody beats the market (except for a handful of "unicorns")! And by using low-cost market-mimicking index funds, we can outperform 96% of mutual funds and nearly as many hedge funds. Welcome to the front of the performance pack! • Since stock-picking mutual funds are charging us extremely high fees (over 3%, on average), we can drop our investment fees by 80% or even 90%. You could have more than twice as much money when you retire or cut years off the time it will take you to get to financial freedom. Let that soak in for a second!

www.ingramcontent.com/pod-product-compliance
Ingram Content Group UK Ltd.
Pitfield, Milton Keynes, MK11 3LW, UK
UKHW041830200726
13854UKWH00002BA/908

9 798885 219396